National 4

Physics

Arthur Baillie

The Publishers would like to thank the following for permission to reproduce copyright material:

Photo credits p.1 (background) and Unit 1 running head image © Gytis Mikulicius / iStockphoto.com, (inset left) © AndreyPopov/Thinkstock, (inset centre) © Fotolia, (inset right) © Dan Tucker / Alamy; p.2 © Arthur Baillie; p.3 © Arthur Baillie; p.20 © AndreyPopov/Thinkstock; p.42 © dvande/Fotolia; p.43 © emirkoo/Fotolia, p.44 © Fotolia; p.51 © Dan Tucker / Alamy; p.52 © PearlBucknall/Alamy; p.53 © Paul White - UK Industries/Alamy; p.54 (top) © Fenton/Fotolia, (bottom) © OPD/LOOK AT SCIENCES/SCIENCE PHOTO LIBRARY; p.61 (both) © Arthur Baillie; p.69 (background) and Unit 2 running head image © Imagestate Media (John Foxx) /Splash V3060, (inset left) © Arthur Baillie, (inset centre) © Allmag/Fotolia, (inset right) © Jim Wehtje/Photodisc/Getty Images; p.75 (all) © Arthur Baillie; p.76 (all) © Arthur Baillie; p.81 (top) © Isabelle Limbach/iStockphoto/Thinkstock, (bottom) © age fotostock/Alamy; p.82 © auremar/Fotolia, p.88 (top left) © taweepat/Fotolia, (bottom left) © Coloures-Pic/Fotolia.com, (top right) © DR RAY CLARK & MERVYN GOFF/SCIENCE PHOTO LIBRARY, (bottom right) © ivansmuk/Thinkstock; p.89 © Allmag/Fotolia; p.90 (left) © LOUISE MURRAY/SCIENCE PHOTO LIBRARY, (right) © Fotokon/Fotolia; p.91 © Jim Wehtje/Photodisc/Getty Images; p.92 (left) © Mark A. Johnson/Alamy, (right) © BSIP SA/Alamy; p.98 © GUSTOIMAGES/SCIENCE PHOTO LIBRARY; p.99 © AMELIE-BENOIST/BSIP/SCIENCE PHOTO LIBRARY; p.102 © Arthur Baillie; p.105 (background) and Unit 3 running head image © StockTrek/Photodisc/Getty Images, (inset left) © Stocktrek Images, Inc./Alamy, (inset centre) © geogphotos/Alamy, (inset right) © NASA - Yuri Arcurs/Fotolia; p.110 (left) © Greg Balfour Evans/Alamy, (right) © Justin Kase zsixz/Alamy; p.118 © TMPhoto / Alamy; p.119 (left) © sciencephotos/Alamy, (right) © Pete Stone/CORBIS; p.120 (top) © sciencephotos/Alamy, (bottom) © Oleksiy Maksymenko Photography/Alamy; p.121 (top) © Editorial Image, LLC/Alamy, (bottom) © RiseAboveDesign/Thinkstock; p.122 © Arthur Baillie; p.125 © Stocktrek Images, Inc./Alamy; p.126 © National Geographic Image Collection/Alamy; p.128 (top) © nmlfd/Thinkstock, (bottom) © geogphotos/Alamy; p.130 © Photodisc/Getty Images; p.132 © Stocktrek Images/Thinkstock; p.135 (left) © Matt McPhee/Fotolia, (top right) © M.Rosenwirth/Fotolia, (bottom right) © Tristan3D/Fotolia; p.136 © Rastan/Thinkstock; p.137 © ESA/ATG medialab; Comet image: ESA/Rosetta/Navcam; p.138 (top left) © NASA - Yuri Arcurs/Fotolia, (bottom left) © HO/AFP/Getty Images.

Every effort has been made to trace all copyright holders, but if any have been inadvertently overlooked the Publishers will be pleased to make the necessary arrangements at the first opportunity.

Whilst every effort has been made to check the instructions of practical work in this book, it is still the duty and legal obligation of schools to carry out their own risk assessments.

Although every effort has been made to ensure that website addresses are correct at time of going to press, Hodder Gibson cannot be held responsible for the content of any website mentioned in this book. It is sometimes possible to find a relocated web page by typing in the address of the home page for a website in the URL window of your browser.

Hachette UK's policy is to use papers that are natural, renewable and recyclable products and made from wood grown in sustainable forests. The logging and manufacturing processes are expected to conform to the environmental regulations of the country of origin.

Orders: please contact Bookpoint Ltd, 130 Park Drive, Milton Park, Abingdon, Oxon OX14 4SE. Telephone: (44) 01235 827720. Fax: (44) 01235 400454. Lines are open 9.00–5.00, Monday to Saturday, with a 24-hour message answering service. Visit our website at www.hoddereducation.co.uk. Hodder Gibson can be contacted direct on: Tel: 0141 848 1609; Fax: 0141 889 6315; email: hoddergibson@hodder.co.uk

© Arthur Baillie 2015

First published in 2015 by
Hodder Gibson, an imprint of Hodder Education,
An Hachette UK Company,
2a Christie Street
Paisley PA1 1NB

Impression number   5 4 3 2 1
Year   2019 2018 2017 2016 2015

All rights reserved. Apart from any use permitted under UK copyright law, no part of this publication may be reproduced or transmitted in any form or by any means, electronic or mechanical, including photocopying and recording, or held within any information storage and retrieval system, without permission in writing from the publisher or under licence from the Copyright Licensing Agency Limited. Further details of such licences (for reprographic reproduction) may be obtained from the Copyright Licensing Agency Limited, Saffron House, 6–10 Kirby Street, London EC1N 8TS.

Cover photo © NASA/JPL-Caltech/K. Su (University of Arizona)
Illustrations by Integra Software Services Pvt. Ltd., Pondicherry, India
Typeset in 11/14 pt Minion Pro Regular by Integra Software Services Pvt. Ltd., Pondicherry, India
Printed in Slovenia

A catalogue record for this title is available from the British Library
ISBN: 978 1 4718 4860 5

Contents

Unit 1 Electricity and Energy
1 Electrical circuits — 2
2 Resistance — 13
3 Electrical systems and components — 20
4 Digital processes — 30
5 Electrical power — 35
6 Electromagnetism — 40
7 Generation and distribution of electricity — 49
8 Gas laws and the kinetic theory — 60

Unit 2 Waves and Radiation
9 Wave characteristics — 70
10 Sound — 75
11 Electromagnetic spectrum — 87
12 Nuclear radiation — 94

Unit 3 Dynamics and Space
13 Speed and acceleration — 106
14 Relationship between forces, motion and energy — 118
15 Satellites — 128
16 Cosmology — 135

National 4 Added Value Unit — 142

Rearranging physics equations — 145

Data sheet — 146

Relationship sheet — 147

Key areas for National 4 Physics — 148

Index — 151

Answers — 153

Introduction

This book is designed to act as a valuable resource for pupils studying SQA National 4 Physics. It provides a core text that adheres closely to the SQA specification. Each unit of the book matches a mandatory unit of the syllabus. Each chapter corresponds to a number of mandatory course key areas. In addition to the core text, the book contains a variety of special features: a list of the knowledge and understanding covered in each chapter, investigations, worked examples, physics in action, key facts and physics equations and end of chapter questions.

Each unit ends with a set of exam practice questions to foster the development of the mandatory subject skills outlined in the course arrangements. The questions are designed to prepare students for National 4 assessment, where they will be expected to demonstrate their ability to solve problems, select relevant information, present information, process data, plan experimental procedure, evaluate experimental design, draw valid conclusions and make predictions and generalisations.

Unit 1

Electricity and Energy

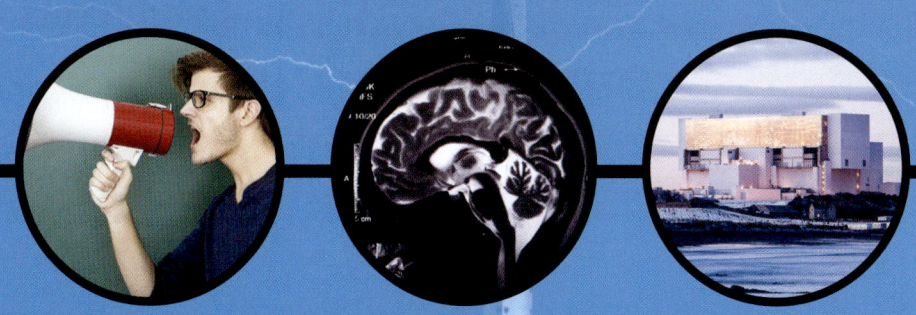

Electricity and Energy Unit 1

 Electrical circuits

Learning outcomes

At the end of this chapter you should be able to:
1. Draw and identify the circuit symbols for a battery, lamp, switch and fuse.
2. State that a battery is a source of electrical energy.
3. Describe a series circuit.
4. State that current is a flow of charge.
5. State that an ammeter is used to measure current.
6. Draw and identify the circuit symbol for an ammeter.
7. Draw a circuit diagram showing the correct position of an ammeter in the circuit.
8. State that in a series circuit, the current is the same at all points.
9. Describe a parallel circuit.
10. State that the sum of currents in parallel branches is equal to the current drawn from the supply.
11. State that voltage is a measure of the energy transferred by a charge.
12. State that a voltmeter is used to measure voltage.
13. Draw and identify the circuit symbol for a voltmeter.
14. Draw a circuit diagram showing the correct position of a voltmeter in a circuit.
15. State that the sum of the voltages across components in series is equal to the voltage of the supply.
16. State that the voltages across two components in parallel are the same for both components.
17. State practical applications of series and parallel circuits.

What is electricity?

Electricity is a form of energy associated with stationary or moving charges in a material.

Electric current

Consider a lamp connected by wires to a battery.

Figure 1.1 A simple electrical circuit

The lamp lights. This is due to negative charges called electrons from the negative terminal of the battery moving through the wires and lamp to the positive terminal of the battery. This movement, or flow, of negative charges is called an **electric current** (or current for short). A current is a movement of electrons. Current is usually given the symbol I. As the electrons move through the lamp, electrical energy is changed into heat and light.

Conductors and insulators

Negative charges (electrons) can only move from the negative terminal to the positive terminal of a battery if there is an electrical path between the terminals. Materials that allow electrons to move through them easily to produce an electric current are known as **conductors**. Materials that do not allow electrons to move through them easily are called **insulators**.

Electrical circuits

> **Investigation**
>
> Set up the circuit shown in Figure 1.2. Place different materials, for example copper, an iron nail, paper, wood, etc., in the gap to test whether the material conducts electricity and allows the lamp to light. Make a table of your results using the headings 'conductors' and 'insulators'.
>
>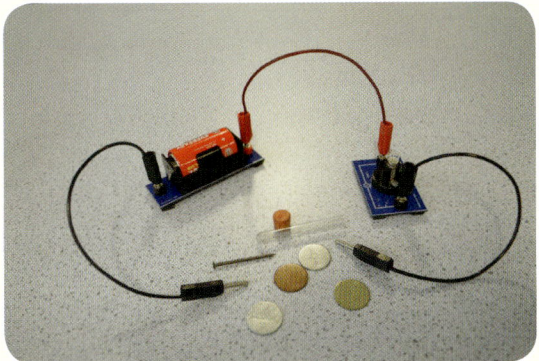
>
> **Figure 1.2** A circuit to test for conductors and insulators

Conductors are mainly metals, such as copper, gold and silver.

Glass, plastic, wood and air are examples of insulators.

Circuit symbols

So that items or **components** such as a battery, a switch, a lamp and some wires (conductors) are easily recognised when drawn in a diagram, circuit symbols are used. The circuit symbols for a battery, switch and lamp are shown in Figure 1.3. Figure 1.4 shows the circuit diagram for a lamp and a switch connected by wires to a battery.

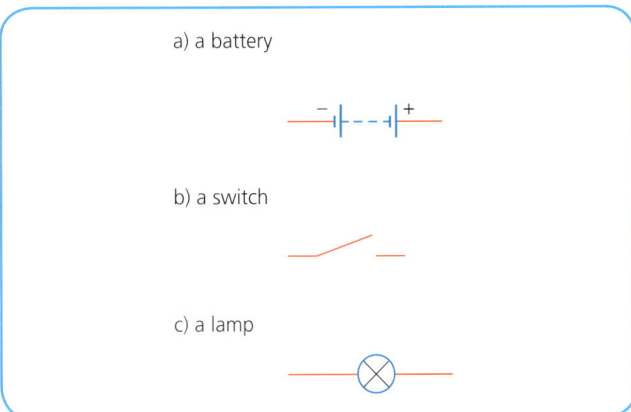

Figure 1.3 Some circuit symbols

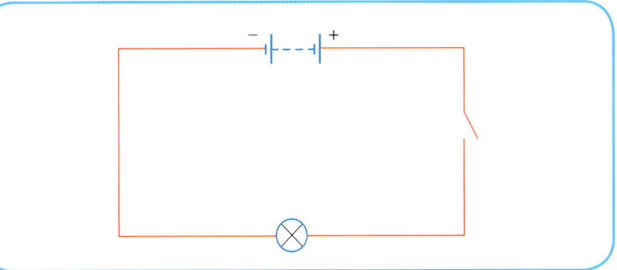

Figure 1.4

The lamp will only light when:
- there is a source of electrical energy – a battery or power supply is connected
- there is a complete electrical path (when the switch is closed and all the wires are connected) for the electrons to move around the circuit.

Types of circuit

Electrical components, such as lamps, can be connected in **series** or in **parallel**.

Figure 1.5 shows three lamps connected in series.

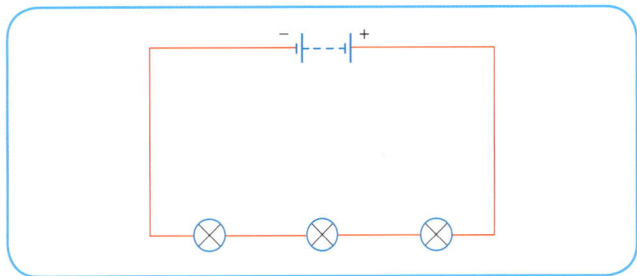

Figure 1.5 A series circuit

Notice that there is only **one** electrical path from the negative terminal to the positive terminal of the battery.

Figure 1.6 shows three lamps connected in parallel.

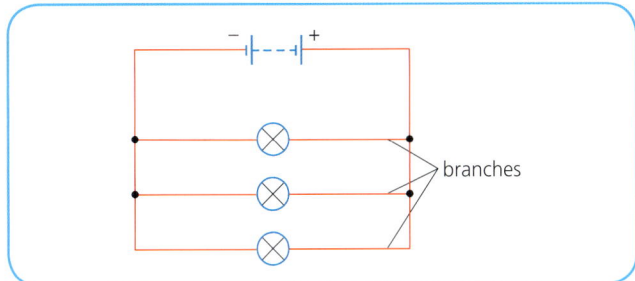

Figure 1.6 A parallel circuit

Notice that there is **more than one** electrical path from the negative terminal to the positive terminal of the battery. These alternative paths are called **branches**.

3

Electricity and Energy

Unit 1

Measuring current

An electric current is a flow of charge (negative charges called electrons). Electric current is measured in amperes, often shortened to amps (A). An **ammeter** is used to measure electric current. The circuit symbol for an ammeter is shown in Figure 1.7. Figure 1.8 shows how an ammeter is connected to an electrical circuit.

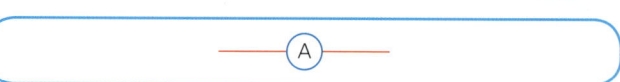

Figure 1.7 Circuit symbol for an ammeter

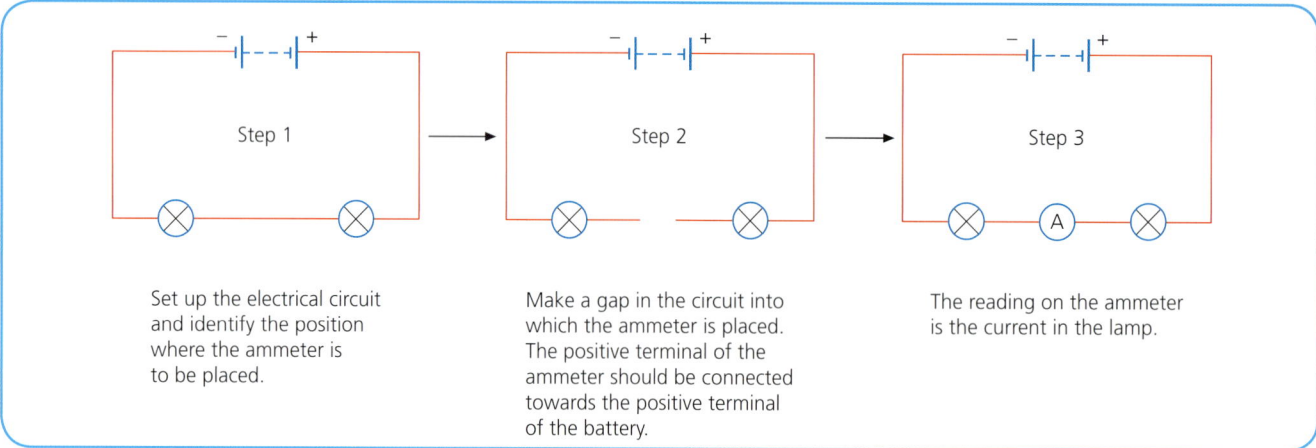

Step 1: Set up the electrical circuit and identify the position where the ammeter is to be placed.

Step 2: Make a gap in the circuit into which the ammeter is placed. The positive terminal of the ammeter should be connected towards the positive terminal of the battery.

Step 3: The reading on the ammeter is the current in the lamp.

Figure 1.8 Connecting an ammeter in an electrical circuit

Note: An ammeter measures the current *in* a component.

Measuring current in a series circuit

Investigation

Set up a circuit with three lamps connected in series as shown in Figure 1.9.

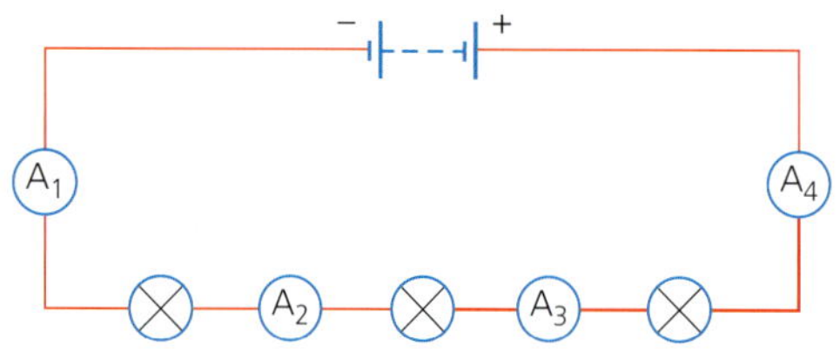

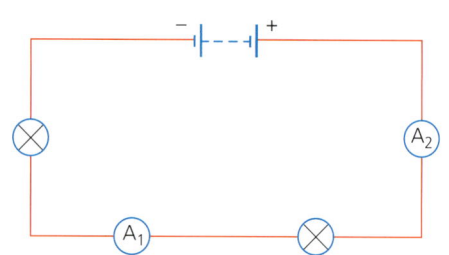

Figure 1.9 Measuring current in a series circuit

Place an ammeter in the circuit, using the instructions in Figure 1.8, to measure the current at position A_1.

Repeat for positions A_2, A_3 and A_4.

What do you notice about the readings recorded at A_1, A_2, A_3 and A_4?

For a series circuit the current is the same at all points. (You do not lose current in any type of circuit.)

Worked example

Example

Two lamps are connected in an electrical circuit as shown in Figure 1.10.

Figure 1.10

a) Are the lamps connected in series or in parallel?
b) The reading on ammeter A_1 is 0.15 A. What is the reading on ammeter A_2?

Solution

a) Series (as only one electrical path)
b) A_2 = 0.15 A (since the lamps are connected in series, the current is the same at all points)

Electrical circuits

A parallel circuit

> **Investigation**
>
> Set up a circuit with two lamps connected in parallel as shown in Figure 1.11.
>
>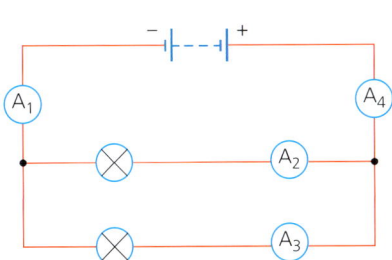
>
> **Figure 1.11** Measuring current in a parallel circuit
>
> Place an ammeter in the circuit, using the instructions in Figure 1.8, to measure the current at position A_1.
> Repeat for positions A_2, A_3 and A_4.
> What do you notice about the readings recorded at A_1, A_2, A_3 and A_4?
> If you add together the reading on A_2 and the reading on A_3, what is the answer the same as?

Circuit current = current in the branches added up.
This is true for any parallel circuit.

Voltage

In Figure 1.1 a lamp is connected to a battery. In this electrical circuit, the battery changes chemical energy (from the substances inside it) into electrical energy. This electrical energy is carried by the charges (electrons) that move round the circuit and is given up as heat and light as they pass through the wire (filament) of the lamp. The voltage of the battery is a measure of the electrical energy given to the negative charges passing through the battery.

Measuring voltage

Voltage is measured in volts (V). Voltage is usually given the symbol V. A **voltmeter** is used to measure voltage. The circuit symbol for a voltmeter is shown in Figure 1.13.

Figure 1.13 Circuit symbol for a voltmeter

Figure 1.14 (on page 6) shows how a voltmeter is connected to an electrical circuit.

Note: A voltmeter measures the voltage *across* a component. Voltage gives us an idea of how much energy is transferred by the charge passing through the component. A bigger voltage means that the charge transfers more energy.

Worked example

Example

Three lamps are connected in parallel as shown in Figure 1.12.
What are the readings on ammeters A_1 and A_2?

Solution

$A_1 = A_5 = 0.6$ A (both ammeters measure the main circuit current)
$A_1 = A_2 + A_3 + A_4$ (since lamps are connected in parallel)
$0.6 = A_2 + 0.2 + 0.2$
$A_2 = 0.2$ A

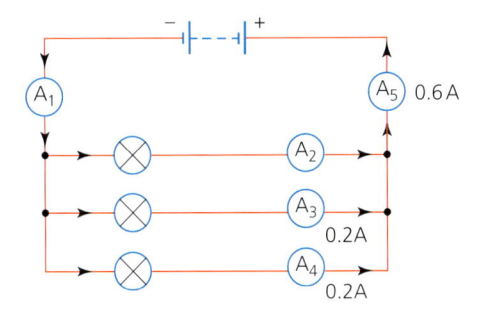

Figure 1.12

Electricity and Energy

Unit 1

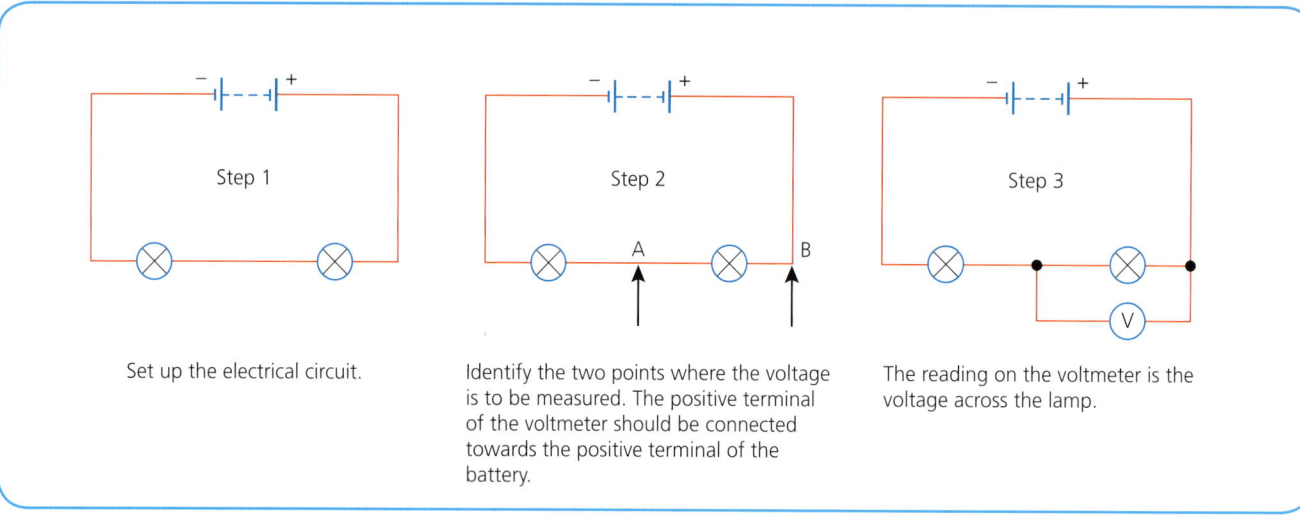

Figure 1.14 Connecting a voltmeter in an electrical circuit

Voltage in a series circuit

Investigation

Set up a circuit with three identical lamps connected in series as shown in Figure 1.15.

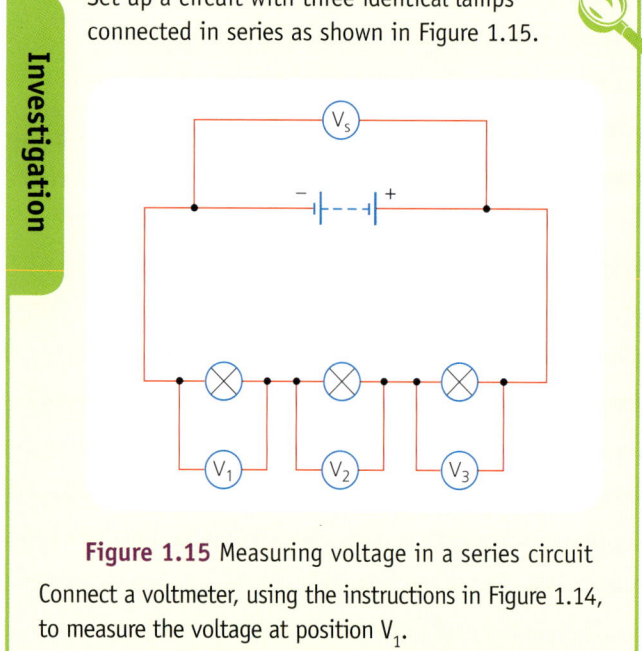

Figure 1.15 Measuring voltage in a series circuit

Connect a voltmeter, using the instructions in Figure 1.14, to measure the voltage at position V_1.

Repeat for positions V_2, V_3 and V_S (the supply voltage). What do you notice about the readings recorded at V_1, V_2, V_3 and V_S?

The supply voltage is equal to the sum of the voltages round the circuit. This is true for any series circuit.

Worked example

Example

Three identical Christmas tree lamps are connected in series to a 9 volt battery.

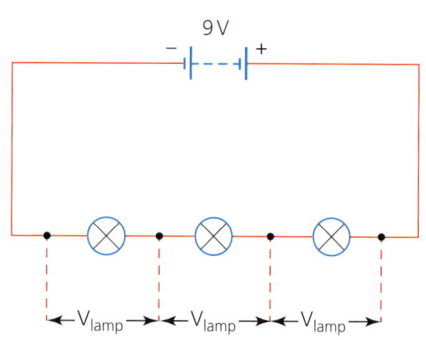

Figure 1.16

What is the voltage across each lamp?

Solution

Since the lamps are connected in series and are identical, the supply voltage is split up equally between the three lamps:

$V_{supply} = V_1 + V_2 + V_3$

$V_{supply} = V_{lamp} + V_{lamp} + V_{lamp}$

$9 = 3 \times V_{lamp}$

$V_{lamp} = \dfrac{9}{3} = 3\,V$

Electrical circuits

Voltage in a parallel circuit

Investigation

Set up a circuit with two lamps connected in parallel as shown in Figure 1.17.

Connect a voltmeter, using the instructions in Figure 1.14, to measure the voltage at position V_1. Repeat for positions V_2 and V_S (the supply voltage).

What do you notice about the readings recorded at V_1, V_2 and V_S?

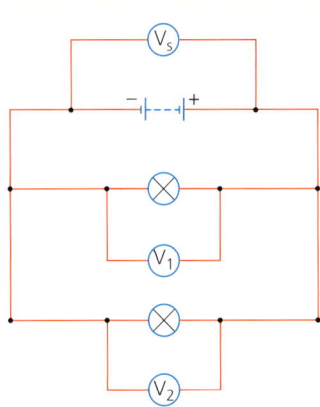

Figure 1.17 Measuring voltage in a parallel circuit

Voltages across parallel branches are the same. This is true for any parallel circuit.

Worked examples

Example 1

Three identical lamps are connected to a 12 volt supply as shown in Figure 1.18.

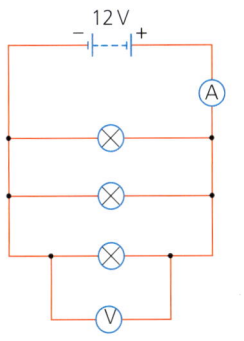

Figure 1.18

a) Are the lamps connected in series or parallel?
b) The current in each lamp is 1.5 A. Calculate the reading on the ammeter.
c) State the value of the reading on the voltmeter.

Solution

a) Parallel (since more than one path)
b) Reading on ammeter = 1.5 + 1.5 + 1.5 = 4.5 A (since current in main part of circuit = current in branches added up)
c) 12 V (since voltages across parallel branches are the same)

Example 2

Three non-identical lamps, P, Q and R, are connected to a 4.5 volt supply as shown in Figure 1.19.

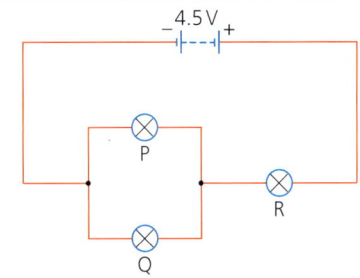

Figure 1.19

The voltage across lamp P is 1.5 V.

a) Are lamps P and Q connected in series or parallel?
b) Is lamp R connected in series or parallel?
c) What is the voltage across lamp Q?
d) What is the voltage across lamp R?

Solution

a) Parallel (since more than one path between P and Q)
b) Series (since only one path in this part of the circuit)
c) P and Q are connected in parallel, so they have the same voltage across them. Voltage across Q = 1.5 V
d) Voltage across R is 3 V, since voltages in a series circuit add up.

7

Electricity and Energy

A practical series circuit – a hedge trimmer

Figure 1.20 shows how a hedge trimmer is wired.

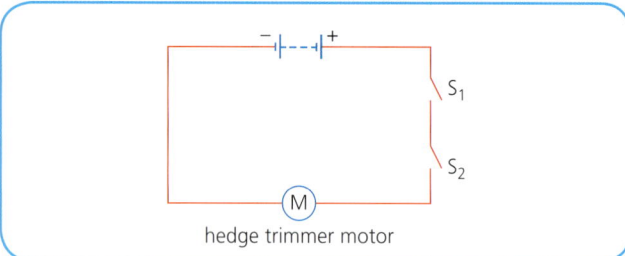

Figure 1.20 Circuit diagram for the wiring of a hedge trimmer

Only when switches S_1 and S_2 are both closed will the motor operate. The hedge trimmer has two switches connected in series so that:

- the person using the hedge trimmer has to use both hands to close each switch (one hand for each switch)
- the person's fingers are always kept safely away from the moving hedge trimmer blades.

A practical parallel circuit – car wiring

Figure 1.21 shows how the sidelights and headlights in a car are wired.

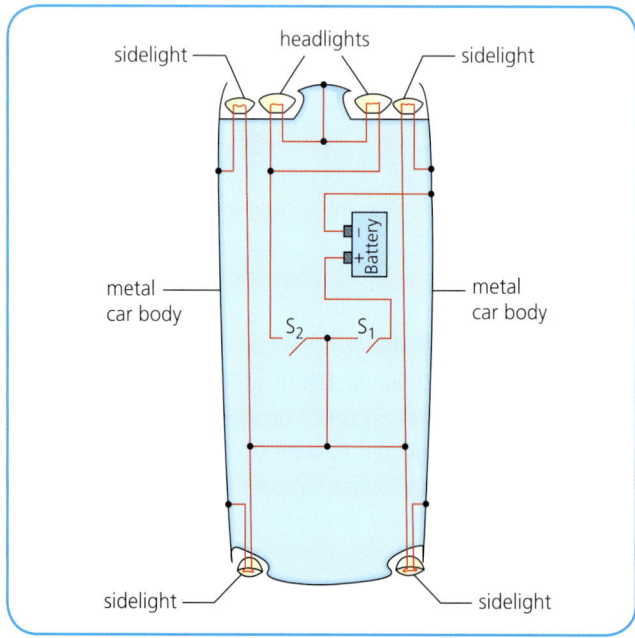

Figure 1.21 Circuit diagram for the wiring of the lights in a car

When S_1 is closed the sidelights come on. When S_1 and S_2 are both closed, the headlights and the sidelights are both on.

The lights are wired in parallel so that:

- all lamps have the same voltage
- if one lamp breaks then the others continue to light.

Fuse

A fuse is used in practical electrical circuits to protect the cables (wires) from overheating. The fuse will melt and break the electrical circuit if the current becomes too high. The circuit symbol for a fuse is shown in Figure 1.22.

Figure 1.22

Power supplies

Sometimes we use a power supply instead of a battery as a source of electrical energy.

A d.c. power supply is similar to a battery. Figure 1.23 shows the symbol for a d.c. power supply. As with a battery, charges (electrons) flow from the negative terminal to the positive terminal when the circuit is complete.

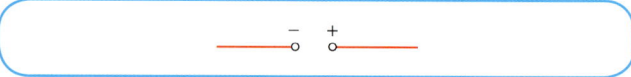

Figure 1.23 Circuit symbol for a d.c. power supply

An a.c. power supply is an alternating supply. This means that the voltage changes from positive to negative and back again. In a complete circuit this means that charges (electrons) flow clockwise, then anticlockwise, then clockwise again and so on round the circuit. Figure 1.24 shows the symbol for an a.c. power supply.

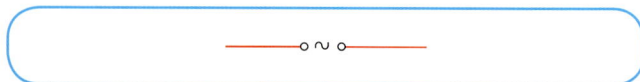

Figure 1.24 Circuit symbol for an a.c. power supply

Figure 1.25 shows two alternative circuit symbols for a variable (voltage) d.c. power supply.

Figure 1.25 Circuit symbols for a variable d.c. power supply

> ### Physics in action
>
> #### What is an electric shock?
> If a voltage is applied to your body, there will be a current in your body. This current can override the tiny electrical signals that make the nerves and muscles work correctly. The current can also cause burning. The bigger the current and the longer there is a current in your body, the greater the damage to your body, especially your heart.

Key facts and physics equations: electrical circuits

- Current is a flow of charge. Current is measured in amperes (A) using an ammeter. An ammeter is connected in series with an electrical component, such as a lamp, to measure the current *in* the component.
- Voltage is measured in volts (V) using a voltmeter. A voltmeter is connected in parallel with an electrical component, such as a lamp, to measure the voltage *across* the component.
- In the series circuit shown in Figure 1.26:
  - the current is the same at all positions – the current does not split up, so $I_1 = I_2 = I_3 = I_4$
  - the supply voltage is equal to the sum of the voltages around the circuit, so $V_S = V_1 + V_2 + V_3$

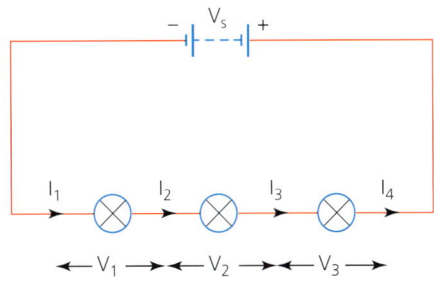

Figure 1.26 A series circuit

- For the parallel circuit shown in Figure 1.27:
  - the current splits up – the circuit current is equal to the sum of the currents in the branches, so $I = I_1 + I_2$
  - the voltage across lamps connected in parallel is the same, so $V_1 = V_2$ and in this case $V_S = V_1 = V_2$.

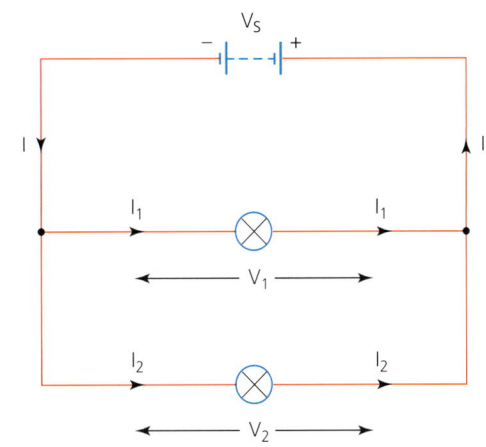

Figure 1.27 A parallel circuit

Electrical circuits

9

Electricity and Energy

Unit 1

End-of-chapter questions

1. Name the components shown in Figure 1.28.

   a)    d)

   b)    e)

   c)    f)

   Figure 1.28

2. In the following sentences the words represented by the letters A, B, C, D, E, F and G are missing.
   A battery is connected to a lamp. The battery is a ___A___ of electrical energy. Negative charges, called ___B___, move from the negative terminal to the ___C___ terminal of the battery. This movement of charge is called a ___D___. Current is measured in ___E___. The electrical energy of the battery is converted into ___F___ and ___G___ by the lamp.
   Match each letter with the correct word below.
   amperes, current, electrons, heat, positive, light, source

3. In the following sentences the words represented by the letters A, B, C, D, E and F are missing.
   When electrical components are connected in series there is ___A___ electrical path. In a ___B___ circuit there is more than one electrical path – the alternative paths are called ___C___. An ammeter is used to measure ___D___ and is connected in ___E___. A ___F___ is used to measure voltage and is connected in parallel.
   Match each letter with the correct word below.
   branches, current, one, parallel, voltmeter, series

4. For each circuit shown in Figure 1.29, state whether the lamps are connected in series or parallel.

a)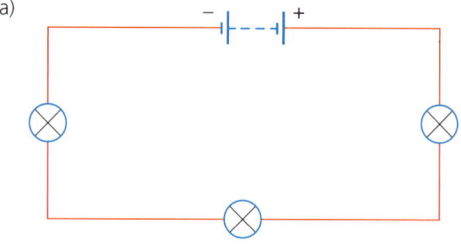

b)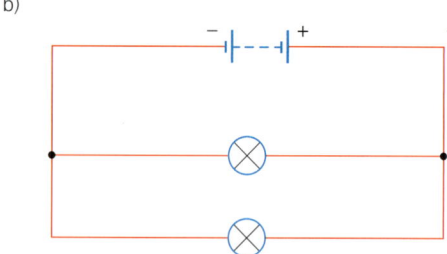

c)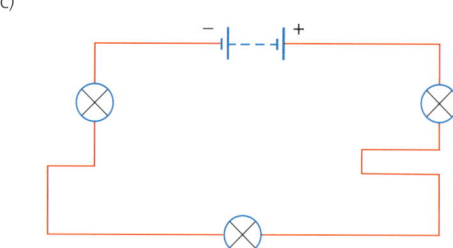

d)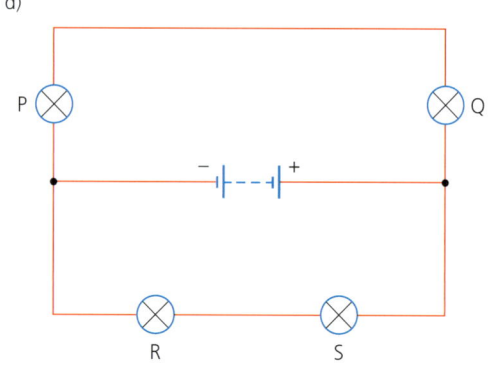

Figure 1.29

5 A student draws the circuit shown in Figure 1.30.

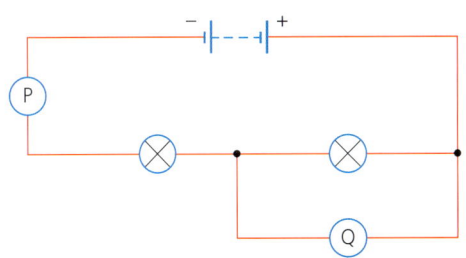

Figure 1.30

Name the type of meter labelled a) P and b) Q.

6 Redraw each of the diagrams in Figure 1.31 to show how:
   a) an ammeter is connected to measure the current in lamp Y
   b) a voltmeter is connected to measure the voltage across lamp Z.

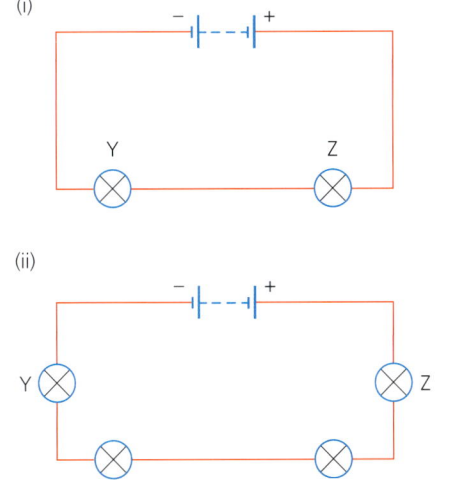

Figure 1.31

7 In the circuits shown in Figure 1.32, what are the readings displayed on ammeters:
   a) A_1, A_2, A_3
   b) A_4, A_5 and A_6?

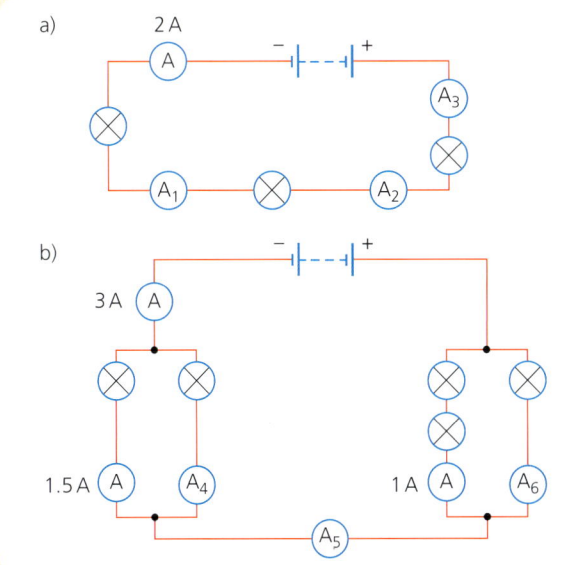

Figure 1.32

8 In the circuit shown in Figure 1.33, what is the reading displayed on voltmeter V_1?

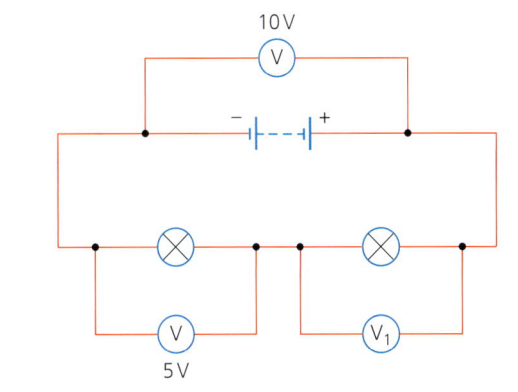

Figure 1.33

Electricity and Energy

9 In the circuits shown in Figure 1.34, what are the readings displayed on:
   a) ammeters A_1 and A_2
   b) voltmeters V_1 and V_2?

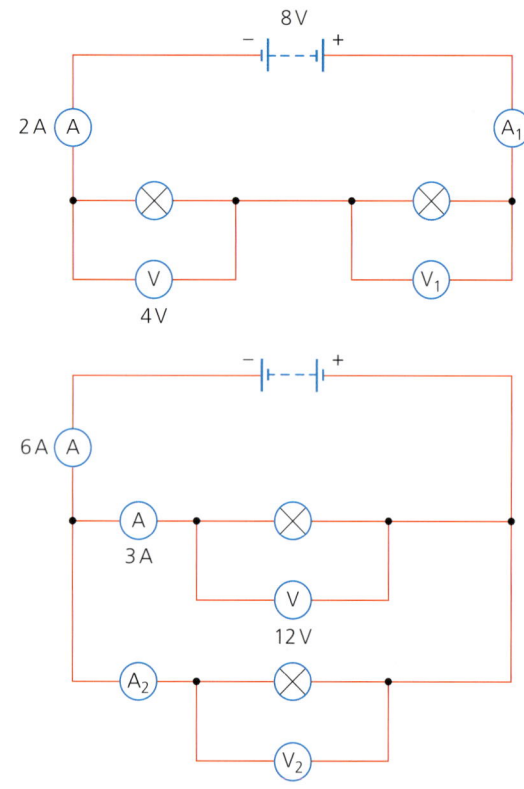

Figure 1.34

10 Draw the circuit symbol for: a) a switch, b) a lamp, c) an ammeter, d) a battery, e) a voltmeter, f) a fuse.

Resistance

Learning outcomes

At the end of this chapter you should be able to:
1. State that resistance is a measure of the opposition a circuit component has to current.
2. State that an increase in the resistance of a circuit leads to a decrease in the current in the circuit.
3. State that resistance is measured in ohms (Ω).
4. State that a resistor converts electrical energy into heat.
5. Draw and identify the circuit symbol for a resistor and a variable resistor.
6. Give two practical uses of a variable resistor.
7. State that an ohmmeter is used to measure resistance.
8. Describe how to use an ohmmeter to measure the resistance of a component.
9. Carry out calculations involving the relationship between current, voltage and resistance.
10. Carry out calculations involving resistors connected in series.
11. State that lamps, heaters and motors convert electrical energy into other forms of energy.

Investigation

Set up the circuit shown in Figure 2.1.

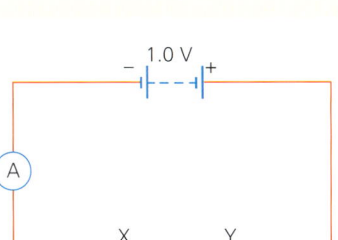

Figure 2.1 Measuring the current in different values of resistor

Place resistors with different values (from 1 ohm to 10 ohms) between points X and Y. Switch the power on **for no more than 10 seconds** (otherwise the resistor will overheat!). Take the reading on the ammeter, and then switch off.

Repeat for different values of resistor. Draw up a table of your results.

Draw a graph of current against resistance.

Resistance

When an electric current passes through a wire, the moving electrons collide with the particles that make up the wire. These collisions impede the flow of charge in the circuit. This reduces the current in the circuit. The effect of the electron-particle collisions is called resistance. The resistance of a component is a measure of the opposition to current in the component.

The larger the resistance, the smaller the current.

The smaller the resistance, the larger the current.

Resistance is measured in ohms (Ω).

An **ohmmeter** can be used to measure resistance. The circuit symbol for an ohmmeter is shown in Figure 2.2.

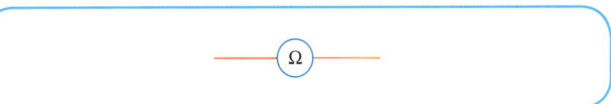

Figure 2.2 Circuit symbol for an ohmmeter

Electricity and Energy

Investigation

Use an ohmmeter to measure the resistance of a 10 cm length of wire. Repeat for 20, 30, 40, 50, 60, 70, 80, 90 and 100 cm lengths of the wire. Draw up a table of your results.

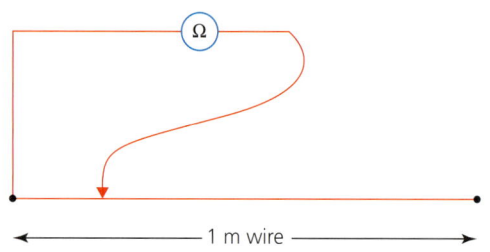

Figure 2.3 Using an ohmmeter to measure the resistance of different lengths of a wire

Draw a graph of resistance of wire against the length of wire.

For most materials, resistance depends on the:

- length of the piece of material – the longer the material, the higher the resistance
- thickness of the piece of material – the thinner the material, the higher the resistance
- type of material – the better the conductor, the lower the resistance (for example, copper is a better conductor than iron)
- temperature of the material – the higher the temperature, the higher the resistance.

For a particular resistor, the resistance value remains constant for different currents, provided the temperature of the resistor does not change.

Physics in action

The strain gauge

A strain gauge is used to measure the strain experienced by structures such as buildings, bridges and aircraft. The strain gauge consists of a very fine wire mounted on a backing sheet. The gauge is connected to the structure under test. As the shape of the structure changes, the wire is stretched. As the wire stretches, it gets longer and thinner – its resistance increases. By measuring the change in resistance, physicists can calculate the strain exerted in the structure.

A resistor (a circuit component just like a lamp or switch) is simply a piece of material that opposes current. A resistor with a resistance that can be changed is known as a **variable resistor**. The resistance is normally changed by altering the length of the wire in the resistor (the longer the wire, the higher the resistance). Variable resistors are often used as volume controls, for example on a radio. Another use for variable resistors is in dimmer switches for lights – the brightness of the lights is varied by changing the resistance.

The circuit symbols for a resistor and a variable resistor are shown in Figure 2.4.

Figure 2.4 Circuit symbols for a) a resistor and b) a variable resistor

Figure 2.5 shows an ohmmeter being used to measure the resistance of a resistor. When using an ohmmeter to measure the resistance of a component, there should be no current in the component.

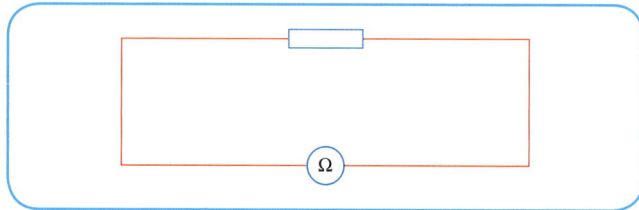

Figure 2.5 Measuring the resistance of a resistor using an ohmmeter

Resistance

Investigation

Copy the table shown below.

Resistor	Resistance (Ω)	Voltage across resistor (V)	Current in resistor (A)	V/I
P				
Q				
R				
S				

Use an ohmmeter to measure the resistance of a resistor P. Write the resistance of P in your table.

Repeat for resistors Q, R and S.

Set up the circuit shown in Figure 2.6.

Connect resistor P between points X and Y. Measure the voltage across P and the current in P. Complete the table for resistor P.

Repeat for resistors Q, R and S.

Complete the last column of the table by calculating the value of voltage divided by current (V/I) for each resistor.

What do you notice about the resistance of the resistor as measured by the ohmmeter in column 2 and the value of V/I in column 5?

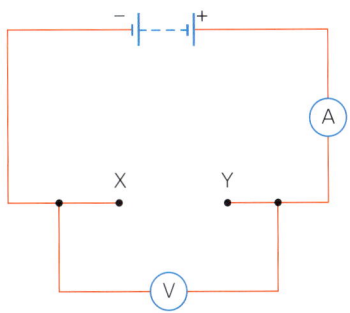

Figure 2.6 Measuring the current in a resistor and the voltage across a resistor

The resistance of a resistor can also be measured using an ammeter and a voltmeter as shown in Figure 2.7. In this method the voltage across the resistor and the current in the resistor have to be measured.

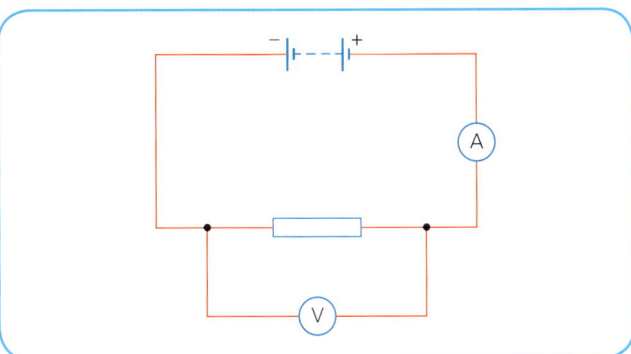

Figure 2.7 Measuring the resistance of a resistor using an ammeter and a voltmeter

The resistance of the resistor can then be calculated using:

$$\text{resistance of resistor} = \frac{\text{voltage across resistor}}{\text{current in resistor}}$$

i.e. $R = \dfrac{V}{I}$

This is known as **Ohm's law**. Ohm's law is normally written as:

$$\text{voltage across resistor} = \text{current in resistor} \times \text{resistance of resistor}$$

i.e. $V = IR$

Using the 'maths' triangle (see Rearranging physics equations on page 145) for Ohm's law gives:

$$V = I \times R \qquad I = \frac{V}{R} \qquad R = \frac{V}{I}$$

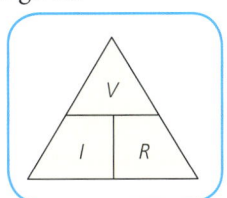

15

Electricity and Energy

Unit 1

Worked examples

Example 1
The current in a resistor is 0.15 A. The resistance of the resistor is 20 Ω. Calculate the voltage across the resistor.

Solution

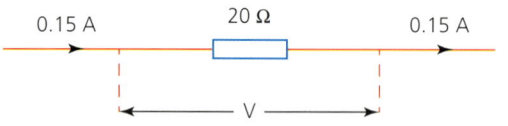

Figure 2.8

$V = IR = 0.15 \times 20 = 3$ V

Example 2
The voltage across a lamp is 12 V. The current in the lamp is 1.5 A. Calculate the resistance of the lamp.

Solution

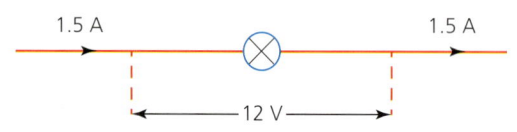

Figure 2.9

$V = IR$

$R = \dfrac{V}{I} = \dfrac{12}{1.5} = 8$ Ω

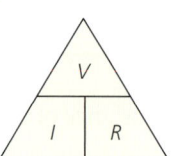

Example 3
The resistance of an electrical component is 30 Ω. The voltage across the component is 6.0 V. Calculate the current in the component.

Solution

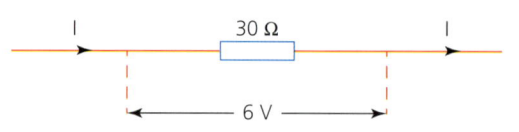

Figure 2.10

$V = IR$

$I = \dfrac{V}{R} = \dfrac{6}{30} = 0.2$ A

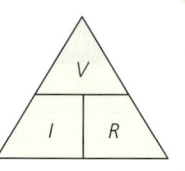

Example 4
A student sets up the circuit shown in Figure 2.11.

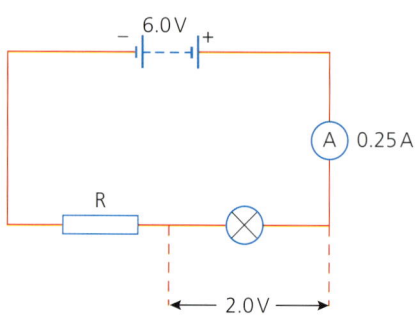

Figure 2.11

a) What is the current in resistor R?
b) What is the voltage across resistor R?
c) Calculate the resistance of resistor R.

Solution

a) 0.25 A (since this is a series circuit, the current is the same at all points)

b) 4 V (voltage in a series circuit splits up, i.e. $V_{supply} = V_R + V_{lamp}$)

c) $V = IR$

$R = \dfrac{V}{I} = \dfrac{4}{0.25} = 16$ Ω

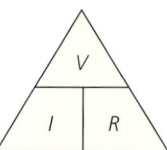

Resistance

Investigation

Use an ohmmeter to measure the resistance of a resistor R_1, as shown in Figure 2.12.

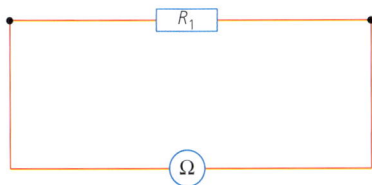

Figure 2.12

Use the ohmmeter to measure the resistances of two other resistors R_2 and R_3.

Now connect resistors R_1, R_2 and R_3 in series. Measure the total resistance R_T of the three resistors in series by connecting the ohmmeter between A and B as shown in Figure 2.13.

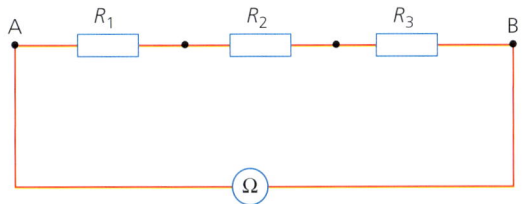

Figure 2.13

Record your results for R_1, R_2, R_3 and R_T in a table. What do you notice about the value of R_T and the values of R_1, R_2 and R_3?

The total resistance of a number of resistors connected in series is equal to the sum of the individual resistors i.e. $R_T = R_1 + R_2 + R_3 + \ldots$

Adding resistors in series increases the total resistance of the circuit and so the circuit current will decrease.

Worked example

Example

Three resistors are connected as shown in Figure 2.14. Calculate the resistance between X and Y.

Figure 2.14

Solution

$R_{XY} = R_1 + R_2 + R_3 = 10 + 8 + 15 = 33\ \Omega$

Energy conversions

When there is an electric current in a resistor, some of the electrical energy is changed into heat in the resistor (wire). There are a number of electrical devices, or appliances, in our homes that use this energy change. For example, the heating element in a kettle changes electrical energy into heat in the wire inside the element. Other electrical appliances change electrical energy into a form that is useful for what we are doing and in many cases into other forms of energy that are not so useful. For instance, a lamp changes electrical energy into heat and light. The most useful, and main, energy change for a lamp is the change of electrical energy into light.

Some other examples of the main energy change for household appliances are:

- The heater element (resistor) in a toaster changes electrical energy into heat.
- A lamp changes electrical energy into light.
- The motor in a washing machine changes electrical energy into kinetic (movement) energy.
- A radio changes electrical energy into sound.

Key facts and physics equations: resistance

- A variable resistor is a resistor with a resistance that can be changed.
- Variable resistors are used as volume controls on radios. They are also used in dimmer switches, where the variable resistor is used to alter the brightness of a light.
- The resistance of a resistor can be measured using an ohmmeter.
- Voltage across resistor = current in resistor × resistance of resistor
  i.e. $V = IR$
- Voltage is measured in volts (V), current in amperes (A) and resistance in ohms (Ω).
- In a series circuit the total resistance (R_T) is found using $R_T = R_1 + R_2 + R_3 + \ldots$
- In a resistor, electrical energy is changed into heat.

Electricity and Energy

End-of-chapter questions

1 Name the components shown in Figure 2.12.

Figure 2.15

2 State two practical uses of a variable resistor.

3 In the following sentences the words represented by the letters A, B, C, D, E and F are missing.
The opposition to current is called ___A___.
Resistance can be measured using an ___B___ and is measured in ___C___. Increasing the resistance of a circuit ___D___ the current in the circuit. When there is a current in a resistor, ___E___ energy is changed into ___F___.
Match each letter with the correct word below.
decreases, electrical, heat, ohmmeter, ohms, resistance

4 In the table shown, calculate the value of each missing quantity.

Voltage (V)	Current (A)	Resistance (Ω)
a)	2	115
b)	0.05	100
10	c)	4
5	d)	50
10	2	e)
12	4	f)

5 There is a current of 1.5 A in a 5.0 Ω resistor. Calculate the voltage across the resistor.

6 A 1.5-volt battery is connected to a torch lamp. The resistance of the lamp, when lit, is 7.5 Ω. Calculate the current in the lamp.

7 A lamp is connected to a 12-volt supply. When lit, the current in the lamp is 2.0. A. Calculate the resistance of the lamp.

8 An electrical circuit is shown in Figure 2.16.

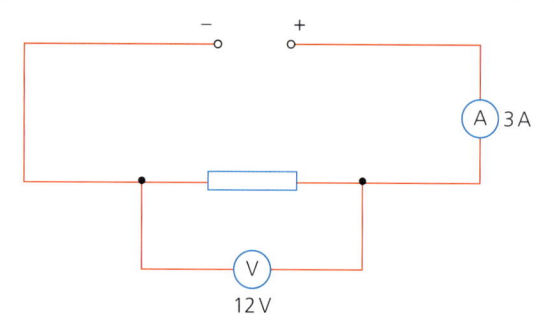

Figure 2.16

Calculate the resistance of the resistor.

9 Two electrical circuits, circuit A and circuit B, are shown in Figure 2.17.

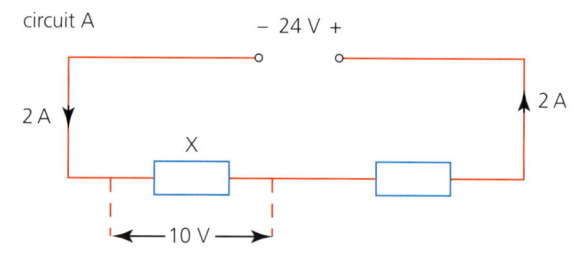

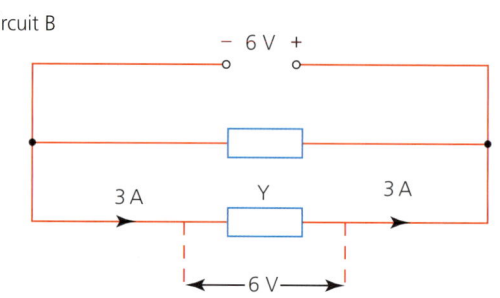

Figure 2.17

a) Which circuit shows the electrical components connected in series?
b) Calculate the resistance of resistor X.
c) Calculate the resistance of resistor Y.

10 The element of a cooker is connected to the 230 V mains supply. The element has a resistance of 46 Ω.
   a) Calculate the current in the cooker element.
   b) State the energy change for the cooker element.
11 Two resistors of value 33 Ω and 82 Ω are connected in series. Calculate the total resistance of the circuit.
12 Three resistors of value 10 Ω, 15 Ω and 30 Ω are connected in series. Calculate the total resistance of the circuit.
13 Name three electrical appliances in the home that change electrical energy into heat.
14 Draw the circuit symbol for: a) a switch, b) a lamp, c) an ammeter, d) a resistor, e) a voltmeter, f) a variable resistor.
15 The graph in Figure 2.18 shows how the voltage, V, across a resistor varies with the current, I, in the resistor.
   a) Draw a circuit that could be used to obtain the information shown in the graph.
   b) Use the graph to find the resistance of the resistor.

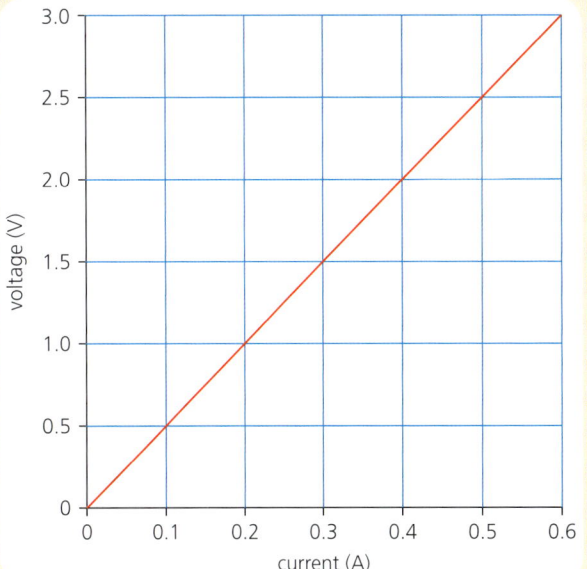

Figure 2.18

Electricity and Energy

Unit 1

3 Electrical systems and components

Learning outcomes

At the end of this chapter you should be able to:
1. State that an electronic system consists of three parts: input, process and output.
2. Distinguish between digital and analogue signals.
3. Identify analogue and digital signals from waveforms viewed on an oscilloscope.
4. Describe the energy transformations involved in the following input devices: microphone, solar cell.
5. Identify from a list an appropriate input device for a given application.
6. State that the resistance of a thermistor changes with temperature and the resistance of an LDR decreases with increasing light intensity (brightness).
7. Carry out calculations using V = IR for the thermistor and the LDR.
8. State that an output device changes electrical energy into another form of energy.
9. Identify from a list an appropriate output device for a given application.
10. Draw and identify the symbol for an LED.
11. State that an LED will light only if connected one way round in a circuit.
12. Explain the need for a series resistor with an LED.
13. State that different numbers can be produced by lighting appropriate segments of a seven-segment display.
14. Give examples of digital output devices and analogue output devices.

Figure 3.1 A person using a loudhailer

A simplified view of a loudhailer system would be:

- sound waves are changed into weak electrical signals
- the weak electrical signals are then made bigger by a processing device
- the larger electrical signals are then converted into sound.

Notice that it is convenient to break the loudhailer system into three parts:

1. the microphone that picks up the sound waves and converts them into weak electrical signals – known as the **input**
2. the processing device that boosts the weak electrical signals – known as the **process**
3. the loudspeaker that converts the electrical signals to sound – known as the **output**.

In fact, all electronic systems can be broken into these three parts – input, process and output. The input section starts the system working, the process section alters the input so as to produce the required output and the output section gives the desired result.

Since all electronic systems use electrical signals, devices are required to convert one form of energy (for example, light, heat, sound, etc.) into electrical energy at the input stage and to do the opposite at the output stage. For example, a microphone converts sound into electrical energy and a loudspeaker converts electrical energy into sound.

An electronic system may be drawn as a **block diagram** (see Figure 3.2). The arrows show how information is passed (electrically) from one block to another.

Electrical systems

Electronics is the area of physics that deals with the control of electrons in an electrical circuit or electrical system. It usually involves the use of processing devices or electrical components.

An **electrical system** is a collection of electrical components connected together to perform a particular function, for example a loudhailer.

Electrical systems and components

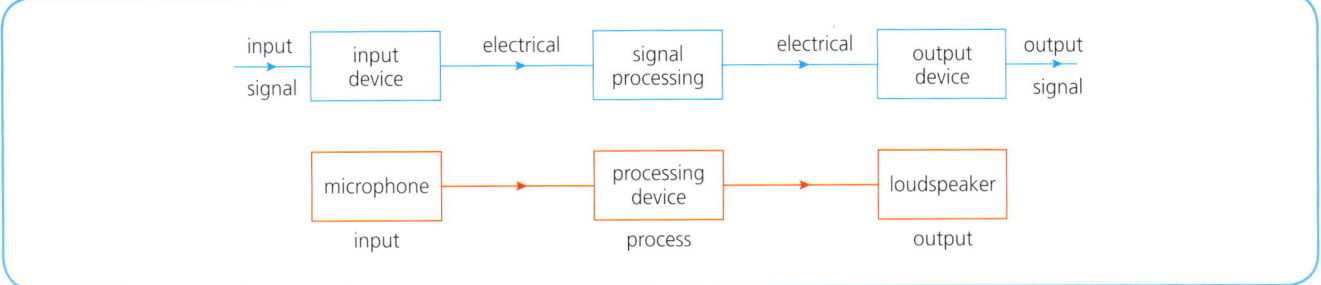

Figure 3.2 Block diagram for a loudhailer

Analogue signals and digital signals

The signals used by electronic systems are of two types: **analogue** or **digital**. Figure 3.3 shows the traces displayed on an oscilloscope screen with an analogue signal and a digital signal.

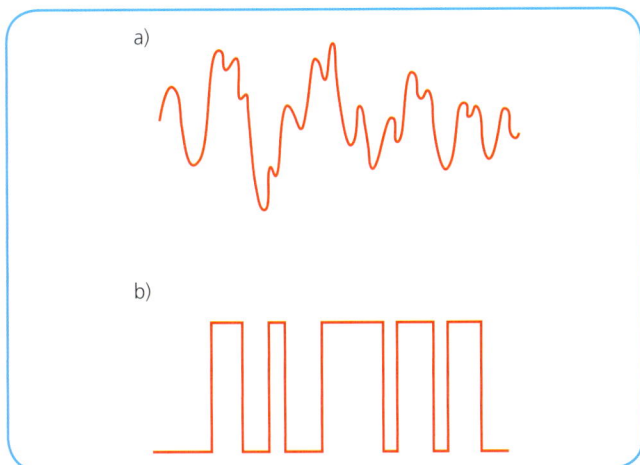

Figure 3.3 a) An analogue signal; b) a digital signal

Figure 3.3a) shows a typical electrical signal from the microphone of a telephone when a person is speaking. The trace has a continuous range of values. This type of signal is called an analogue signal. Most input devices produce analogue signals.

Figure 3.3b) shows a typical electrical signal from a CD player. The trace has a series of electrical pulses, each with the same amplitude (height of signal). This type of signal is called a digital signal. In a digital signal the trace is either at a maximum value (called a **high** or **logic '1'**) or a minimum value (called a **low** or **logic '0'**).

An analogue signal has a continuous range of values. A digital signal can have only one of two possible values.

Many electrical systems consist of both digital and analogue signals. An analogue signal produced by an input device may be converted into a digital signal in the process unit. For example, many telephone systems change the human voice (an analogue signal) into a digital signal, which can be transmitted over long distances, and then back into an analogue signal (sound) that can be heard.

Input devices

There are a number of input devices available for different applications. Most input devices change some form of energy into electrical energy or produce a change in an electrical signal.

The microphone

> **Investigation**
>
> Connect a microphone to an oscilloscope as shown in Figure 3.4. Whistle a quiet note and then a louder note into the microphone. Look at the trace obtained on the oscilloscope screen in each case.
>
>
>
> Figure 3.4 A microphone connected to an oscilloscope
>
> What is the energy change that takes place in the microphone?

21

Electricity and Energy

A microphone can be connected to an oscilloscope. As louder notes are played into the microphone, the trace on the oscilloscope increases in amplitude.

A **microphone** is an input device that changes sound into electrical energy. The louder the sound, the greater the electrical energy produced.

The solar cell

Connect a solar cell to a voltmeter as shown in Figure 3.5. Cover the solar cell with your hand and then place the solar cell in bright light. Look at the reading on the voltmeter in each case.

Figure 3.5 A solar cell connected to a voltmeter

What is the energy change that takes place in the solar cell?

A solar cell can be connected to a voltmeter. When the solar cell is exposed to more light, the reading on the voltmeter increases.

A **solar cell** is an input device that changes light into electrical energy. The brighter the light shining on the solar cell, the greater the electrical energy produced.

The thermistor

Connect a thermistor to an ohmmeter as shown in Figure 3.6. Place the thermistor in a beaker of cold water and then in warm water. Look at the reading on the ohmmeter in each case.

Figure 3.6 A thermistor connected to an ohmmeter

A thermistor can be connected to an ohmmeter. When the thermistor is heated, the reading on the ohmmeter decreases.

A **thermistor** is an input device. When the temperature of a thermistor increases, the resistance of the thermistor decreases.

Worked example

Example

A circuit is set up as shown in Figure 3.7.

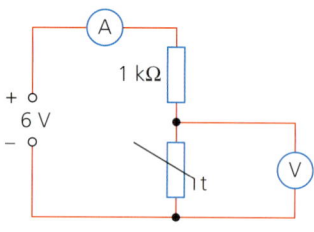

Figure 3.7

The thermistor is at a temperature of 20 °C. The reading on the voltmeter is 2.0 V. The reading on the ammeter is 0.004 A.

a) Calculate the resistance of the thermistor at 20 °C.
b) The temperature of the thermistor is increased to 30 °C.
  (i) State a possible value for the reading now displayed on the ammeter.
  (ii) Justify your choice for the reading on the ammeter.

Solution

a) $V_{thermistor} = (IR)_{thermistor}$

$R_{thermistor} = \dfrac{V}{I} = \dfrac{2}{0.004} = 500\ \Omega$

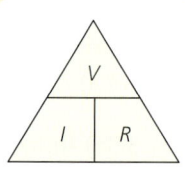

b) (i) 0.005 A (any value greater than 0.004 A)
  (ii) As the temperature of the thermistor has increased, the resistance of the thermistor must have decreased. The total resistance of the circuit will be less. Since there is less opposition to the current, the current in the circuit will increase.

Electrical systems and components

The light-dependent resistor (LDR)

> **Investigation**
>
> Connect a light-dependent resistor (LDR) to an ohmmeter as shown in Figure 3.8. Cover the LDR with your hand and then place the LDR in bright light. Look at the reading on the ohmmeter in each case. 
>
> **Figure 3.8** An LDR connected to an ohmmeter

A light-dependent resistor can be connected to an ohmmeter. When the light-dependent resistor is exposed to more light, the reading on the ohmmeter decreases.

A **light-dependent resistor (LDR)** is an input device. As the light gets brighter (light intensity increases), the resistance of the LDR decreases.

> **Worked example**
>
> ### Example
> A circuit is set up as shown in Figure 3.9.
>
>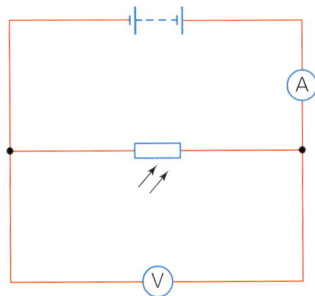
>
> **Figure 3.9**
>
> Light is shone on the LDR. The reading on the voltmeter is 2.5 V. The reading on the ammeter is 0.002 A. Calculate the resistance of the LDR at this light level.
>
> #### Solution
>
> $V_{LDR} = (IR)_{LDR}$
>
> $R_{LDR} = \dfrac{V}{I} = \dfrac{2.5}{0.002} = 1250\ \Omega$
>
>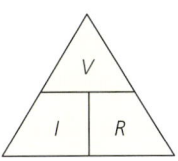

A switch

> **Investigation**
>
> Connect a switch to an ohmmeter as shown in Figure 3.10. Look at the readings on the ohmmeter when the switch is open and closed.
>
>
>
> **Figure 3.10** A switch connected to an ohmmeter

A switch can be connected to an ohmmeter. When the switch is open, there is an air gap between the contacts of the switch and the ohmmeter reading is very, very high. The resistance of an open switch is so big that it cannot be measured (we call it infinite).

When the switch is closed, the contacts touch and the ohmmeter reading is zero (or very close to zero).

A **switch** is an input device.

Summary of input devices

Microphone – changes sound into electrical energy.

Solar cell – changes light into electrical energy.

Device	Conditions	Resistance
thermistor	low temperature	high
	high temperature	low
LDR	dark	high
	light	low
switch	open	very, very high
	closed	zero

Table 3.1 Input devices

Electricity and Energy

Output devices

There are a number of output devices available for different applications. Output devices change electrical energy into another form of energy.

The loudspeaker

> **Investigation**
>
> Connect a loudspeaker to a signal generator as shown in Figure 3.11. Change the amplitude (loudness) and frequency controls on the signal generator.
>
>
>
> Figure 3.11 A signal generator connected to a loudspeaker
>
> What is the energy change that takes place in the loudspeaker?
>
> Name two appliances in your home that contain a loudspeaker.

A loudspeaker is usually an analogue output device that changes electrical energy into sound. A radio and a television are examples of electronic systems that contain a loudspeaker.

Buzzer

> **Investigation**
>
> Connect a buzzer to a battery and a switch as shown in Figure 3.12. Close the switch.
>
>
>
> Figure 3.12 A d.c. power supply connected to a switch and a buzzer
>
> Open the switch. Reverse the connections to the buzzer. Close the switch. What effect, if any, does this have?
>
> What is the energy change that takes place in the buzzer?
>
> Name one appliance in your home that could contain a buzzer.

A buzzer is usually a digital output device (i.e. it is either 'on' or 'off') that changes electrical energy into sound energy. A microwave is an example of an electronic system that often contains a buzzer.

The electric motor

> **Investigation**
>
> Connect an electric motor to a variable d.c. power supply (set at 2 V) and a switch, as shown in Figure 3.13. Close the switch.
>
>
>
> Figure 3.13 A variable d.c. power supply connected to a switch and a motor
>
> Open the switch. Reverse the connections to the motor. Close the switch. What effect, if any, does this have?
>
> Open the switch. Increase the voltage to 3 V. Close the switch. What effect, if any, does this have?
>
> What is the energy change that takes place in the electric motor?
>
> Name one appliance in your home that contains an electric motor.

An electric motor is an analogue output device that changes electrical energy into kinetic (movement) energy. The speed of the motor increases as the voltage is increased. The direction of rotation of the motor can be reversed by reversing the connections to the d.c. power supply.

An electric motor could be a digital output device if the motor was connected to a d.c. supply and a switch. The motor would then be either 'on' when the switch was closed or 'off' when the switch was open.

Vacuum cleaners and washing machines contain mains-operated electric motors.

The relay

> **Investigation**
>
> Connect a relay to a battery and a switch, S, as shown in Figure 3.14. Close switch S. 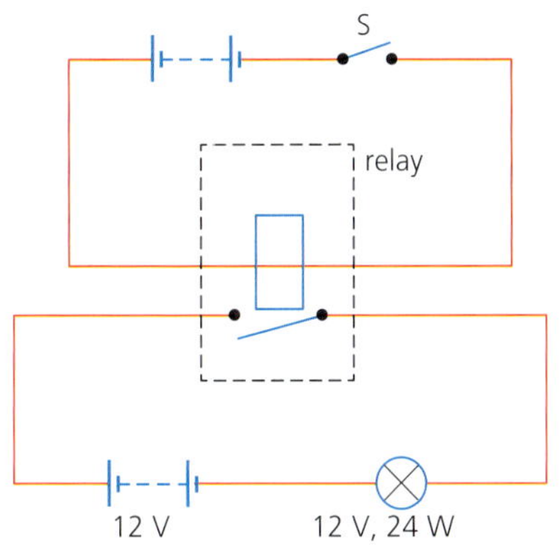
>
> [circuit diagram with battery 12 V, switch S, relay, and lamp 12 V, 24 W]
>
> **Figure 3.14** A relay circuit
>
> Open switch S. Reverse the connections to the relay. Close switch S. What effect, if any, does this have?
>
> What is the energy change that takes place in the relay?
>
> Name one appliance in your home that could contain a relay.

A relay is a switch operated by an electromagnet (see Chapter 6). A coil of wire, when carrying an electric current, provides the magnetic field required to close the switch contacts in the relay shown in Figure 3.14. When switch S is closed, there is a current in the coil surrounding the relay switch. The switch contacts close, completing the lower electrical circuit and thus allowing the lamp to light. When S is opened, the relay switch contacts open and the lamp goes out.

The advantage of a relay is that a small current in one circuit is able to control another circuit containing a device such as a lamp, electric bell or motor that requires a larger current. The relay is a digital output device that changes electrical energy into movement energy – the opening or closing of a switch. A washing machine and microwave are examples of appliances that contain a relay.

The solenoid

> **Investigation**
>
> Connect a solenoid to a battery and a switch as shown in Figure 3.15. Close the switch. 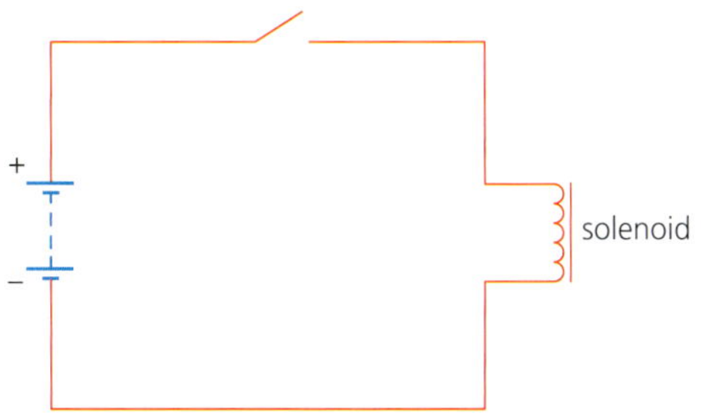
>
> [circuit diagram with battery and solenoid]
>
> **Figure 3.15** A solenoid circuit
>
> What is the energy change that takes place in the solenoid?
>
> Name a device or system that could contain a solenoid.

A solenoid consists of a coil of wire surrounding a metal core. When there is no current in the coil of wire, a strong spring pushes the metal core away from the coil. However, when there is a large enough current in the coil, the magnetic field produced attracts the metal core into the coil.

When the switch in Figure 3.15 is closed, the metal core moves into the coil and is held there. When the switch is opened, the metal core moves out of the coil and then stops. A solenoid is a digital output device that changes electrical energy into movement in a straight line. Solenoids are used in the central locking system of a car.

Electricity and Energy

The filament lamp

> **Investigation**
>
> Connect a lamp to a variable d.c. power supply (set at 2 V) and a switch, as shown in Figure 3.16. Close the switch.
>
>
>
> **Figure 3.16** A variable d.c. power supply connected to a switch and a lamp
>
> Open the switch. Reverse the connections to the lamp. Close the switch. What effect, if any, does this have?
>
> Open the switch. Increase the voltage to 3 V. Close the switch. What effect, if any, does this have?
>
> What is the energy change that takes place in a lamp?

A filament lamp consists of a thin wire (filament) in a glass container. When there is a large enough current in the wire, electrical energy is changed into heat and light in the filament.

A lamp can be connected to a variable d.c. voltage supply. Increasing the voltage across the lamp increases the current in the lamp and so the lamp gets brighter. No difference is observed when the connections from the d.c. power supply to the lamp are reversed. The filament in the lamp requires a relatively large current to light properly and gets very hot in operation.

A filament lamp can be an analogue or a digital output device. They are analogue devices when used with a dimmer circuit (the brightness changes) and digital devices when they are switched 'on' or 'off'. Filament lamps change electrical energy into heat and light. They are often used to light our homes, although more efficient compact fluorescent lamps and light-emitting diode lamps are replacing them as they convert less electrical energy into heat.

The light-emitting diode (LED)

> **Investigation**
>
> Connect a light-emitting diode (LED) to a variable d.c. power supply (set at 2 V), a resistor and a switch, as shown in Figure 3.17. Close the switch.
>
>
>
> **Figure 3.17** A variable d.c. power supply connected to a switch, resistor and an LED
>
> Open the switch. Reverse the connections to the LED. Close the switch. What effect, if any, does this have?
>
> Open the switch. Increase the voltage to 3 V. Close the switch. What effect, if any, does this have?
>
> Open the switch. Reverse the connections to the LED. Close the switch. What effect, if any, does this have?
>
> What is the energy change that takes place in the LED?
>
> Name one device that contains an LED.

Light-emitting diodes are made by joining two special materials (called semiconductors) together to produce a junction. When there is a current in the junction, electrical energy is changed into light. However, too large a current – or indeed too high a voltage – will destroy the junction. To prevent this, a resistor must be connected in series with the LED.

Figure 3.17 shows an LED and a resistor connected to a variable d.c. voltage supply. Increasing the voltage across the LED increases its brightness. The LED does not light when the connections from the supply are reversed. The LED only requires a small current in order to light and does not get hot in operation. LEDs are available that emit red, green, yellow, blue and white light.

An LED is usually used as a digital output device, i.e. it is either 'on' or 'off'. An LED changes electrical energy into light. LEDs are used in televisions, hi-fis, instrument panels and to light our homes.

The seven-segment display

> **Investigation**
>
> Connect a seven-segment display to a battery. Open and close the seven switches to display the decimal numbers zero to nine.
>
> What is the energy change that takes place in the seven-segment display?
>
> Name one device that contains a seven-segment display.

A seven-segment display consists of seven LEDs arranged in a rectangular package as shown in Figure 3.18. Any number in the range zero to nine can be produced by lighting a number of the individual LEDs. For example, the number one is displayed by lighting LEDs connected to terminals b and c, and number three is displayed by lighting the LEDs connected to a, b, c, d and g.

Some calculators use seven-segment displays that are LED displays. Other calculators use liquid crystal displays (LCDs), again of the seven-segment display type.

The seven-segment display is a digital output device that changes electrical energy into light. Seven-segment displays are used in some televisions, hi-fis, instrument panels and calculators.

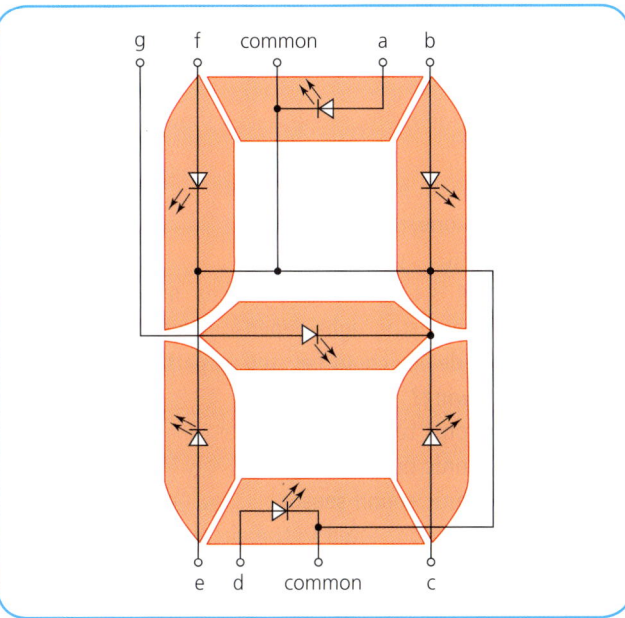

Figure 3.18 Part of a seven-segment display showing each of the seven LEDs (a to g)

> ### Physics in action
>
> Some cars are fitted with LED clusters instead of filament lamps for use as side and brake lights. LED clusters contain a number of ultra-bright LEDs. The main advantages compared with filament lamps are low power consumption, long life and reliability.
>
> A torch uses a light source to change chemical energy stored in the battery into light. Torches that use a filament lamp as the light source are generally bulky and heavy. This is due to the size and number of batteries required to power the lamp. However, torches that use an LED or LEDs consume less power than a filament lamp, so the batteries can be smaller and fewer, giving a more compact and lighter torch.

Key facts and physics equations: electrical systems and components

- All electronic systems can be broken down into three parts – input, process and output.
- An analogue signal has a continuous range of values.
- A digital signal has two possible values. The signal is either at a maximum value, called a high or logic '1', or at a minimum value, called a low or logic '0'.
- Most input devices change some form of energy into electrical energy or produce a change in an electrical signal.
- There are various input devices. Examples include microphones, solar cells, thermistors, light-dependent resistors (LDRs) and switches.
- A microphone changes sound into electrical energy.
- A solar cell changes light into electrical energy.
- The resistance of a thermistor decreases as the temperature increases.
- The resistance of an LDR decreases with increasing light level.
- An open switch has a very, very high (infinite) resistance and a closed switch has zero resistance.
- An output device changes electrical energy into some other form of energy.
- There are various output devices. Examples include loudspeakers, buzzers, electric motors, relays, solenoids, lamps, light-emitting diodes (LEDs) and seven-segment displays.

Electricity and Energy

- The relay, solenoid and seven-segment display are all digital output devices.
- The loudspeaker, buzzer, electric motor, light-emitting diode (LED) and lamp can be analogue or digital output devices. When the output device is either 'on' or 'off', the device is digital. However, if the output signal to the output device varies in value then the device is analogue.
- A loudspeaker and a buzzer change electrical energy into sound.
- An electric motor changes electrical energy into kinetic (movement) energy.
- A lamp and an LED change electrical energy into light.
- LEDs will only light up when connected to a d.c. power supply the correct way round.
- A resistor should always be connected in series with an LED. This protects the LED from damage caused by too high a current in the LED (or too high a voltage across the LED).

End-of-chapter questions

1. The output signals from four devices are displayed on the oscilloscope screens shown in Figure 3.19.

   diagram P
   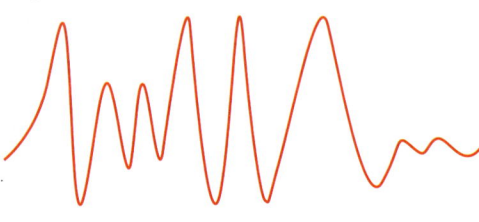

   diagram Q

   diagram R

   diagram S
   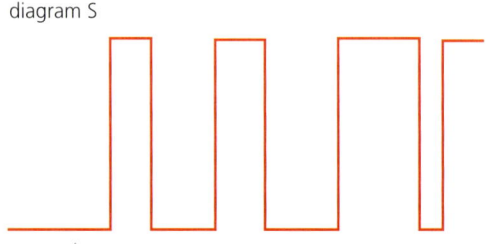

   Figure 3.19

   a) Which of the oscilloscope traces show digital signals?
   b) Which of the oscilloscope traces show analogue signals?

2. What is the main energy change for:
   a) a microphone?
   b) a solar cell?

3. The following is a list of input devices: microphone, solar cell, thermistor, light-dependent resistor (LDR). Which input device could be used as part of a circuit for the following?
   a) an electronic temperature sensor
   b) an electronic light meter
   c) an electronic sound sensor

4. A thermistor is connected in the circuit shown in Figure 3.20. The reading on the ammeter is 0.0036 A. The reading on the voltmeter is 1.8 V. The thermistor is at a temperature of 18 °C.

   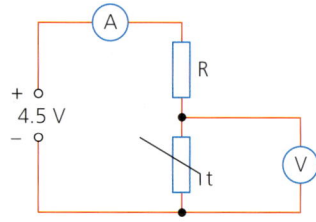

   Figure 3.20

   a) Calculate the resistance of the thermistor.
   b) Calculate the resistance of the resistor, R.
   c) The temperature of the thermistor rises to 20 °C. Suggest a suitable value for the reading now displayed on the ammeter.

5 State the main energy change for the following output devices:
   a) electric motor
   b) LED
   c) loudspeaker.
6 Which LEDs in Figure 3.21 must be lit in order to display the numbers:
   a) 2
   b) 5
   c) 7?

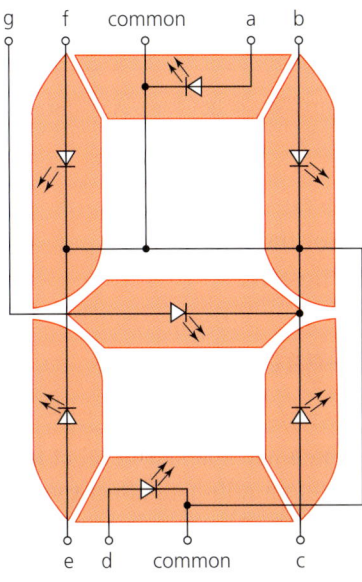

Figure 3.21

7 The following is a list of output devices: buzzer, lamp, motor, relay. Which output device from the list could be used to:
   a) indicate that the required cooking time for an oven is complete?
   b) move the conveyor belt at a supermarket checkout?
   c) stop and start the movement of the conveyor belt at a supermarket checkout?

8 A shop sells the following electrical devices: electric motor, light-dependent resistor (LDR), light-emitting diode (LED), loudspeaker, microphone, relay, solenoid and thermistor.
   a) (i) From the above list, name two digital output devices.
      (ii) From the above list, name two input devices.
      (iii) State the useful energy change that takes place in a microphone.
   b) A thermistor is connected in the circuit shown in Figure 3.22.

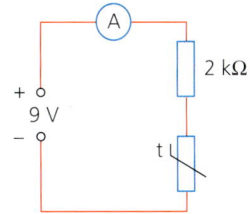

Figure 3.22

The graph shows how the resistance of the thermistor changes as the temperature changes.

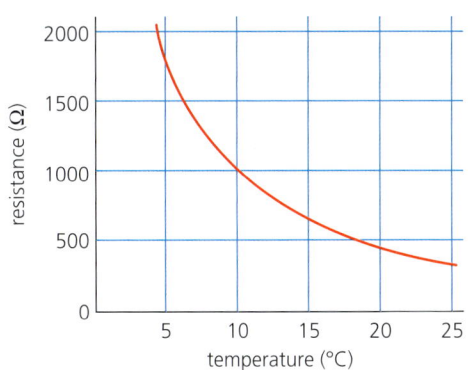

Figure 3.23

During the day the temperature of the thermistor rises.
   (i) What happens to the reading on the ammeter?
   (ii) Explain your answer.

Electricity and Energy

Unit 1

4 Digital processes

Learning outcomes

At the end of this chapter you should be able to:
1. Draw and identify the symbols for an AND-gate, OR-gate and NOT-gate.
2. State that logic gates may have one or more inputs and that a truth table shows the output for all possible input combinations.
3. State that high voltage = logic '1' and low voltage = logic '0'.
4. Draw the truth tables for an AND-gate, OR-gate and NOT-gate.
5. Explain how to use combinations of digital logic gates for control in simple situations.

Digital processing devices: logic gates

Logic gates are digital devices that frequently obtain analogue signals as their inputs. These analogue inputs have to be converted into a digital form by the gate before it is able to carry out its task.

The inputs and outputs from a gate are voltages that may either be 'high' (close to the supply voltage) or 'low' (near to zero volts). These are referred to as logic '1' and logic '0'.

A table known as a **truth table** shows how the output of the gate varies with the input or inputs. A truth table is a shorthand way to show the behaviour of an electronic system.

The NOT (or inverter) gate

> **Investigation**
>
> Connect the input of a NOT-gate to logic '0' and then to logic '1'. Note the output in each case.
>
> Why is this gate called a NOT-gate?

Figure 4.1 shows the circuit symbol and truth table for a **NOT-gate**.

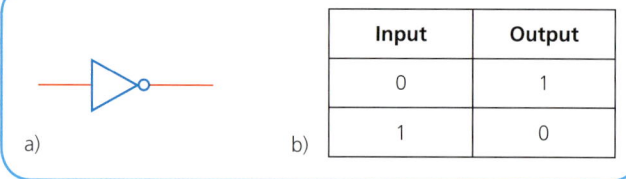

Input	Output
0	1
1	0

Figure 4.1 a) Circuit symbol for a NOT-gate b) Truth table for a NOT-gate

From the truth table it can be seen that the output of a NOT-gate is **not** the same as the input. A NOT-gate is also called an **inverter**.

The AND-gate

> **Investigation**
>
> Investigate how the logic level of inputs A and B of an AND-gate affect the output.
>
> Why is this gate called an AND-gate?

The circuit symbol and truth table for an **AND-gate** are shown in Figure 4.2.

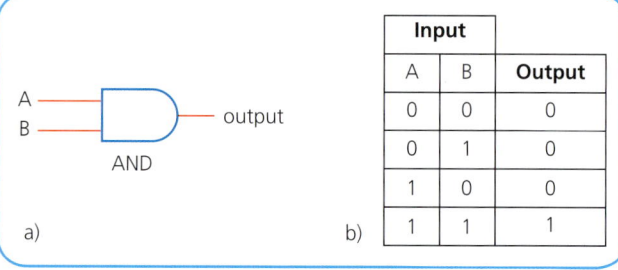

Input A	Input B	Output
0	0	0
0	1	0
1	0	0
1	1	1

Figure 4.2 a) Circuit symbol for an AND-gate b) Truth table for an AND-gate

30

Digital processes

From the truth table, it can be seen that the output of an AND-gate will be logic '1' (high) only when inputs A **and** B are logic '1' (high).

The OR-gate

> **Investigation**
>
> Investigate how the logic level of inputs A and B of an OR-gate affect the output.
>
> Why is this gate called an OR-gate?

The circuit symbol and truth table for an **OR-gate** are shown in Figure 4.3.

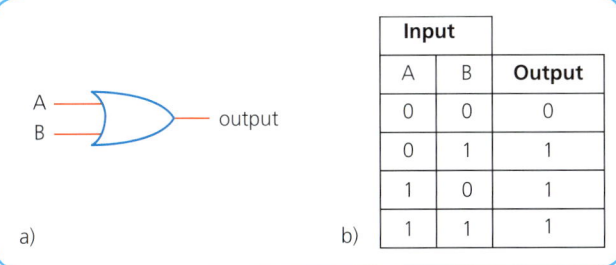

Figure 4.3 a) Circuit symbol for an OR-gate b) Truth table for an OR-gate

From the truth table, it can be seen that the output of an OR-gate will be logic '1' (high) when either of the inputs A **or** B is logic '1' (high).

AND-, OR- and NOT-gates may be combined together to form a sophisticated electronic system.

In the following examples you may assume that:

- a light sensor gives a logic '1' in light and a logic '0' in dark
- a temperature sensor gives a logic '1' when warm and a logic '0' when cold
- a switch gives a logic '1' when closed and a logic '0' when open.

Worked examples

Example 1

a) Draw a logic diagram for a system where an LED will light when a car engine gets too hot. The lamp should only operate when the ignition of the car is switched on (logic '1').
b) Construct a truth table for this system.

Solution

a) Requires LED to be on (1) when the ignition is on (1) **and** the engine is too hot (1).

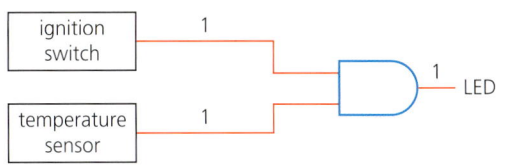

Figure 4.4

b)

Temperature sensor	Ignition switch	LED
cold (0)	off (0)	off (0)
cold (0)	on (1)	off (0)
hot (1)	off (0)	off (0)
hot (1)	on (1)	on (1)

Example 2

a) Draw a logic diagram for a system that will switch on the pump of a central heating system when the house is cold and the central heating is switched on (logic '1').
b) Construct a truth table for this system.

Solution

a) Requires a pump to be on (1) when the central heating is on (1) **and** the temperature is cold (0) (**not** warm (1)).

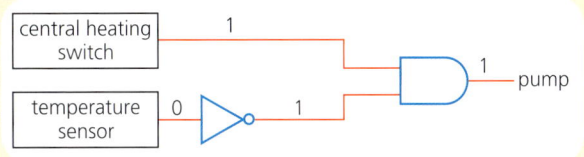

Figure 4.5

31

Electricity and Energy

b)

Central heating switch	Temperature sensor	NOT temperature sensor	Pump
off (0)	cold (0)	(1)	off (0)
off (0)	warm (1)	(0)	off (0)
on (1)	cold (0)	(1)	on (1)
on (1)	warm (1)	(0)	off (0)

Example 3

a) Draw a logic diagram for a system that will turn on a heater in a greenhouse when it gets cold at night. The heater should be switched off (logic '0') during the day.

b) Construct a truth table for this system.

Solution

a) Requires a heater to be on (1) when it is cold (0) (**not** warm (1)) **and** dark (0) (**not** light (1)).

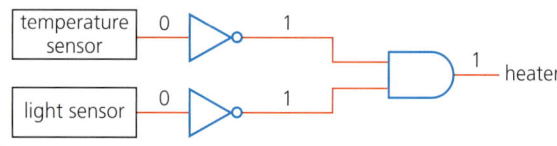

Figure 4.6

b)

Light sensor	NOT light sensor	Temperature sensor	NOT temperature sensor	Heater
dark (0)	(1)	cold (0)	(1)	on (1)
dark (0)	(1)	warm (1)	(0)	off (0)
light (1)	(0)	cold (0)	(1)	off (0)
light (1)	(0)	warm (1)	(0)	off (0)

Key facts and physics equations: digital processes

- A digital signal has two possible values. The signal is either at a maximum value, called a high or logic '1', or at a minimum value, called a low or logic '0'.
- Logic gates are digital processing devices – NOT-gate (or inverter), AND-gate and OR-gate.
- Logic gates use logic '1' to represent a high voltage level and logic '0' to represent a low voltage level.
- A truth table shows how the output from a gate or system varies with the input or inputs.
- The circuit symbols and truth tables for NOT-gate, AND-gate and OR-gate are shown in Figures 4.7 to 4.9.

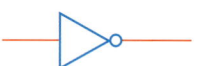

Figure 4.7 Circuit symbol for NOT-gate

Figure 4.8 Circuit symbol for AND-gate

Figure 4.9 Circuit symbol for OR-gate

Digital processes

End-of-chapter questions

1. The terms 'high voltage' and 'low voltage' are used with logic gates. Which of these terms refers to logic '1' and which to logic '0'?

2. a) Draw the circuit symbol for a NOT-gate.
   b) The table shows the possible inputs for a NOT-gate.

Input	Output
0	
1	

   Copy and complete the table to show the correct outputs.

3. a) Draw the circuit symbol for an AND-gate.
   b) The table shows the possible inputs for an AND-gate.

Input A	Input B	Output
0	0	
0	1	
1	0	
1	1	

   Copy and complete the table to show the correct outputs.

4. a) Draw the circuit symbol for an OR-gate.
   b) The table shows the possible inputs for an OR-gate.

Input A	Input B	Output
0	0	
0	1	
1	0	
1	1	

   Copy and complete the table to show the correct outputs.

5. State an alternative name for the logic gate known as an inverter.

6. Part of an electronic circuit is shown in Figure 4.10.

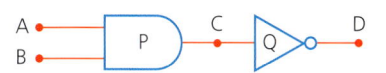

   Figure 4.10

   a) What name is given to:
      (i) gate P
      (ii) gate Q?
   b) The table shows the possible logic levels of inputs A and B.

A	B	C	D
0	0		
0	1		
1	0		
1	1		

   Copy and complete this table to show the logic levels of C and D.

7. Part of an electronic circuit is shown in Figure 4.11.

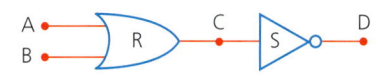

   Figure 4.11

   a) What name is given to:
      (i) gate R
      (ii) gate S?
   b) The table shows the possible logic levels of inputs A and B.

A	B	C	D
0	0		
0	1		
1	0		
1	1		

   Copy and complete the table to show the logic levels of C and D.

Electricity and Energy

Unit 1

8. Part of an electronic circuit is shown in Figure 4.12.

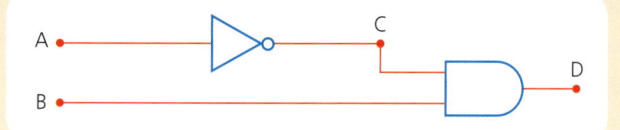

Figure 4.12

The table shows the possible logic levels of inputs A and B.

A	B	C	D
0	0		
0	1		
1	0		
1	1		

Copy and complete this table to show the logic levels of C and D.

9. A student is asked to design a circuit to remind a car driver that the car lights have been left on after the ignition switch has been switched off. A buzzer is to sound when the lights are on but only when the ignition is switched off.
The light switch sensor gives logic '1' when the lights are on.
The ignition switch gives logic '1' when switched on.
The buzzer is switched on by logic '1'.
Draw a suitable logic diagram, naming the logic gates involved.

10. The logic diagram for the operation of a car interior lamp is shown in Figure 4.13.

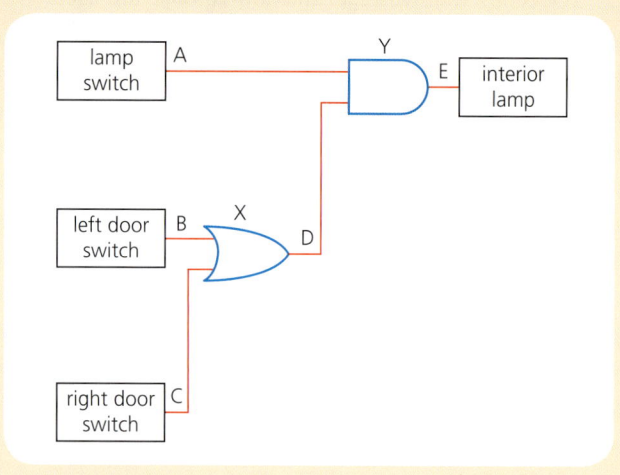

Figure 4.13

The interior lamp will come on when either door is open provided the lamp switch is on.
The lamp switch gives logic '1' when it is switched on and logic '0' when switched off.
Either door switch gives logic '1' when a door is opened and logic '0' when a door is closed.
The lamp lights with logic '1'.

a) (i) Name logic gate X.
   (ii) Name logic gate Y.
b) Copy and complete the truth table for the switch system when the lamp is on.

A	B	C	D	E
1	0	0		
1	0	1		
1	1	0		
1	1	1		

5 Electrical power

Learning outcomes

At the end of this chapter you should be able to:
1. State that when there is an electrical current in a component, there is an energy transformation.
2. Carry out calculations involving the relationship between power, energy and time.
3. State that in a lamp electrical energy is transformed into heat and light.
4. State that the energy transformation in an electrical heater occurs in the resistance wire.
5. Carry out calculations using:
$$\text{efficiency} = \frac{\text{useful energy output}}{\text{total energy input}} \times 100\%$$
6. Carry out calculations using:
$$\text{efficiency} = \frac{\text{useful power output}}{\text{total power input}} \times 100\%$$

Energy conversions

The electrical appliances we use in our homes, industry and schools use **electrical energy** from the mains supply or from batteries. They change electrical energy into a form that is useful for what we are doing (and in many cases into other forms of energy that are not so useful). For instance, a lamp changes electrical energy into heat and light. The most useful energy change for a lamp is the change from electrical energy into light.

The list below shows the main energy change for a number of household appliances:

- A kettle changes electrical energy into **heat**.
- A radio changes electrical energy into **sound**.
- A lamp changes electrical energy into **light**.
- A washing machine changes electrical energy into **kinetic** (movement) **energy**.

Most electrical appliances are fitted with a **rating plate**. Figure 5.1 shows the rating plates for three common household appliances. The rating plate gives information about the appliance – the voltage (the number with the letter 'V' after it) and frequency (the number with the letters 'Hz' after it) required to operate it, and the power rating (the number with the letter 'W' after it).

230 V ~
350 W
☐ 50 Hz

food mixer rating plate

230 V ~
50 Hz
2200 W
Made in Gt. Britain

kettle rating plate

230 V ~ 950 W
50 Hz
Made in Gt. Britain

toaster rating plate

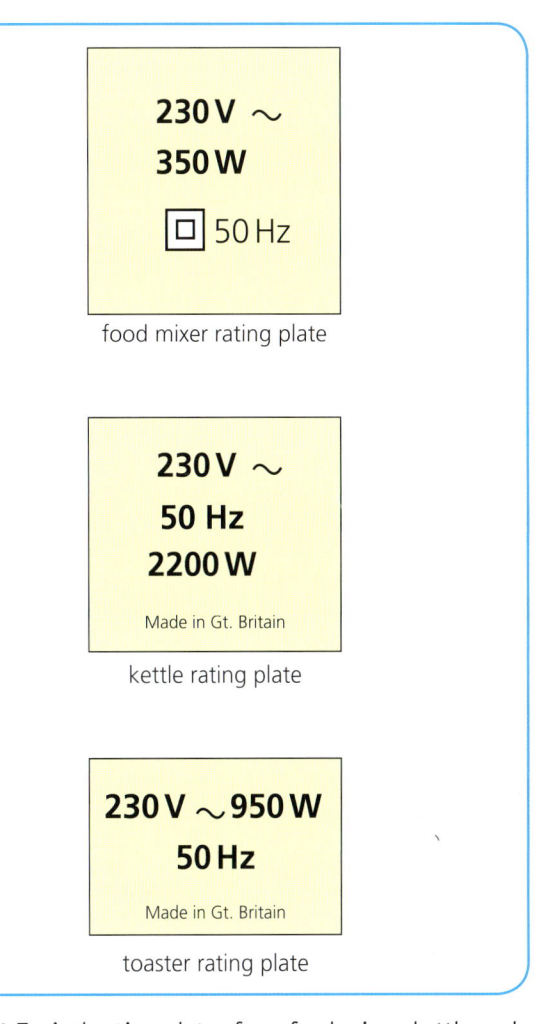

Figure 5.1 Typical rating plates for a food mixer, kettle and toaster

Table 5.1 shows the power ratings for the three appliances in Figure 5.1.

Appliance	Power rating (watts)
food mixer	350
kettle	2200
toaster	950

Table 5.1 Power ratings for a food mixer, kettle and toaster

The electric kettle has the highest power rating at 2200 watts and the food mixer has the lowest power rating at 350 watts.

35

Electricity and Energy

Unit 1

Power

Investigation

A joulemeter is a meter that measures the energy used by a component.

Set up the circuit shown in Figure 5.2.

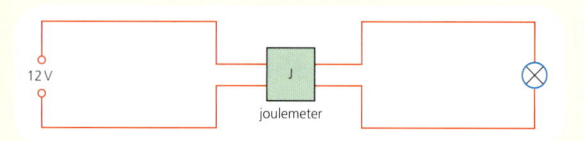

Figure 5.2 Measuring the power rating of a lamp

Reset the joulemeter to zero. Switch on the lamp for 100 seconds.

Note the final reading on the joulemeter – how much energy was used by the lamp in 100 seconds?

How much energy was used by the lamp in 1 second?

Compare the energy used in 1 second by the lamp with the power rating of the lamp (this is marked on the lamp) – what do you notice?

Repeat the above method for a lamp with a different power rating.

When there is an electric current in a wire, the electrons making up the current collide with the atoms of the wire. These collisions make the atoms vibrate more and this results in the wire becoming hotter, i.e. electrical energy has been changed into heat in the wire. The amount of heat produced depends on the value of the current and the value of the resistance of the wire. Heating elements for kettles and toasters change electrical energy into heat in the resistance wire making up the element.

A lamp transfers electrical energy into heat and light in a resistance wire called the filament. The energy transferred in 1 second is known as the power rating of the lamp.

Power is the energy transferred in 1 second.

$$\text{Power} = \frac{\text{energy transferred}}{\text{time taken}}$$

$$P = \frac{E}{t}$$

where P = power, measured in watts (W)

E = energy transferred, measured in joules (J)

t = time taken, measured in seconds (s).

Using the 'maths' triangle (see Rearranging physics equations on page 145) for this equation gives:

$$P = \frac{E}{t} \qquad E = P \times t \qquad t = \frac{E}{P}$$

1 watt means that 1 joule of energy is transferred each second.

Worked examples

Example 1

A lamp uses 45 000 joules of energy in a time of 900 seconds. Calculate the power rating of the lamp.

Solution

$$P = \frac{E}{t} = \frac{45\,000}{900} = 50 \text{ watts}$$

Example 2

The power rating of a kettle is 2200 watts. The kettle is switched on for 150 seconds. Calculate the energy transferred by the kettle in this time.

Solution

$P = \dfrac{E}{t}$

$E = P \times t = 2200 \times 150$

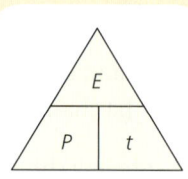

$E = 330\,000$ joules

Example 3

The power rating of a vacuum cleaner is 900 W. The vacuum cleaner is switched on and transfers 270 000 J of energy. Calculate how long the vacuum cleaner is switched on for.

Solution

$P = \dfrac{E}{t}$

$t = \dfrac{E}{P} = \dfrac{270\,000}{900} = 300 \text{ s}$

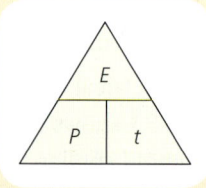

Electrical power

We are charged for the amount of electrical energy that appliances use. From the power equation, the electrical energy that an electrical appliance uses ($E = P \times t$), and therefore the cost, depends on the power rating of the appliance and the length of time the appliance is in use:

- cost increases as power rating increases
- cost increases as the time the appliance is used for increases.

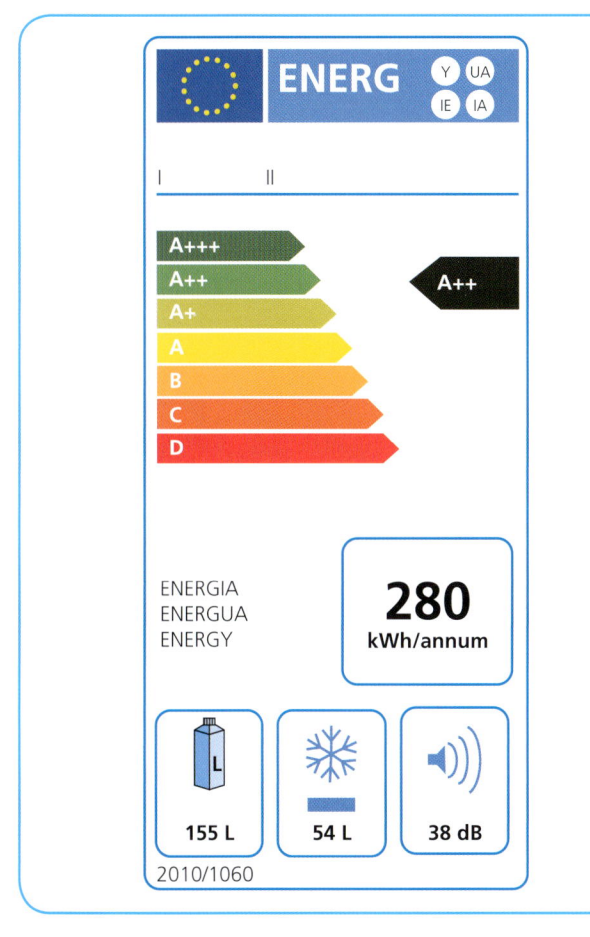

Figure 5.3 EU energy label for a refrigerator

Energy efficiency labels are to be found on new appliances for sale, such as washing machines, fridges and freezers. They allow customers to compare how much electrical energy similar appliances will use (A+++ being the most efficient). For instance, a washing machine that has an energy efficiency A++ rating will use less electrical energy (and cost less to use) than a machine with an energy efficiency C rating (for doing the same number and type of washes). The expected annual electricity used (in kW) by the appliance is also shown on the label.

Worked example

A shop sells two types of lamp, lamp X and lamp Y. The power rating of lamp X is 50 W. The power rating of lamp Y is 5.0 W. When connected to the mains supply, both lamps give out the same amount of light and appear equally bright.
a) Which lamp is more efficient at producing light?
b) It costs £7.50 to use lamp X for 1000 hours. What is the cost of using lamp Y for 1000 hours?

Solution

a) Lamp Y (both lamps are equally bright so they give out the same amount of light, but lamp X is using more energy per second and will be producing a lot more heat than lamp Y).
b) Lamp Y uses a tenth of the power of lamp X.

Cost of using lamp Y for 1000 hours $= \dfrac{1}{10} \times 7.50 = £0.75$

Efficiency

The efficiency of an electrical device or machine is given by:

$$\% \text{ efficiency} = \dfrac{\text{useful energy output}}{\text{total energy input}} \times 100\%$$

As the energy output from a machine is always less than the energy input, the efficiency is always less than 100%. The useful energy we get from a machine is never as much as the energy we put in. This is because some of the energy is transferred into other forms, such as heat and perhaps sound. We say that some of the energy put in to the machine has been 'lost'. However, the total amount of energy remains the same, i.e. the total energy is **conserved**.

Sometimes it is easier to look at the energy being used every second (the power). In this case 'power' replaces 'energy' in the equation:

$$\% \text{ efficiency} = \dfrac{\text{useful power output}}{\text{total power input}} \times 100\%$$

37

Electricity and Energy

Worked examples

Example 1

A woman uses an electric saw to cut some pieces of wood. During use, the saw uses 5000 joules of electrical energy. The useful energy output of the saw is 450 joules. Calculate the efficiency of the saw.

Solution

$$\% \text{ efficiency} = \frac{\text{useful energy output}}{\text{total energy input}} \times 100\%$$

$$= \frac{450}{5000} \times 100\% = 9\%$$

Example 2

A hydroelectric power station is able to produce 54 000 W of electrical power. The power input to the station is 67 500 W. Calculate the efficiency of the power station.

Solution

$$\% \text{ efficiency} = \frac{\text{useful power output}}{\text{total power input}} \times 100\%$$

$$= \frac{54\,000}{67\,500} \times 100\% = 80\%$$

Example 3

The energy produced each second by water passing through the turbine of a hydroelectric power station is 1 000 000 J. The power station produces 750 000 J of electrical energy each second.

a) Calculate the efficiency of the power station.
b) What percentage of the energy input was changed into heat and sound in the power station?

Solution

a) $$\text{Efficiency} = \frac{\text{useful energy output}}{\text{total energy input}} \times 100\%$$

$$= \frac{750\,000}{1\,000\,000} \times 100\% = 75\%$$

b) Energy input changed into heat and sound = 100 − 75 = 25%

Key facts and physics equations: electrical power

- Power = $\frac{\text{energy}}{\text{time}}$, i.e. $P = \frac{E}{t}$
- Power is measured in watts (W), energy in joules (J) and time in seconds (s).
- % efficiency = $\frac{\text{useful energy output}}{\text{total energy input}} \times 100\%$
- % efficiency = $\frac{\text{useful power output}}{\text{total power input}} \times 100\%$

Electrical power

End-of-chapter questions

1. Write down the main energy change that takes place in the following appliances:
   a) electric toaster
   b) washing machine
   c) electric cooker
   d) food mixer.

2. The rating plates of four different appliances are shown below.

Appliance	Rating plate
table lamp	Made in Britain 40 W 230 V
clock	Model No. 3206 230–250 V 7 W
refrigerator	Type F/433 230 V 300 W
electric drill	Model No. 45C Power Drill 230 V/750 W

   a) Which of the above appliances has the lowest power rating?
   b) Each appliance is switched on for 10 minutes. Which of these appliances would use the most energy in 10 minutes?

3. A lamp is plugged into the mains supply and switched on. Write down the energy change that takes place in the lamp.

4. The element of an electric kettle is rated at 2200 watts. How much electrical energy does the kettle use in 1 second?

5. Calculate the missing values in the table.

Power (watts)	Energy transferred (joules)	Time taken (seconds)
a)	1050	30
b)	6000	2000
900	c)	500
2200	d)	120
60	18 000	e)
100	200 000	f)

6. A television is switched on for 720 seconds. During this time it uses 216 000 joules of electrical energy. Calculate the power rating of the television.

7. The power rating of an electric toaster is 900 W. The toaster is switched on and uses 135 000 J of energy. Calculate the time the toaster is switched on for.

8. The power rating of a CD player is 14 W. The CD player is switched on for 1800 s. Calculate the energy the CD player uses in this time.

9. A fluorescent lamp is switched on for 240 s. During this time, it uses 7200 J of electrical energy. The lamp gives out 5760 J of light in this time. Calculate the efficiency of the lamp.

10. A wind turbine on a yacht is used to charge batteries. The wind turbine is able to convert some of the wind's energy into electrical energy. During part of the day, the wind blows steadily giving a power input to the turbine of 20 W. The turbine produces a steady power output of 6.0 W. Calculate the efficiency of the wind turbine.

11. An electric motor was used to raise a mass from the floor. During the lifting, the mass gained 12 J of gravitational potential energy. The electrical energy supplied to the motor during the lifting process was 48 J. Calculate the efficiency of the lifting operation.

12. The power input to a gas-fired power station is 1800 million watts. The power station produces 810 million watts of electrical power. Calculate the efficiency of the power station at producing electricity.

Electricity and Energy

Unit 1

6 Electromagnetism

Learning outcomes

At the end of this chapter you should be able to:

1. State that the region surrounding a magnet is called a magnetic field.
2. State that a magnetic field exists around a current-carrying wire and is controlled by the current in the wire.
3. Give two examples of practical applications that make use of the magnetic effect of a current-carrying wire.
4. Identify circumstances in which a voltage will be induced in a conductor.
5. State the factors that affect the size of the induced voltage, i.e. strength of magnet, number of turns on the coil, and speed of the magnet or coil.
6. Carry out calculations involving the equation $\dfrac{n_S}{n_P} = \dfrac{V_S}{V_P}$.

Magnets

A magnet is able to exert a force on certain materials. The region surrounding the magnet is called a magnetic force field or simply a magnetic field. A magnet (sometimes called a bar or permanent magnet) has a magnetic field that cannot be switched off. The opposite ends, or poles, of a magnet are called north and south (a north pole means a north-seeking pole, i.e. it always tends to point north).

Investigation

Use a bar magnet to find out which materials are attracted to it. Try brass, bronze, glass, iron, nickel, paper, plastic, steel, wood and zinc.

Place a sheet of paper over the bar magnet. Scatter some iron filings on top of the paper. Gently tap the paper and observe the pattern of the iron filings.

Take two bar magnets and place them so that like poles face each other – a north pole faces a north pole or a south pole faces a south pole. What do the magnets 'want' to do?

Now place the two magnets so that opposite poles face each other – a north pole faces a south pole. What do the magnets 'want' to do now?

The shape of the magnetic field surrounding a magnet can be shown by scattering iron filings on a piece of paper placed on top of the magnet. The direction of the magnetic field can be found using a compass. The needle of the compass points away from the north towards the south.

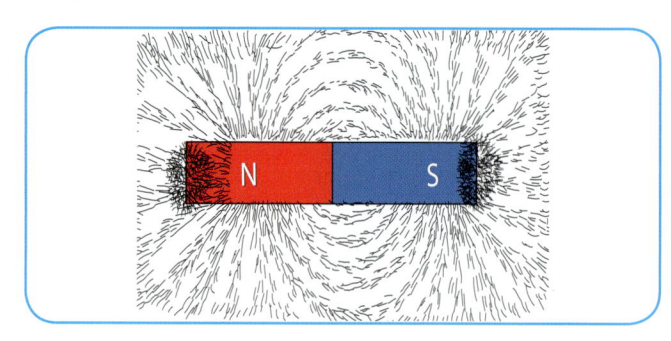

Figure 6.1 Iron filings show the magnetic field line pattern surrounding a permanent magnet

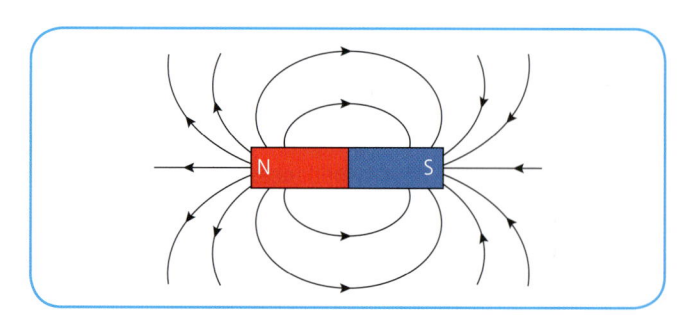

Figure 6.2 Magnetic field lines surrounding a permanent magnet

When two magnets are placed close together, their magnetic fields produce forces that cause:

- a north pole to repel a north pole
- a south pole to repel a south pole
- a north pole to attract a south pole.

In other words, like poles repel and unlike poles attract.

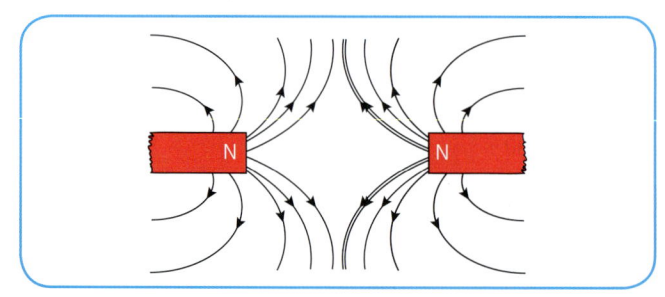

Figure 6.3 Magnetic field lines surrounding two opposing magnets

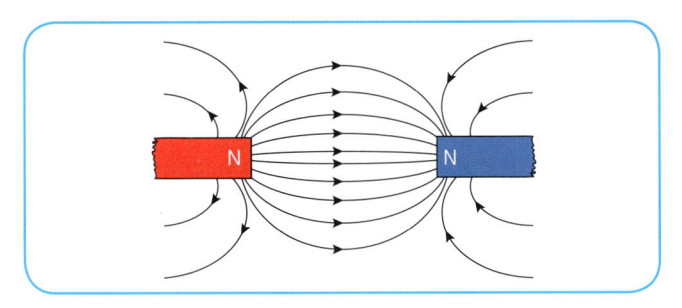

Figure 6.4 Magnetic field lines surrounding two attracting magnets

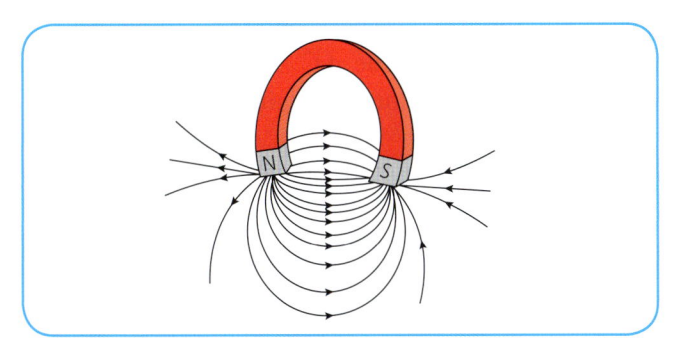

Figure 6.5 Magnetic field lines surrounding a horseshoe magnet

Most materials are not affected by a magnet. However, some metals such as iron and steel are attracted by a magnet.

Some uses of magnets:

- a fridge magnet for holding a shopping list
- magnetic door seals on fridge and freezer doors – as the door of the appliance is closing, the magnetic field from the seal pulls the door fully closed. This prevents warm air from entering the appliance.
- in a house alarm – a reed switch (a magnetically-operated switch) is attached to the doorpost. A magnet, close to the reed switch, is attached to the door. When the door is closed, the magnetic field from the magnet holds the reed switch closed. When the door is opened, the magnet moves away from the reed switch and the reed switch opens. The opening and closing of the reed switch is detected by the alarm circuit.
- in some electric motors – the magnetic field generated by a current-carrying wire in the motor interacts with the magnetic field of a permanent magnet to produce movement.

Electromagnetism and electromagnets

Figure 6.6 shows a long, straight wire passing vertically through a piece of card. A magnetic field surrounds the wire when there is an electric current in the wire.

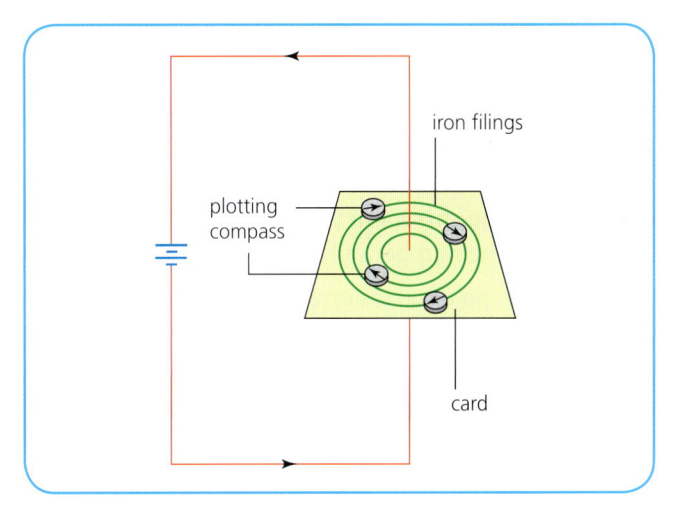

Figure 6.6 Magnetic field lines surrounding a current-carrying wire

Increasing the current in the wire increases the strength of the magnetic field surrounding the wire. Reversing the direction of the current in the wire reverses the direction of the magnetic field around the wire.

Investigation

Take a length of insulated wire about 1.0 m long. Wind **half** the length of wire around a 10-cm-long iron nail. Connect the ends of the wire to a power supply. Set the power supply to 2 V. Switch on the power supply **for no more than 30 seconds** (otherwise the wire will get very hot!). Hold the iron nail close to a metal paper clip, and then switch off. When the supply is switched on, is the paper clip attracted to the nail?

Set the power supply to 4 V, to increase the current in the wire. Switch on the power supply **for no more than 30 seconds**. Again, hold the iron nail close to a paper clip, and then switch off. Is there any difference in the attraction of the paper clip to the nail?

Set the power supply to 2 V. Wind more of the wire onto the nail. Switch on the power supply **for no more than 30 seconds**. Hold the iron nail close to a paper clip, and then switch off. Is there any difference in the attraction of the paper clip to the nail?

Remove the iron nail from the coil. Set the power supply to 2 V. Switch on the power supply **for no more than 30 seconds**. Hold the coils of wire close to a paper clip, and then switch off. Is there any difference in the attraction of the paper clip to the coils of wire?

Electricity and Energy

Unit 1

When there is an electric current in a wire that is coiled around an iron core, the core becomes magnetised and an electromagnet is produced, as shown in Figure 6.7. However, the electromagnet has little strength without the iron core. The iron core is able to concentrate the magnetic field within itself, so giving a stronger magnetic effect.

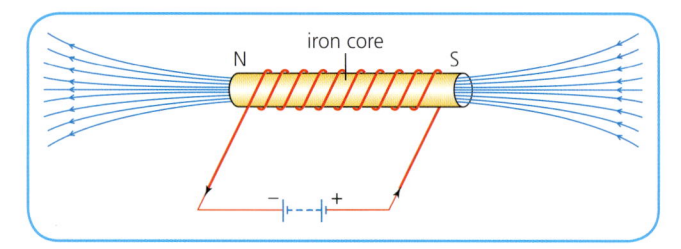

Figure 6.7 Magnetic field lines surrounding an electromagnet

The magnetic field of an electromagnet can be made stronger by:

- increasing the current in the coils of wire
- increasing the number of turns of wire on the core.

When there is no electric current in the coils, there is no magnetic field. This on-off nature of the magnetic field of an electromagnet can be used to lift scrap iron (magnetic field on) and then release it (magnetic field off), as shown in Figure 6.8.

Figure 6.8 Electromagnets can lift heavy objects

Electromagnets are essential parts of many electrical devices.

The electric bell

Figure 6.9a) shows an electric bell. When switch S is pressed it completes the electrical circuit. There is a current in the coils of the electromagnet. The electromagnet becomes magnetised and attracts the soft iron armature or bar. However, when the hammer moves to hit the bell, the electrical circuit is broken at C, as shown in Figure 6.9b). There is no longer a current in the electromagnet and the electromagnet loses its magnetism. The springy metal strip is now able to pull the armature back, and in so doing the electrical circuit is remade at C. This completes the circuit again and continuous ringing occurs as long as switch S is pressed.

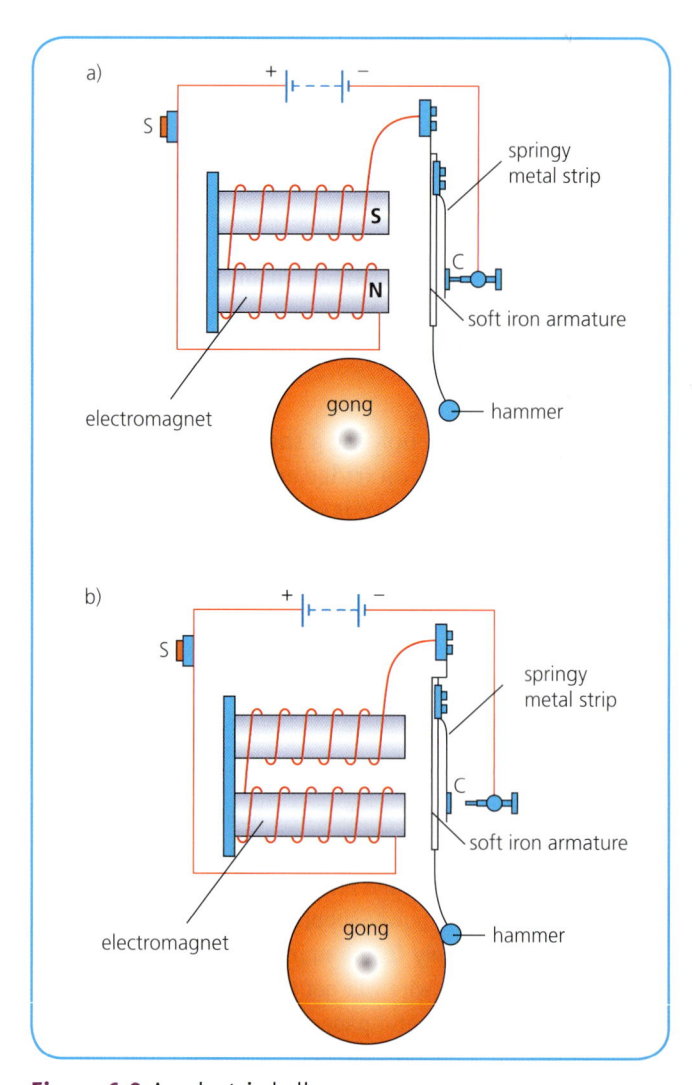

Figure 6.9 An electric bell

Electromagnetism

The magnetic relay

Figure 6.10a) shows an electrically-operated switch called a magnetic relay. When the switch S is closed, there is a small current in the electromagnet. The magnetic field produced pulls the pivoted iron armature towards the iron core of the electromagnet, pushing the contacts closed. This completes the second electrical circuit and the lamp lights (Figure 6.10b)). When the switch S is opened the electromagnet loses its magnetism, releasing the armature. The contacts open, there is no current in the other circuit, and the lamp is unlit.

Relays are very useful devices. They are used when we need a small current in a control circuit to open or close a switch in a main circuit where there will be a large current.

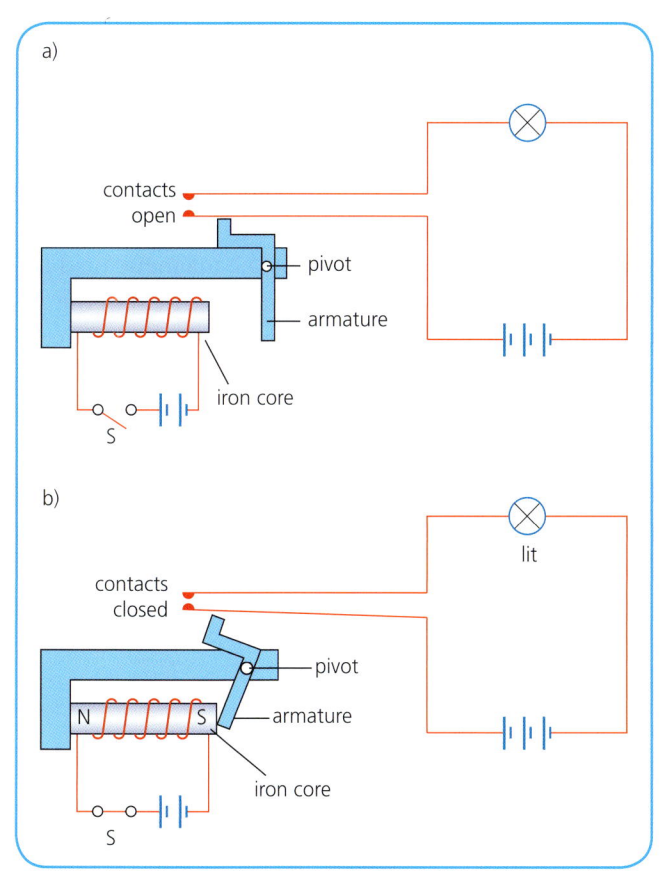

Figure 6.10 A relay

Physics in action

Magnetically levitating (maglev) trains 'float' above the track and can travel much faster than conventional trains. As a result, the duration of long-distance journeys can be reduced. Electromagnets attached to the train are attracted upwards towards the levitation rail. Computers control the current in the electromagnet. This allows the strength of the levitation force to be varied.

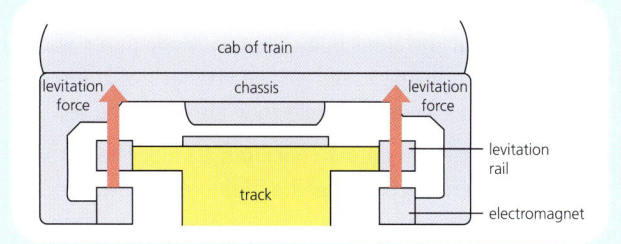

Figure 6.11 A maglev train

The strong magnetic field from a superconducting electromagnet is used in some hospitals to determine what is going on inside the human body. This technique is called magnetic resonance imaging (MRI) and is similar to an X-ray. However, MRI is safer than an X-ray.

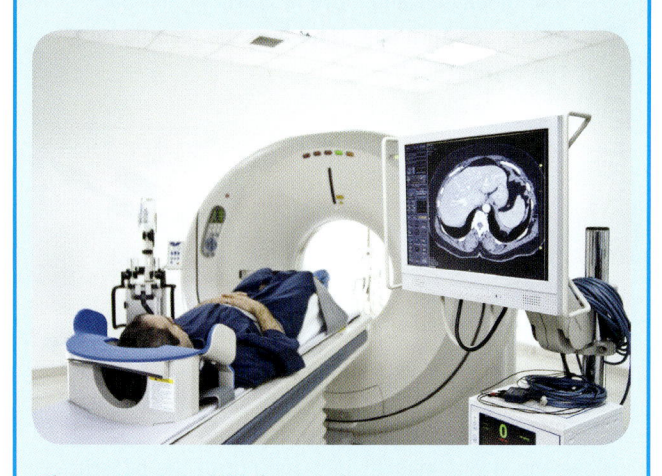

Figure 6.12 An MRI (magnetic resonance imaging) scanner

43

Electricity and Energy

Unit 1

Our bodies contain a lot of water. The way in which water molecules are made up allows them to produce a magnetic field. These magnetic fields are arranged in a totally random manner. When a patient is placed in the strong electromagnetic field of an MRI scanner, the water molecules line up along the magnetic field (just like the iron filings used to show magnetic field lines). A radio signal is then sent through the tunnel of the MRI scanner. This causes the water molecules to spin and emit their own radio signals. The strength of these radio signals depends on the amount of water in the body tissue. This is different for different body tissues. A computer is used to build up an image based on the strength of the radio signals and the length of time they are produced for.

MRI can be used to detect cancerous tissue. The active cells of cancerous tissue need a high blood flow. Blood is mainly water, so cancerous tissue produces a strong signal. MRI can also give excellent images of the brain because of the high blood flow in the brain.

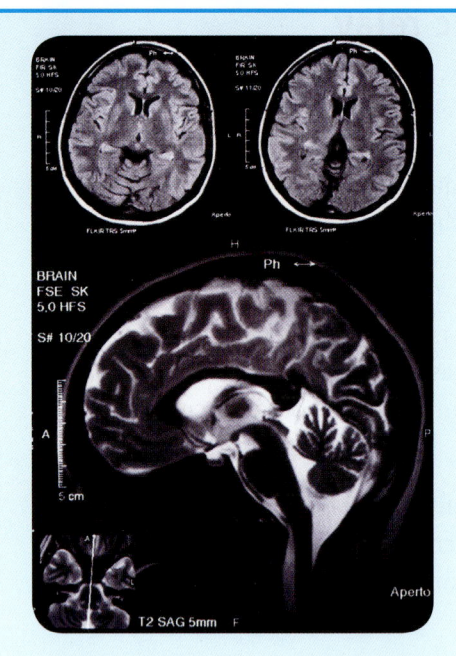

Figure 6.13 An MRI image of the head of a patient

Generating electricity

Investigation

Set up the circuit shown in Figure 6.14. Take a strong magnet and move it slowly in and out of the 625-turn coil. Note how the reading on the voltmeter changes.

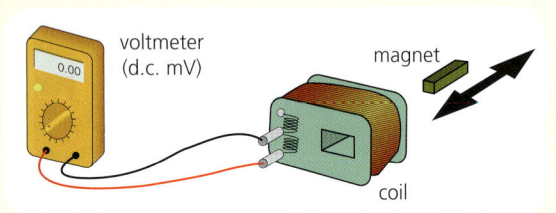

Figure 6.14

Hold the magnet stationary inside the coil. Is there a reading on the voltmeter?

Move the strong magnet into and out of the 625-turn coil quickly. Is there any difference in the reading on the voltmeter? Observe how the reading on the voltmeter changes. Is a.c. or d.c. being produced?

Now move a weaker magnet into and out of the 625-turn coil. How does the reading on the voltmeter compare with when you used the strong magnet?

Now move the strong magnet into and out of a 125-turn coil quickly. How does the reading on the meter compare with when you used the strong magnet and the 625-turn coil?

A bar magnet is suspended from a spring. The magnet can oscillate freely in and out of the coil as shown in Figure 6.15. The coil of wire is connected to a voltmeter. The magnet moves up and down through the coil of wire and as it does this the magnetic field in the coil changes. The changing magnetic field in the coil causes a changing voltage to be produced across the ends of the coil.

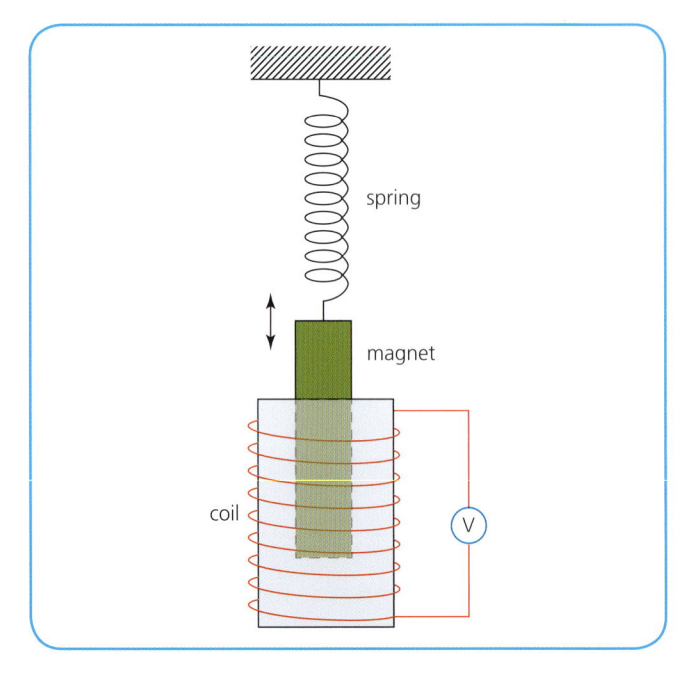

Figure 6.15 A simple electrical generator

The size of this voltage is dependent on:

- the number of turns of wire on the coil – the greater the number of turns, the greater the voltage produced
- the strength of the magnetic field – the stronger the magnetic field, the greater the voltage produced
- the speed of movement – the faster the magnet is moved up or down through the coil, the greater the voltage produced (i.e. the quicker the magnetic field changes, the greater the voltage produced).

> **Investigation**
>
> Turn the handle of a (bicycle) dynamo quickly – what happens to the brightness of the lamp connected to the dynamo?
>
> Turn the handle of a (bicycle) dynamo slowly – what happens to the brightness of the lamp connected to the dynamo?

Figure 6.16 shows a simple electrical generator.

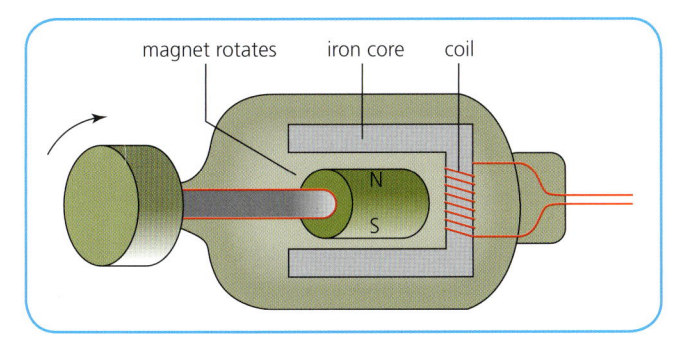

Figure 6.16 A simple electrical generator

An iron core fits closely around a cylindrical permanent magnet, which is made to rotate. As the magnet rotates, the magnetic field near the coil changes and a voltage is produced across the coil. As the magnetic field changes in size and direction, the voltage produced also varies in size and direction, i.e. it is an a.c. voltage.

In power station generators, an electromagnet replaces the permanent magnet, as it can produce a stronger, more compact magnetic field than a permanent magnet. The electromagnet rotates while the coils and their iron core are stationary. A high-pressure steam turbine is used to convert a high-speed stream of steam from the boiler into the rotating movement required to turn the electromagnet.

The transformer

A transformer is a device used to change the value of an alternating voltage.

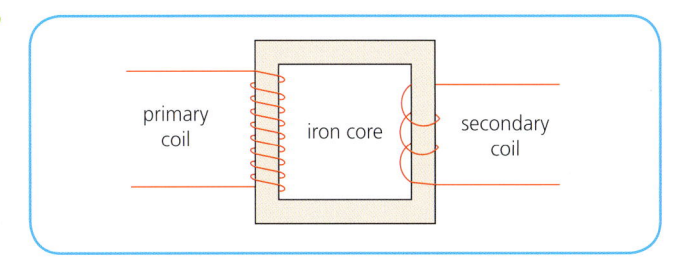

Figure 6.17 Parts of a transformer

The transformer is made of three parts:

1. a primary coil connected to an alternating supply voltage
2. an iron core
3. a secondary coil that is not connected to a supply voltage.

The alternating supply (a.c.) connected to the primary coil causes an alternating current in the primary coil. The alternating current produces a continually changing magnetic field in the primary coil. The iron core transfers this changing magnetic field to the secondary coil. The changing magnetic field in the secondary coil produces an alternating voltage across the secondary coil. This is the output from the transformer. By altering the number of turns of wire on the primary and secondary coils, different output voltages can be obtained.

Electricity and Energy

Unit 1

Investigation

Copy the table shown below.

Primary turns (n_P)	Secondary turns (n_S)	$\dfrac{n_S}{n_P}$	Primary voltage V_P (V)	Secondary voltage V_S (V)	$\dfrac{V_S}{V_P}$
125	500		2		
500	125		2		
125	625		2		
500	500		2		
625	125		2		

Set up the circuit shown in Figure 6.18.

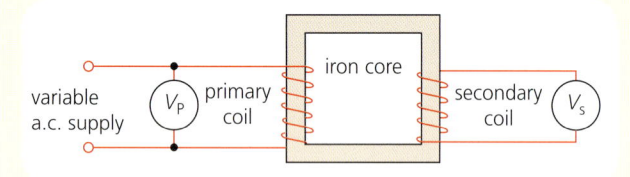

Figure 6.18

For the second row of the table, make the primary coil 125 turns and the secondary coil 500 turns. The voltmeter (set to a.c. voltage) across the primary coil measures the primary voltage, V_P. Adjust the controls on the power supply until the reading on the voltmeter (V_P) is 2 V. The voltmeter (set to a.c. voltage) across the secondary coil measures the secondary voltage, V_S. Record your result for V_S in the second row of the table.

Repeat for the third to sixth rows of the table by altering the values of n_P, n_S and adjust V_P to 2 V – record your result for V_S in each case.

Calculate the values for the third $\left(\dfrac{n_S}{n_P}\right)$ and sixth $\left(\dfrac{V_S}{V_P}\right)$ columns of the table.

What do you notice about the values of $\dfrac{n_S}{n_P}$ and $\dfrac{V_S}{V_P}$ for each row of the table?

For an **ideal** or perfect transformer: $\dfrac{n_S}{n_P} = \dfrac{V_S}{V_P}$

Worked example

Example

A 230 V a.c. supply is connected to the 4600 turn primary coil of an ideal transformer. The voltage across the secondary coil is 6.0 V. Calculate the number of turns on the secondary coil of the transformer.

Solution

Note V_P = 230 V, n_S = 4600 turns and V_S = 6 V

$\dfrac{n_S}{n_P} = \dfrac{V_S}{V_P}$

$\dfrac{n_S}{4600} = \dfrac{6}{230}$

$n_S = \dfrac{6}{230} \times 4600 = 120$ turns

Key facts and physics equations: electromagnetism

- A magnetic field surrounds a magnet.
- A magnetic field surrounds a current-carrying wire.
- The current in a wire controls the magnetic field surrounding the wire.
- An electromagnet consists of a current-carrying wire wrapped around an iron core.
- The magnetic field surrounding an electromagnet allows many electrical devices to operate, for example an electric bell and a relay.
- A voltage can be produced in a coil of wire when the magnetic field near the coil changes.
- The size of the voltage produced can be increased by increasing the strength of the magnetic field, increasing the number of turns on the coil, and increasing how quickly the magnetic field through the coils changes.
- For an ideal transformer $\dfrac{n_S}{n_P} = \dfrac{V_S}{V_P}$.

Electromagnetism

End-of-chapter questions

1. In the following sentences the words represented by the letters A, B, C, D and E are missing.
   A north pole of a magnet repels a ___A___ pole of another magnet. A south pole of a magnet repels a ___B___ pole of another magnet. A north pole of a magnet ___C___ a south pole of another magnet. ___D___ poles repel. ___E___ poles attract.
   Match each letter with the correct word below.
   attracts, like, north, south, unlike

2. A horseshoe magnet is shown in Figure 6.19.

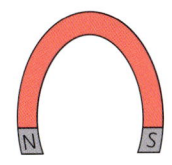

   Figure 6.19

   Copy the magnet and complete your diagram to show the magnetic field lines between the north and south poles.

3. Diagram A in Figure 6.20 shows the direction of four compass needles before a current-carrying wire is placed between them. Diagram B shows the effect that the current-carrying wire has on the needles.

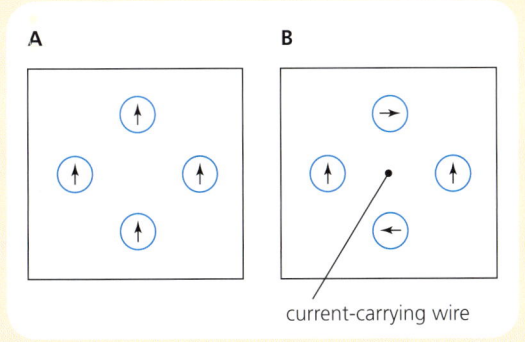

   Figure 6.20

   a) Why do the compass needles move when the current-carrying wire is placed between them?
   b) What would be the effect on the direction of the compass needles in diagram B if the current in the wire:
      (i) was switched off
      (ii) was reversed?

4. A pupil uses a power supply, a length of insulated wire and a nail to produce an electromagnet. She does this by winding a short length of the wire around the nail 30 times. She then attaches the ends of the wire to a 1.5 V d.c. supply. She finds that the electromagnet is able to pick up three paper clips.
   Suggest **two** changes she could make that would allow the electromagnet to lift more paper clips.

5. A circuit is set up as shown in Figure 6.21.

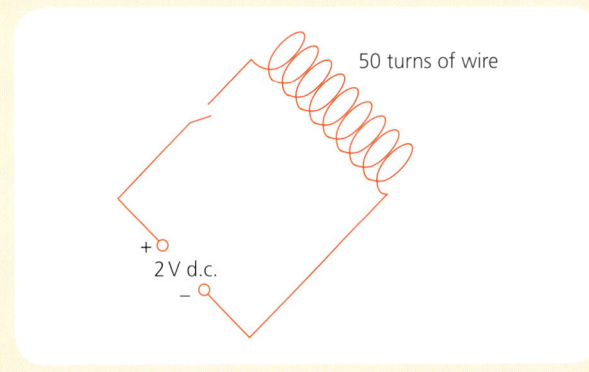

   Figure 6.21

   The switch is closed. The 50 turns of wire now form a weak electromagnet.
   Suggest **three** changes that would increase the strength of the electromagnet.

6. Figure 6.22 shows a loop of wire connected to a voltmeter.

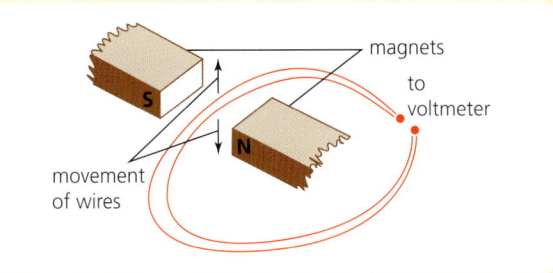

   Figure 6.22

   When the loop of wire is moved between the poles of the magnet, as shown, a reading is obtained on the voltmeter.
   State **three** changes that could be made to increase the reading on the voltmeter.

Electricity and Energy

7 A diagram of a transformer is shown in Figure 6.23.

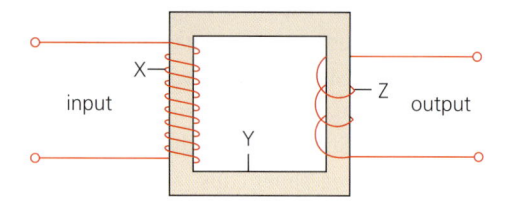

Figure 6.23

Copy the diagram of the transformer. On your diagram, add the correct labels to parts X, Y and Z of the transformer using the list below:
iron core, primary coil, secondary coil

8 Part of an ideal transformer consists of a 4800 turn primary coil. The primary coil is connected to a 16 V a.c. supply. The voltage across the secondary coil is 12 V. Calculate the number of turns on the secondary coil of the transformer.

7 Generation and distribution of electricity

Learning outcomes

At the end of this chapter you should be able to:
1. State that fossil fuels are our main sources of energy at present.
2. State that the reserves of fossil fuels will not last forever, i.e. they are finite.
3. Carry out calculations relating to energy supply and demand.
4. State that radioactive waste is produced by nuclear reactors.
5. Classify renewable and non-renewable sources of energy.
6. Describe the principle and give the advantages of a pumped hydroelectric scheme.
7. Explain the advantages and disadvantages associated with at least three renewable energy sources.
8. Identify from a diagram the energy transformation at each stage of: a thermal power station; a hydro-electric power station; a nuclear power station.
9. Describe qualitatively the transmission of electrical energy by the National Grid system.
10. State that high voltages are used in the transmission of electricity to reduce power loss in the transmission lines.
11. State that transformers are used to change the magnitude of an a.c. voltage.
12. Explain one way of conserving energy related to the use of energy in the home and in transport.
13. State advantages and disadvantages of using nuclear power for the generation of electricity.

Supply and demand

Scotland uses an enormous amount of energy each year in three main ways:
- in heating (homes and buildings)
- for transport (cars, trains, buses and planes)
- to produce electricity.

Figure 7.1 shows the proportions of energy used for these things in 2013.

For Scotland in 2013, a large proportion of this energy came from **fossil fuels** – coal, oil and gas. They are called fossil fuels because they are the remains of plants and animals that lived many millions of years ago. However, burning fossil fuels produces large quantities of carbon dioxide – a greenhouse gas that causes global warming.

Coal is used mainly to generate electrical energy at power stations. Oil is used mainly for transport – cars, trains and aeroplanes. Gas is largely used for heating and for generating electricity.

Fossil fuels are likely to become more expensive as supplies are used up. Once they have been used up, they cannot be replaced, i.e. they are finite.

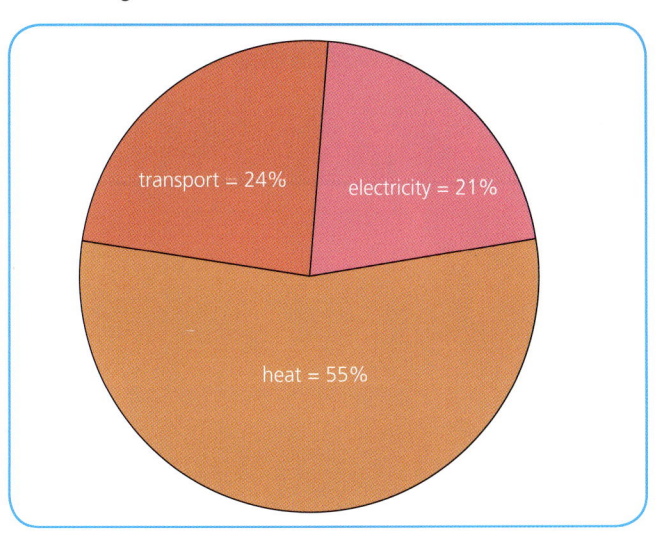

Figure 7.1 Percentages of energy use in Scotland in 2013
(transport = 24%, electricity = 21%, heat = 55%)

Electricity and Energy

Physics in action

Fracking or hydraulic fracturing is a process that has the potential to increase the UK's supplies of oil and gas. Fracking is a process used to release gas and oil from shale (a type of rock that contains quantities of oil and gas). The process is carried out by drilling down into the shale rock and then horizontally along the layer of shale. A high-pressure mixture of water, sand and chemicals is injected into the drill hole. The high pressure creates fractures in the shale rock, which then allows trapped gas and oil to flow to the surface (Figure 7.2).

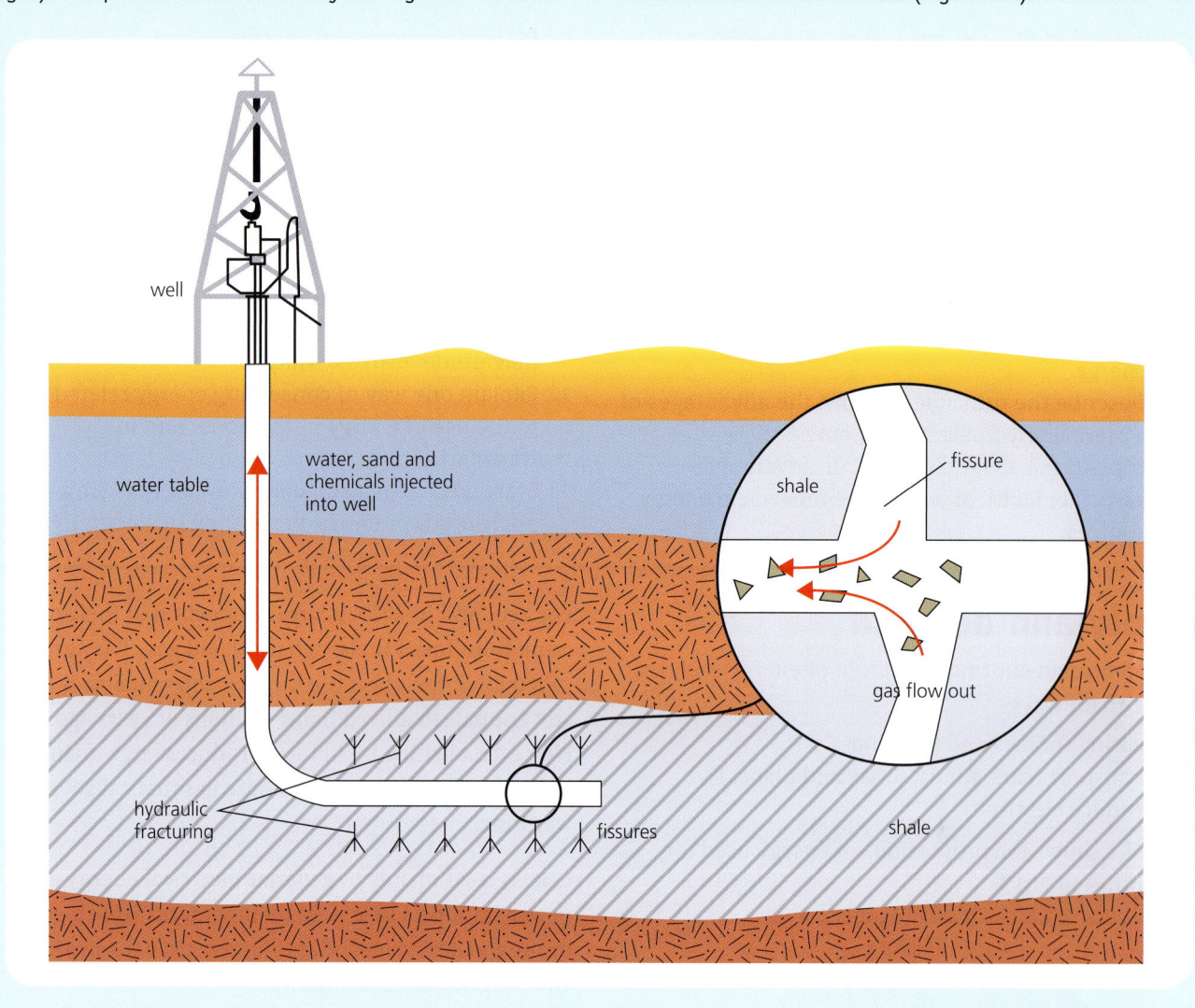

Figure 7.2 Hydraulic fracturing in shale rock to obtain oil and gas

Nuclear power stations are used to generate electricity. Even in small quantities, the uranium fuel used in a nuclear power station can produce large amounts of electrical energy. Known reserves of uranium will last a long time, but are still finite. The radioactive waste produced by nuclear power stations can be extremely dangerous and needs very careful handling and storage for a very long time (see Chapter 12).

Renewable energy sources

Renewables are energy sources that, in theory, are infinite (will not run out). These sources result from:

- the Sun providing the Earth with the energy required to drive weather systems and allow plants to grow
- the tides being a consequence of the gravitational pull of the Sun and Moon
- the Earth having a very hot interior that comes close to the surface in some parts of the world.

Renewable energy sources include hydro, wind, wave, solar, biomass, tidal and geothermal. Renewable energy can be used for heating, transport and to generate electricity.

Figure 7.4 shows the energy sources used to generate electrical energy in Scotland in 2013. It is expected that 100% of the electricity demand equivalent for Scotland will be generated from renewables by 2020.

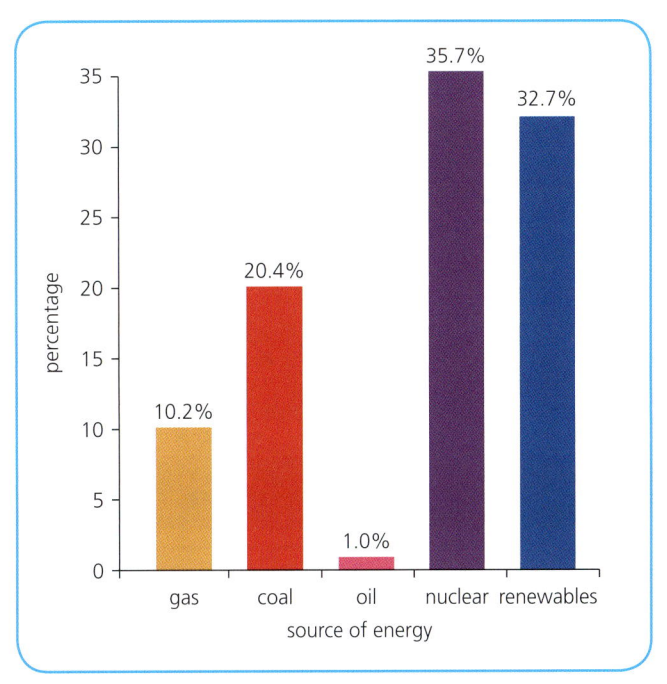

Figure 7.4 Energy sources used to generate electrical energy in Scotland in 2013

Figure 7.3 Torness (near Edinburgh) nuclear power station

Electricity and Energy

Unit 1

Hydroelectric power stations

Water in a high-level dam or reservoir has gravitational potential energy. Hydroelectric power generation makes use of this form of energy. Water flows in a pipe down a steep hill and turns a turbine. The shaft connected to the turbine turns the generator (see Chapter 6) to produce electricity. Figure 7.5 shows a diagram of a hydroelectric power station.

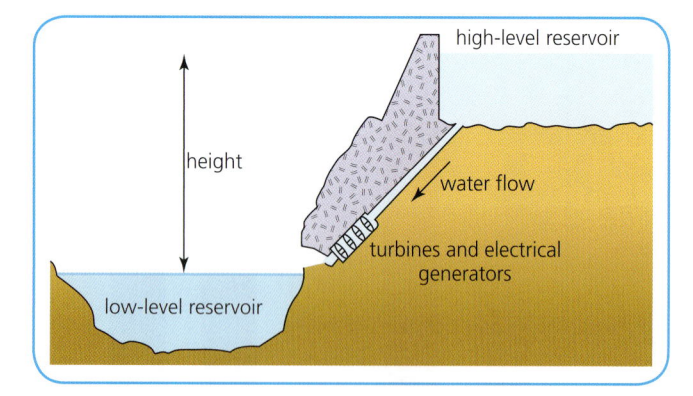

Figure 7.5 A hydroelectric power station

Hydroelectric power is a renewable, reliable and a clean source of energy. However, it can only be used in the hilly parts of the country where there is ample rainfall.

There are also environmental objections to the building of dams as this can result in the flooding of large areas of land, and there is a very small risk of a dam bursting.

Pumped hydroelectric power stations

Electrical energy in large quantities cannot be stored and so it must be used as it is generated. However, demand for electrical energy changes with the time of day and the season of the year.

In a hydroelectric station with pumped storage, surplus electrical energy generated at 'off-peak' periods of the day or night is used to pump water back up from a low-level reservoir to a high-level reservoir. At 'peak' periods of the day when demand for electrical energy is high, the gravitational potential energy of the water in the high-level reservoir is converted back into electrical energy. Although only three units of electrical energy are recovered for every four units supplied, pumped-storage schemes are an economical way of meeting peak demand. They help to increase the overall efficiency of the electrical energy supply system. (The unit used in physics for energy is the **joule** (J). The electrical industry uses kilowatt hours or units of electricity, where 1 kilowatt hour = 1 unit = 3 600 000 joules.)

Figure 7.6 Pitlochry hydroelectric power station

Generation and distribution of electricity

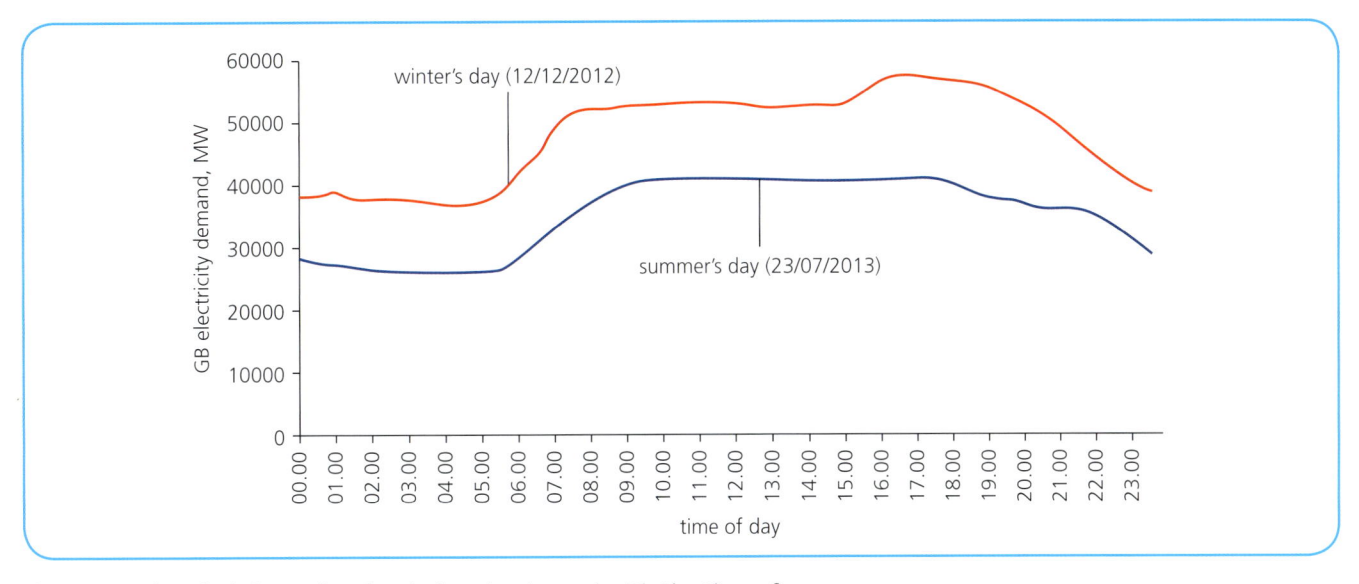

Figure 7.7 Electrical demand varies during the day and with the time of year

Wind power

In past centuries, windmills were used mainly to mill grain or pump water. The windmill converted the energy of the wind into rotational energy using wooden sails.

Today modern wind turbines convert the energy of the wind into electrical energy. These turbines are situated in windy locations, such as hilltops, in what are called **wind farms**. A wind turbine uses specially-shaped blades. When the wind is strong enough, the blades of the turbine begin turning and this rotation is transferred to a generator to produce electricity. As the wind speed increases, the rotation of the blades increases. However, if this rotation is too great the wind turbine will be damaged. To prevent this, the blades of the turbine are turned so they are out of the high wind.

The wind is a renewable and clean source of energy. Conditions for wind energy in Scotland are favourable. The prevailing winds are strong, especially in winter when energy demand is at its greatest. However, the wind cannot always be relied on to blow and so it is difficult to maintain a constant supply of electricity. In addition, wind generators can be unsightly and since the best locations are generally in areas of great natural beauty, there are environmental objections.

Figure 7.8 Whitelees (near Glasgow) wind farm

Electricity and Energy

Unit 1

Figure 7.9 Solar cells on houses generate electricity during daylight hours

Solar power

Sunlight can be used to generate electricity using solar cells (see Chapter 3) similar to those found in solar-powered calculators.

The heat in sunlight (even on a dull Scottish day) is sufficient to heat water in panels (called solar panels) on the roofs of houses and so provide heating for the house.

Solar power is a renewable and clean source of energy. However, it is difficult and expensive to convert large amounts of solar energy into useful forms such as electrical energy. This conversion can only take place during daylight hours.

Biomass (plants)

Biomass is created by harvesting any organic material, such as wood. The biomass is converted into heat, electricity or transport fuel. To generate electricity, the biomass is burned. Properly looked-after forests can provide a sustainable source of energy.

Biomass is a renewable source of energy, but growth is slow and large areas of land are required to provide large amounts as a fuel.

Wave power

The wind causes waves to form on the sea. The energy in the waves can be extracted using various devices. Wave energy is more reliable than the wind, since the waves continue long after the wind that produced them has died away.

Figure 7.10 A Pelarmis wave machine

There are a number of different methods of producing electrical energy from the energy of the waves. The Pelarmis wave machine uses a long series of semi-submerged cylinders, linked by hinged joints. As a wave moves along the cylinders, the cylinders move up and down relative to one another. This up and down motion causes hydraulic oil to pass through a turbine. The turbine is connected to a generator to produce electricity.

Wave power is a renewable and clean source of energy. However, there are difficulties with the construction, maintenance and energy conversion of wave-energy devices. It will be some years before large-scale devices are available in significant numbers.

Tidal power

The tides (the movement of water around the Earth) are caused by the gravitational pull of the Moon and Sun. Tidal power, unlike wave and especially wind power, is a predicable source of clean, renewable energy. Scotland has a large number of sites that are suitable for extracting electrical energy from the tides, such as the Pentland Firth. Devices with designs similar to a wind turbine are submerged in the water. The tide causes the blades to turn and this rotation is transferred to a generator to produce electricity.

Figure 7.11 A horizontal axis tidal turbine

Tidal power is a renewable and clean source of energy. However, there are significant cost and environmental objections to such schemes. It will be some years before these are available in significant numbers.

Geothermal power

The heat inside the Earth can be extracted when water is pumped into a bore hole (injection well). The water is heated and boils. The steam formed is extracted (via a production well) and can be used for heating and to generate electricity.

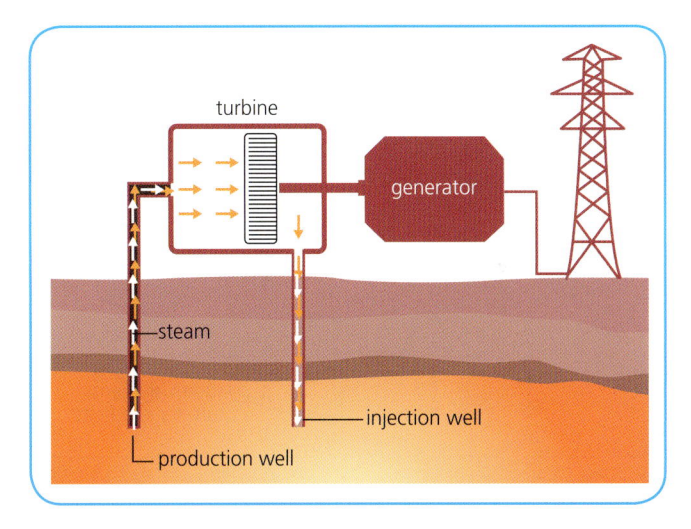

Figure 7.12 A geothermal power station

Geothermal energy is a renewable and clean source of energy, but it is dependent on suitable sites. The extraction of geothermal energy can present considerable technical difficulties.

Table 7.1 summarises the main renewable and non-renewable energy sources.

Renewable energy sources	Non-renewable (finite) energy sources
hydroelectric	coal
wind	oil
solar	gas
biomass (plants)	nuclear
wave	
tidal	
geothermal	

Table 7.1

Electricity and Energy

Power stations

Electrical energy is mostly generated in large power stations using coal, gas, oil or nuclear fuel. Figure 7.13 shows a thermal (fossil-fuelled) power station. The chemical energy of the coal, natural gas or oil is changed into heat when the fuel is burned. The heat produced changes water in a boiler into steam at high pressure. The steam drives the turbine (which changes the kinetic energy of the steam into kinetic energy of rotation) at high speed. This drives the generator, which produces electrical energy. Steam leaving the turbine enters the condenser, which turns it back into water. The water is then pumped back to the boiler under pressure. Cooling towers are required to cool the large quantities of water needed by the condenser. Only about 35% of the fuel's energy (the energy input to the power station) is converted into electrical energy. The remaining 65% is 'lost' as waste heat. A large proportion of this waste heat is transferred to the atmosphere by the cooling towers.

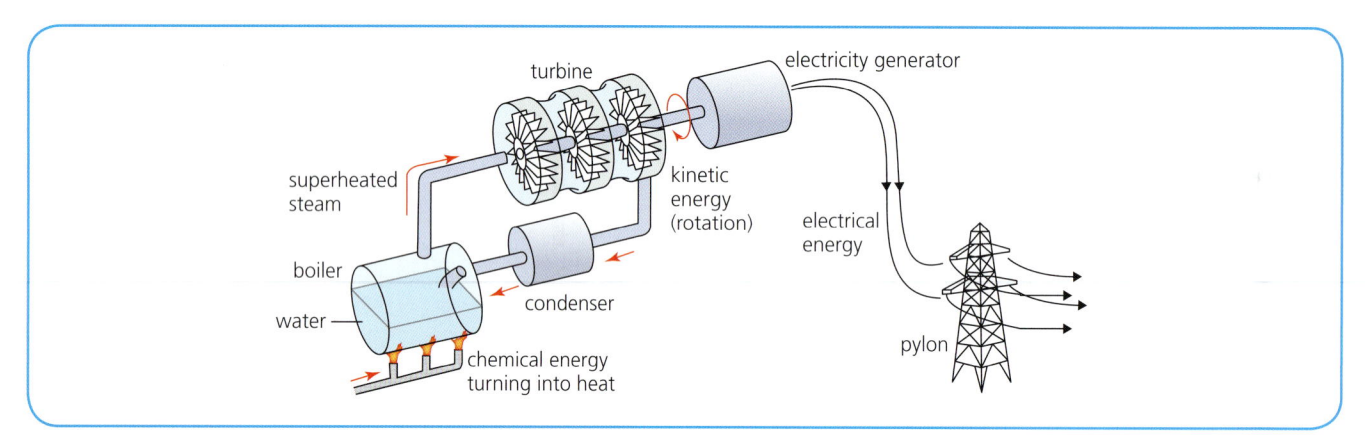

Figure 7.13 A fossil-fuelled power station

In a nuclear power station, a reactor replaces the boiler used in a conventional power station. The nuclear energy of some of the uranium fuel is changed to heat. A gas then carries the heat produced by the uranium fuel in the reactor to a heat exchanger. The heat exchanger transfers heat from the gas to the water, which turns into steam. The steam is used to turn turbines, just as it is in a conventional power station.

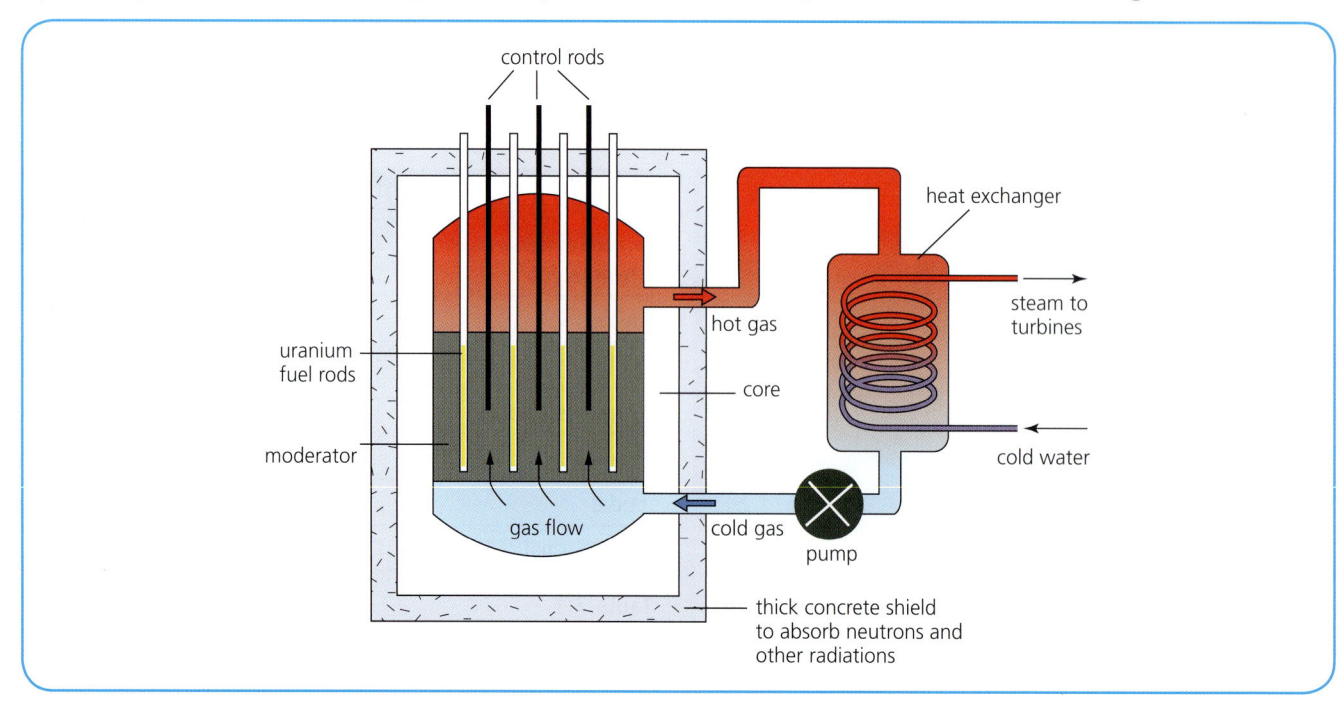

Figure 7.14 A nuclear power station

A nuclear power station requires much less fuel than the equivalent coal-fired power station. This is because 1 kilogram of uranium fuel produces about 200 000 times more energy than 1 kilogram of coal.

Nuclear power stations do not produce greenhouse gases but do produce radioactive waste, which can be very dangerous to us and the environment. This waste has to be safely stored for many years.

Combined heat and power

Combined heat and power (CHP) stations not only generate electricity but also supply hot water to heat buildings in district heating schemes. The hot water is piped to local houses and other buildings, passed through radiators and returned, cooler, to the power station for re-heating. About 25% of the energy input to the power station is converted into electrical energy and 50% is usefully used to heat homes and offices, leaving about 25% as waste heat.

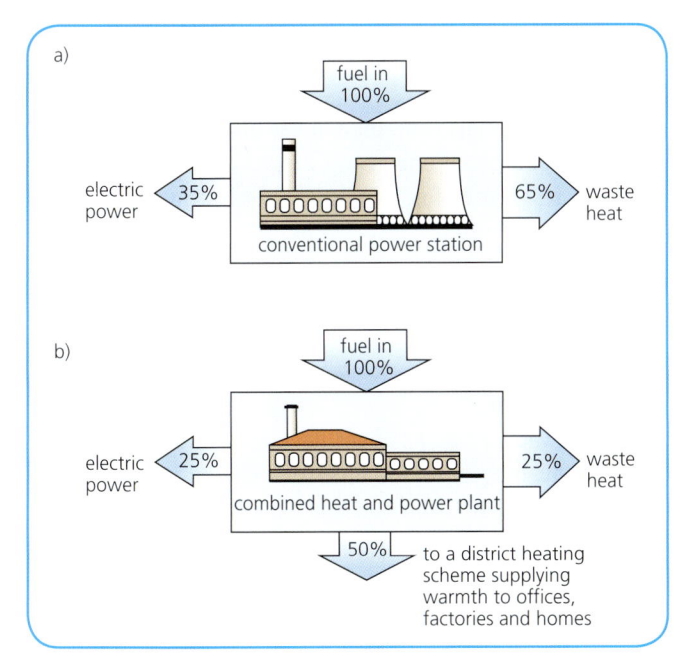

Figure 7.15 Efficiencies of a) conventional and b) combined heat and power stations

Efficiency

The efficiency (see Chapter 5) of an electrical device or machine is given by:

$$\% \text{ efficiency} = \frac{\text{useful energy output}}{\text{total energy input}} \times 100\%$$

$$\% \text{ efficiency} = \frac{\text{useful power output}}{\text{total power input}} \times 100\%$$

Transmitting electrical energy

Figure 7.16 shows how electrical energy generated at a power station is distributed through the National Grid transmission system to our homes.

The generator at the power station produces a voltage at 25 000 volts. For efficient transmission over long distances, this voltage is increased by a device called a (step-up) transformer (see Chapter 6) to 275 000 volts (or 400 000 volts for the National Grid system). At the end of the transmission lines a (step-down) transformer reduces this voltage for distribution to consumers.

Model power line

Figure 7.17 shows an experiment to demonstrate why transformers are required in the transmission of electrical energy.

In Figure 7.17a) electrical energy is transmitted directly along the transmission lines. Lamp Y is not as brightly-lit as lamp X. This is because some of the electrical energy in the transmission lines is changed into heat. The amount of energy changed into heat every second (the power loss) in the transmission lines depends on the current in the transmission lines and the resistance of the transmission lines.

In Figure 7.17b) the voltage is increased (stepped up) before transmission, and reduced (stepped down) at the far end of the transmission lines. In this case lamp Y is much brighter than before, indicating that much less heat has been produced per second in the transmission lines.

Electricity and Energy

Unit 1

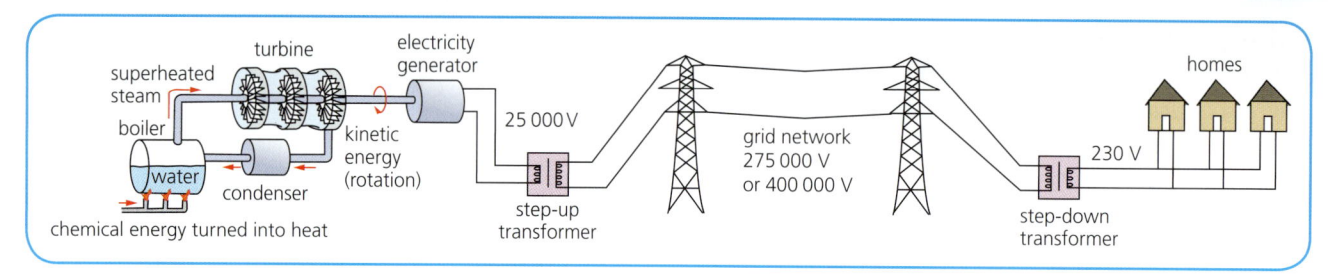

Figure 7.16 Power transmission and distribution

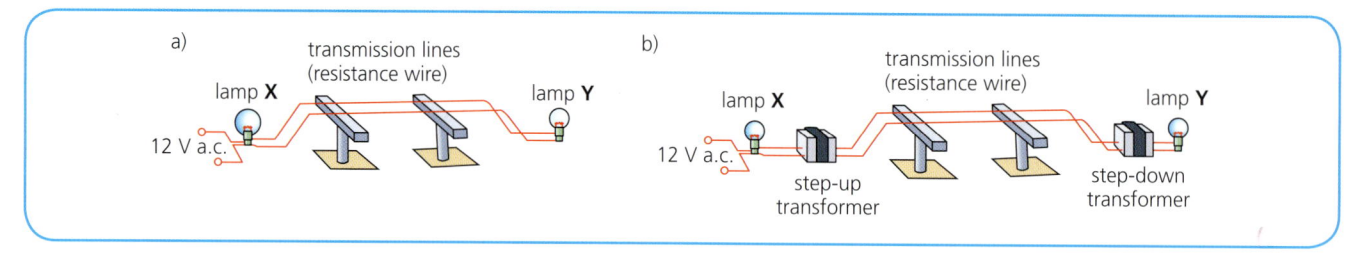

Figure 7.17 Power transmission a) without transformers and b) with transformers

When electrical power is transmitted along transmission lines, it is important to keep the power loss as low as possible. This is done by reducing both the current in the transmission lines and the resistance of the transmission lines. In practice there is a limit to how low the resistance of the transmission lines can be economically made. However, transformers make it possible to reduce the size of the current in the transmission lines by increasing the voltage. Transformers are therefore essential when electrical energy is to be transmitted over large distances.

Conserving energy

The gas and electricity companies produce information that explains how we can save energy (and therefore money) in our homes. Some examples are draught-proofing around windows and doors, unplugging appliances that are not being used (even chargers continue to use electricity when they aren't charging), and replacing filament lamps with energy-efficient fluorescent or LED (light-emitting diode) lamps.

There are a number of ways that energy can be saved in our everyday lives. Examples include sharing a car, using public transport instead of a car, walking or cycling.

> **Key facts and physics equations: generation and distribution of electricity**
>
> - The fossil fuels coal, oil and gas are currently our main sources of energy.
> - The reserves of fossil fuels will not last for ever, i.e. they are finite.
> - Burning fossil fuels produces carbon dioxide, a greenhouse gas.
> - Examples of renewable energy sources are hydroelectric, wind, solar, biomass, wave, tidal and geothermal.
> - Renewable energy sources have advantages and disadvantages, for example solar energy is non-polluting but is difficult and expensive to produce in large amounts.
> - Thermal power stations change the chemical energy of the fuel (coal, gas or oil) into electrical energy (chemical to heat to kinetic to electrical).
> - A nuclear power station changes the nuclear energy of the uranium fuel into electrical energy (nuclear to heat to kinetic to electrical).
> - A nuclear power station produces radioactive waste.
> - The size of an a.c. voltage can be changed by a transformer.
> - High voltages are used in the transmission of electrical power, as this reduces the current in the transmission lines, which reduces the power loss in the transmission lines.

End-of-chapter questions

1. The main sources of Britain's energy are the fossil fuels.
   a) Name three fossil fuels.
   b) Why are they called 'fossil fuels'?
2. Give one way in which energy could be conserved in:
   a) the home
   b) transport.
3. List the following sources of energy under the headings 'renewable' and 'non-renewable': biomass, coal, gas, oil, solar, water, wind.
4. Explain the difference between renewable and non-renewable energy sources.
5. Give one advantage and one disadvantage of the following sources of energy:
   a) wind
   b) solar
   c) wave.
6. A wind farm consists of 30 large wind generators. Each generator can produce 1.5 million units of electrical power.
   a) Suggest a suitable location for the wind farm.
   b) How much electrical power is the wind farm capable of generating?
7. The output power from a wave generator is on average 10 000 units per metre. An island requires 20 000 000 units of electrical power. Calculate the total length of wave generators required to supply power to the island.
8. The input power to a transformer is 25 watts. The output power from the transformer is 23 watts. Calculate the efficiency of the transformer.
9. A small generator produces 24 000 watts of power. A transmission system delivers the power to a device. The power reaching the device is 18 000 watts. Calculate the efficiency of the transmission system.
10. The power input to a model transmission system is 60 W. The power output from the transmission system is 42 W. Calculate the efficiency of the transmission system.
11. The power input to a hydroelectric power station is 1 000 000 W. The power output from the station is 750 000 W. Calculate the efficiency of the power station.
12. The power input to a gas-fired power station is 1800 units. The power station produces 846 units of electrical power. Calculate the efficiency of the power station in producing electricity.

Electricity and Energy

Unit 1

8 Gas laws and the kinetic theory

Learning outcomes

At the end of this chapter you should be able to:
1. Describe how the kinetic model accounts for the pressure exerted by a gas.
2. Explain the pressure-volume, pressure-temperature and volume-temperature laws qualitatively in terms of a kinetic model.

We are unable to see what makes up a gas with the human eye, or indeed with a very powerful light microscope. But if we were able to 'see' the gas, what would it look like?

Scientists came up with a 'theory' or 'model' of what they think a gas looks like, known as the **kinetic model of a gas**. In this model the gas can be thought of as being made up of tiny particles (similar to billiard balls) called atoms or molecules. These particles are in continuous motion.

In a gas, the particles are moving very fast in all directions. They are very far apart (compared to their size) so that the forces of attraction between them can be neglected. This accounts for the fact that a gas will spread throughout a room. The gas particles are in random motion – they do not move in any particular direction.

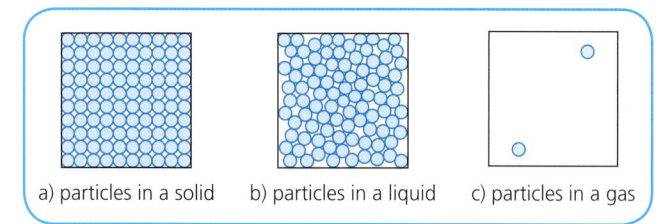

a) particles in a solid   b) particles in a liquid   c) particles in a gas

Figure 8.1 States of matter

Gas pressure

Kinetic theory assumes that the particles of a gas are moving in all directions (random motion). Evidence for this is provided by the motion of smoke particles in a smoke cell. The smoke particles have a jerky, irregular motion, which is known as Brownian motion. The random motion is caused by the bombardment of the smoke particles by the invisible air particles. The air particles are moving in all directions. They collide with the smoke particles and so cause the jerky, irregular motion.

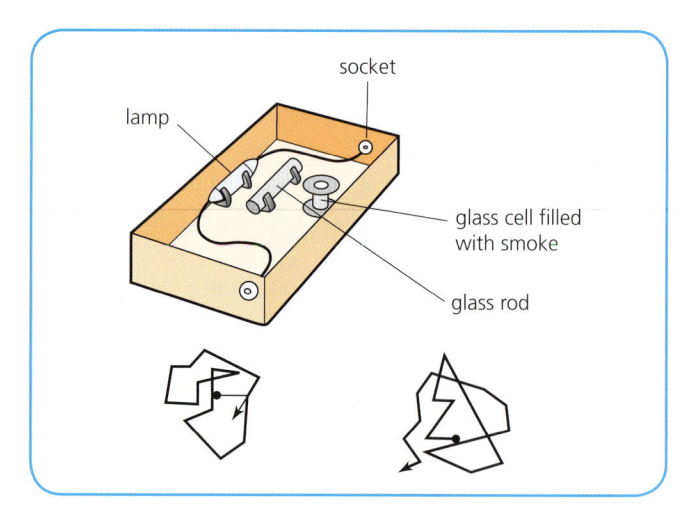

Figure 8.2 A Brownian smoke cell and the random motion of two smoke particles in the cell

A greatly magnified 'picture' or model of the particles making up a gas in a small container is shown in Figure 8.3. In this 'model', each small metal sphere represents a particle of gas. The spheres are made to move rapidly by the vibrating plate at the base. Each time a sphere hits the piston (the square piece of black plastic), it exerts a small upwards force on the piston. However, a large number of spheres hit (or bombard) the piston every second. This bombardment is able to give a large enough upwards force to push the piston part of the way up the tube. When the spheres collide with the piston, the pressure on the piston is due to the force exerted by the metal spheres on the piston.

Gas laws and the kinetic theory

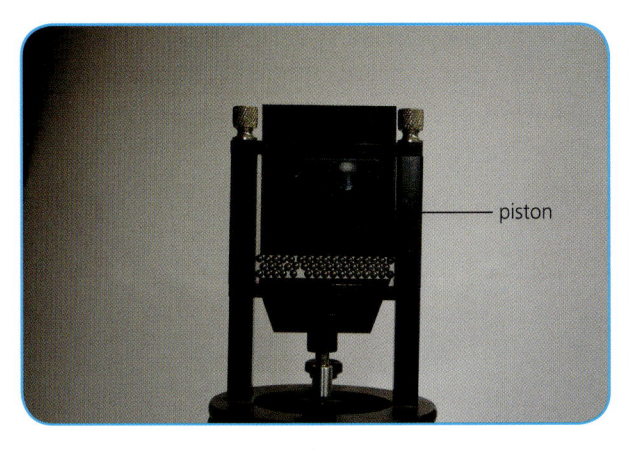

Figure 8.3 'Gas' particles bombarding the walls of a container

From the above, the pressure exerted by a gas on the surface it is in contact with is due to the force of the particles on the surface when they collide with the surface. The pressure exerted by a gas is produced by particle bombardment.

The kinetic model of a gas assumes that the tiny gas particles are in constant random motion. The pressure exerted by a gas on the walls of its container is due to the bombardment of the container walls by the fast-moving gas particles (about 500 metres per second for air at room temperature). The particles hit the walls of the container and rebound, exerting a force on the wall. The pressure is a result of these forces on the area of the wall.

Pressure depends on the number of collisions made by the particles with the walls each second, and on the force of each collision. In other words, pressure depends on particle bombardment:

- A gas is made up of tiny particles.
- The particles of a gas move around in all directions (random motion).
- The particles of a gas collide elastically with each other and with the container walls. ('Elastically' means that the speed of the particles is not changed by the effect of the collisions.)
- The pressure exerted by a gas is caused by the particles colliding with the container walls, i.e. it is due to particle bombardment of the container walls.
- The pressure depends on the force of each collision with the walls and the number of collisions made with the walls every second.

Note: A gas will always flow from an area of higher pressure to an area of lower pressure until the pressures become the same.

A gas

There are three things that can change for a fixed mass of gas:

- the pressure exerted by the gas
- the volume occupied by the gas
- the temperature of the gas.

Pressure and volume

> **Investigation**
>
> Take a plastic syringe. Pull the piston halfway out. Now close off the end of the syringe with your thumb and push the piston in. What happens to the pressure of the gas?
>
> Take the syringe and pull the piston halfway out. Now close off the end of the syringe with your thumb. Now pull the piston outwards. What happens to the pressure of the gas?

The apparatus shown in Figure 8.4 is used to find out what happens to the pressure exerted by a gas and the volume occupied by the gas, with the gas temperature remaining constant. The gas used in the experiment is air. The mass of the air is fixed (no air is added or leaves the cylinder during the experiment).

61

Electricity and Energy

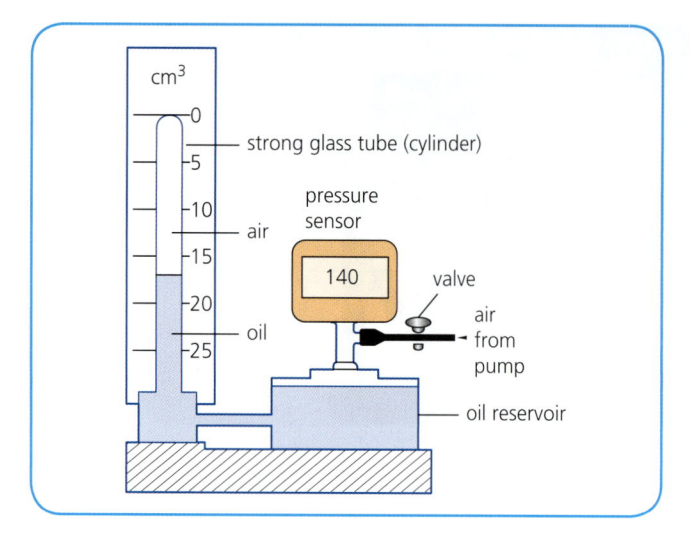

Figure 8.4 Pressure against volume apparatus

The air in the cylinder is first compressed using a foot pump. During the compression the temperature of the air rises as work is being done on it. The air is allowed to return to room temperature before any readings are taken. The air in the cylinder is allowed to expand slowly by opening the valve. The pressure of the air at appropriate volumes is noted and recorded as shown in the table.

Pressure (units)	300	250	200	150	100
Volume (units)	8.0	9.6	12	16	24

Table 8.1 Pressure against volume results

Notice that as the volume of the gas increases, the pressure decreases.

> ### Physics in action
>
> When you breathe your chest cavity expands, which allows the lungs to expand. Since the volume of the lungs has increased, the pressure in the lungs decreases. The outside pressure is then greater than the pressure in the lungs and this forces air into the lungs.

Pressure and temperature

The apparatus shown in Figure 8.5 is used to find out what happens to the pressure exerted by a gas and the temperature of the gas while at constant volume. The gas used in this experiment is air. The mass of the gas is fixed (no air enters or leaves the flask during the experiment).

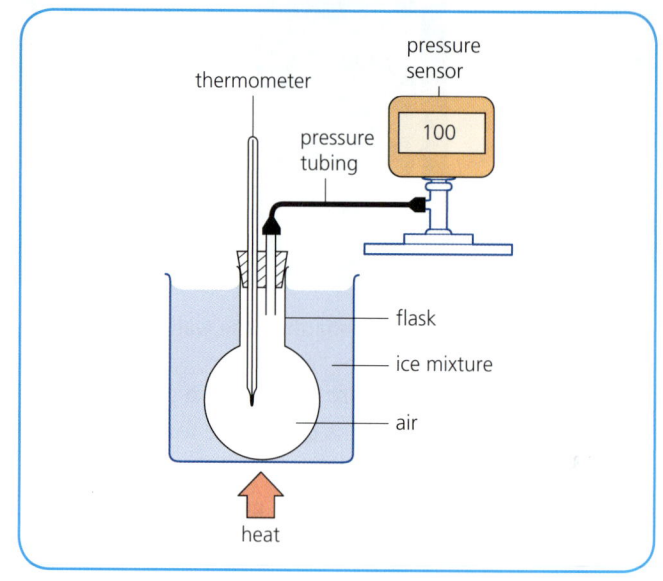

Figure 8.5 Pressure against temperature apparatus

The ice mixture is heated slowly. Readings of the pressure and temperature of the gas are taken at regular intervals and recorded in the table.

Pressure (units)	100	110	120	130	140
Temperature (°C)	0	25	50	75	100

Table 8.2 Pressure against temperature results

Notice that as the temperature of the gas increases, the pressure increases.

> ### Physics in action
>
> The pressure of a car tyre increases during a journey because the temperature of the air in the tyre increases.
>
> It can be very dangerous when a pressurised aerosol can (even an 'empty' one), such as a hairspray aerosol, is heated excessively. This may happen when an aerosol can is burned along with other waste materials. When the can is heated, the pressure of the gas inside the can will increase. If the pressure becomes too high then the can will rupture – i.e. it explodes.

Gas laws and the kinetic theory

Volume and temperature

> **Investigation**
>
> Carefully measure the circumference of a blown-up balloon. Now place the balloon in a freezer and leave it there for 15 minutes.
>
> Remove the balloon from the freezer and quickly measure its circumference.
>
> How does the size (volume) of the balloon change as the air in the balloon returns to room temperature?

The apparatus shown in Figure 8.6 is used to find out what happens to the volume and the temperature of a gas while at a constant pressure. The gas used in this experiment is air. The mass of the air is fixed (no air is added to or leaves the capillary tube during the experiment). The air in the cylinder is at a constant pressure since the air above the bead of mercury is always at atmospheric pressure.

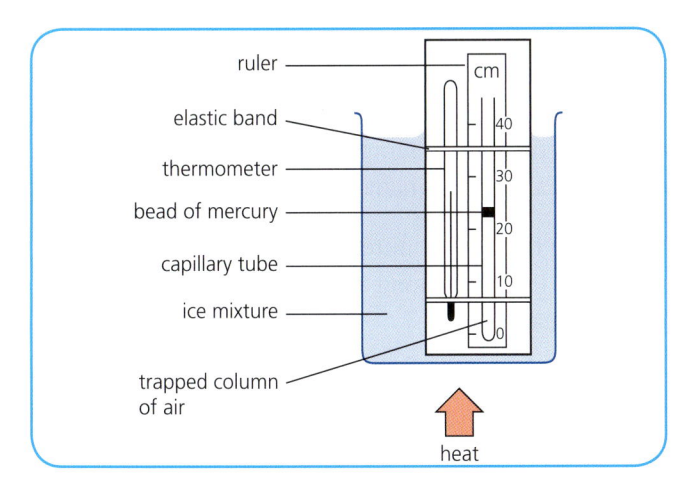

Figure 8.6 Volume against temperature apparatus

The ice mixture is heated slowly. Readings of the volume and temperature of the gas are taken at regular intervals and recorded in the table.

Volume (units)	60.0	64.5	69.0	73.5	78.0
Temperature (°C)	0	25	50	75	100

Table 8.3 Volume against temperature results

Notice that as the temperature of the gas increases, the volume increases.

Gas pressure and kinetic theory

- The pressure exerted by a gas on its container is a result of the bombardment of the walls by the fast-moving gas particles. The particles hit the walls and rebound, exerting a force on the wall. The pressure is the result of these forces. Since the number of particles is very large and they are moving very fast, the number of collisions with the walls per second is very, very large. As a result the series of tiny forces is smoothed out into a steady push on the container walls.
- The particles of the gas collide elastically with each other and with the container walls. ('Elastically' means that during the collisions the speed of the particles does not change.)
- The temperature of a gas depends on the average kinetic energy of the particles. When a gas is heated, the temperature of the gas increases. This means that the average kinetic energy of the gas particles increases and so their speed increases. The gas particles will hit the container walls harder (with more force) and more often, so increasing the particle bombardment. This increases the pressure exerted by the gas.

Examples

Consider a fixed mass of gas trapped in a rigid container, which is sealed at one end by a gas-tight movable piston. When the piston is stationary the pressure on both sides is the same and equal to atmospheric pressure.

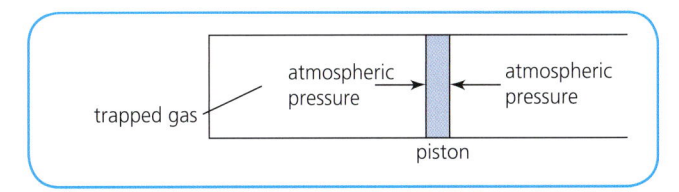

Figure 8.7 A fixed mass of gas trapped in a container by a movable piston

Pressure and temperature (at constant volume)

The volume of gas is kept constant by preventing the piston from moving.

When the trapped gas is heated, the temperature of the gas will rise. The average kinetic energy of the gas particles will increase and so they will speed up. The particles will

63

hit the container walls harder (with greater force) and more often (because they are travelling faster across the same distance), thus increasing the particle bombardment. This causes the pressure exerted by the gas to increase.

As the temperature of the gas increases, so does the pressure exerted by the gas, as long as the volume is unchanged (the law of pressures).

Pressure and volume (at a constant temperature)

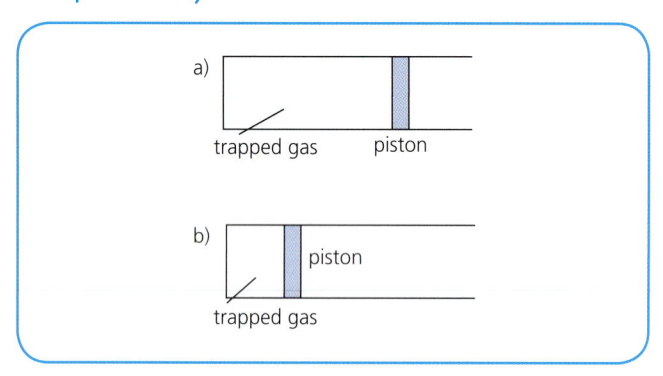

Figure 8.8 a) Before the piston is pushed in; b) after the piston is pushed in

When the piston is moved in, the volume occupied by the gas decreases. When the gas returns to its original temperature, the average kinetic energy of the particles is the same as before, i.e. the particles travel at the same speed. The particles hit the piston with the same force. However, since the volume has decreased, there will be more collisions with the container walls per second (or collisions occur more often). The bombardment of the piston increases and therefore the pressure exerted by the gas increases.

As the volume decreases the pressure exerted by the gas increases, provided the temperature is unchanged.

Volume and temperature (at a constant pressure)

When the trapped gas (in Figure 8.7) is heated, the temperature of the gas rises. The average kinetic energy of the gas particles increases, so they speed up. The particles hit the container walls harder (with greater force) and more often (because they are travelling faster in the same area), thus increasing the particle bombardment. This causes the pressure exerted by the gas on the piston to increase. The piston moves out and the volume occupied by the gas increases. The gas particles then have more distance to travel between collisions. There will now be fewer collisions with the container walls per second (or collisions occur less often) and so the particle bombardment will decrease. This cancels out the increase in particle bombardment due to the increase in temperature. The pressure exerted by the gas is unchanged.

Increasing the temperature of the gas increases the volume of the gas, as long as the pressure exerted by the gas is unchanged.

Physics in action

At normal atmospheric pressure, water boils at 100°C. However, at pressures higher than atmospheric pressure, water boils at a higher temperature. The steam produced will be at a temperature greater than 100°C. In a pressure cooker, due to the higher pressure, the temperature of the steam is about 115°C. The steam is forced through the food, which cooks more rapidly as a result of the higher temperature. This saves energy.

As you climb a high mountain, atmospheric pressure decreases. However, at lower pressures than atmospheric pressure, water boils at a temperature lower than 100°C. So making a cup of tea up a high mountain would mean that your tea would be cooler than normal!

You may have noticed that the volume of a sealed packet of sweets when on board an aeroplane flying at a high altitude is greater than when it was on the ground. The air pressure in the sealed packet will always equal the air pressure outside. However, when the aeroplane is at an altitude, the pressure in the cabin is less than at ground level. This means that the pressure of the air inside the sealed packet is greater than the pressure in the cabin – the volume of the bag increases until the air pressure inside the packet and the air pressure in the cabin are the same.

Gas laws and the kinetic theory

Diving

If you have ever dived or swam to a depth of a few metres in water, you may have felt some pain in your ears. This is due to the pressure on the outside of your eardrums becoming too great.

The deeper under the water you go, the greater the pressure acting on you. At a depth of more than 0.5 metres it is very difficult to breathe. This is because of the extra pressure on your lungs due to the water. You may have noticed that snorkel tubes are quite short. A long snorkel tube would not be any use to you since you would find it almost impossible to breathe air into your lungs.

SCUBA (Self-Contained Underwater Breathing Apparatus) diving enables divers to swim underwater. This is because the air that the diver breathes is adjusted to the same pressure as the surrounding water. Part of the equipment used is called an aqualung.

The aqualung consists of a cylinder of compressed air, a hose, and a mouthpiece unit. On top of the cylinder is a valve. If the air pressure in the hose falls below a certain value, the valve opens and air from the cylinder passes into the hose. The mouthpiece unit contains a demand valve that allows air from the hose to pass into the air chamber. When the diver breathes in air, the pressure on the air chamber falls. The rubber diaphragm is pushed inwards by the pressure of the surrounding water. This allows the demand valve to open. Air is now supplied to the diver at a similar pressure to the pressure in the lungs.

The pressure in the diver's lungs depends on the water pressure outside their body. When a diver uses SCUBA equipment, air is breathed in at the same pressure as the surrounding water. As the diver dives deeper in the water, more and more nitrogen gas from the air supply becomes dissolved in the diver's blood. If the diver returns rapidly to the surface, the nitrogen forms bubbles in the blood (due to the decrease in pressure). When the bubbles form in the diver's blood, the diver is said to have the 'bends'. This condition can cause death. The only way to avoid this problem is to ensure that the pressure of the diver's blood is reduced very slowly. For a deep-sea diver this process may take several days while the diver stays in a decompression chamber.

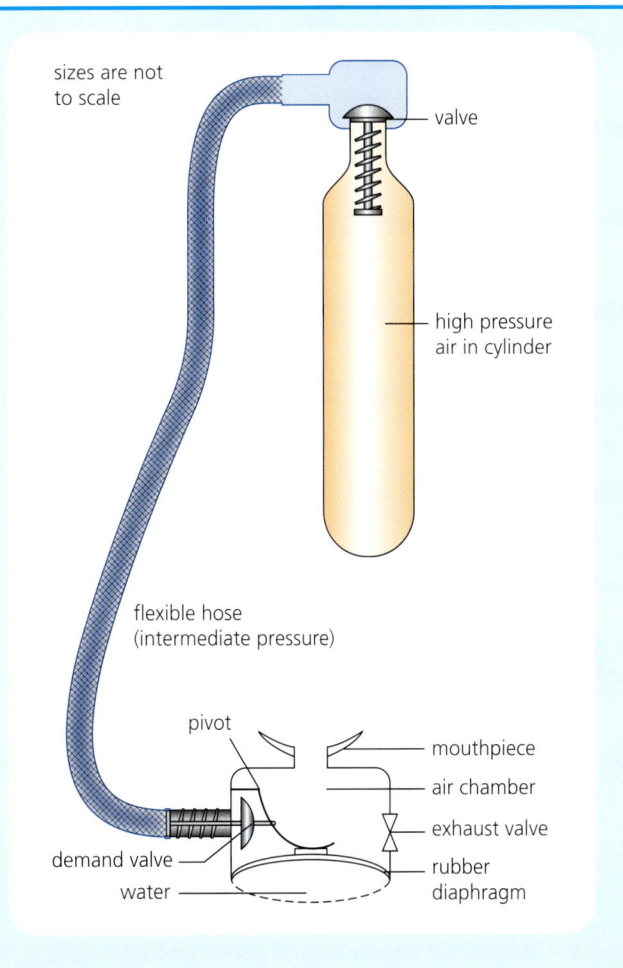

Figure 8.9 An aqualung

Key facts and physics equations: gas laws and the kinetic theory

- The kinetic model explains how the particles of a gas are able to exert pressure due to particle bombardment of the walls of the container.
- Temperature is a measure of the average kinetic energy of the particles making up the substance.
- As the volume of a gas decreases, the pressure increases.
- As the temperature of a gas increases, the pressure increases.
- As the temperature of a gas increases, the volume increases.

Electricity and Energy

Unit 1

End-of-chapter questions

1. A driver, before starting on a long journey, checks the pressure of the air in the tyres on her car. She sets the pressure of the air in the tyres to 31 units. During the journey, the temperature of the air in the tyres increases.
    a) Suggest a value for the pressure of the air in the tyres, in units, at the end of the journey.
    b) Explain your answer.
2. Explain why it is dangerous to throw an aerosol can onto a bonfire.
3. Use the kinetic theory of a gas to explain how the pressure exerted by a fixed volume of gas falls as the temperature of the gas decreases.
4. In some squash balls, the outer layer is made up of a rubber compound and the central core is filled with air. During a game of squash the players hit the ball with a racquet so that it collides with and rebounds from a wall. This happens a number of times during a rally.
    a) State whether the temperature of the air in the squash ball at the end of the game is greater than, the same as, or less than the temperature at the start of the game.
    b) After a game, the squash ball is harder to compress compared to the start of the game. Explain why this is so.

Unit 1 exam practice

1. Some of the main sources of energy used in Great Britain are: coal, hydroelectric, natural gas, nuclear, oil and wind.
    a) From the above list select one source of energy that is not a fossil fuel.
    b) Name a renewable source of energy that is not shown in this list.
    c) State one disadvantage of generating electrical energy from:
        (i) the wind
        (ii) nuclear energy.
2. The figure below shows the time that some sources of non-renewable energy are expected to last, according to one report.

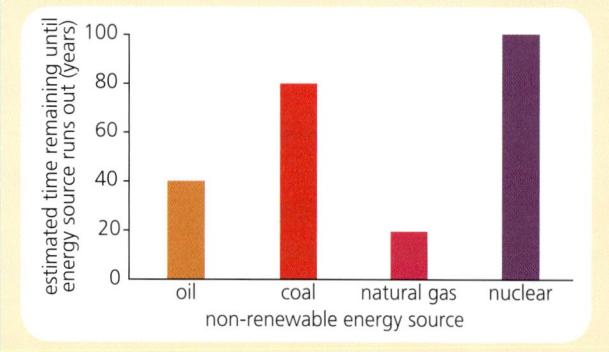

Figure E1.1

Use information from the bar chart to answer the following.
    a) Which source of non-renewable energy will last the longest?
    b) How long will natural gas last for?
    c) State two sources of renewable energy that could be used to replace the non-renewable energy sources.
3. A model transformer is shown below.

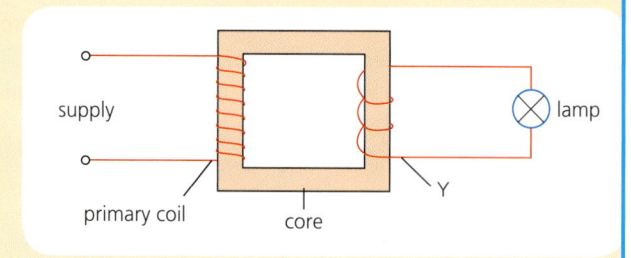

Figure E1.2

    a) Name part Y of the transformer.
    b) The input power to the transformer is 20 W. The output power from the transformer is 18 W. Calculate the efficiency of the transformer.
4. Some information from the rating plates of a games console and a hairdryer are shown below.

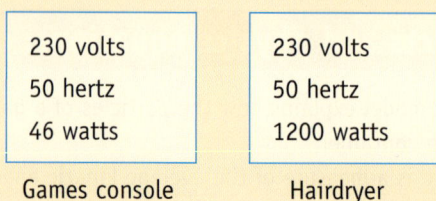

Games console	Hairdryer
230 volts	230 volts
50 hertz	50 hertz
46 watts	1200 watts

    a) State the power rating of the games console.
    b) Both appliances are switched on for 15 minutes. Which appliance will use more energy in this time?

c) The hairdryer is switched on for 10 minutes. Calculate the energy used by the hairdryer in this time.

5 a) A bar magnet is shown below.

Figure E1.3

Copy the diagram. Sketch the shape of the magnetic field around the bar magnet.

b) A simple hand-operated generator is connected to a lamp as shown.

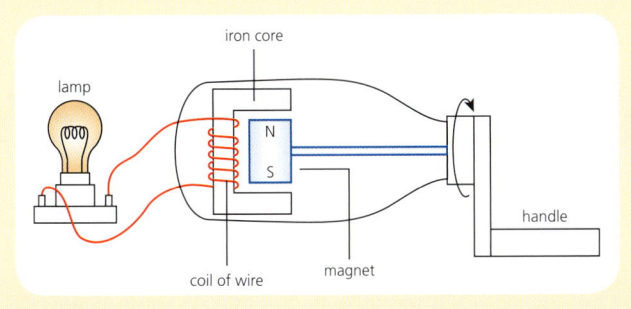

Figure E1.4

(i) Explain how a voltage is produced across the coil of wire when the handle is turned.
(ii) State two ways in which a bigger voltage could be produced by the generator.

6 An anemometer is a device used to measure wind speed. A simple anemometer is shown below.

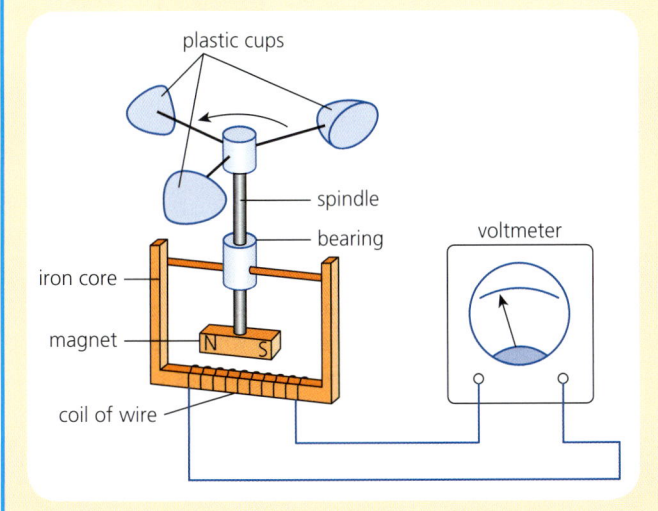

Figure E1.5

When a steady wind blows, the spindle rotates and the pointer on the voltmeter is deflected to give a constant reading.

a) When the spindle rotates, a reading is displayed on the voltmeter. Explain why a reading is displayed on the voltmeter.
b) Give two ways in which this anemometer could be modified so as to produce a larger reading on the same voltmeter.

7 a) A heater is connected to a 230 V supply as shown.

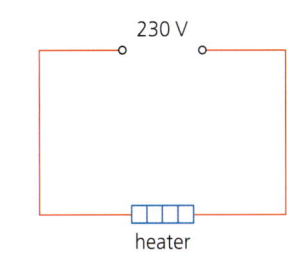

Figure E1.6

The current in the heater is 5.0 A. Calculate the resistance of the heater.

b) Part of a circuit for a two-bar electric fire is shown below.

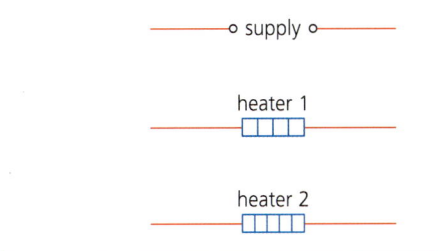

Figure E1.7

Heater 1 and heater 2 are connected in parallel. Copy and complete the diagram to show how two switches can be used to:
(i) switch on only heater 1
(ii) switch on both heater 1 and heater 2.

8 A circuit is set up as shown below.

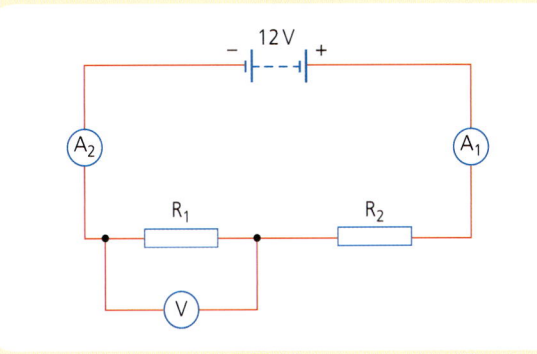

Figure E1.8

Electricity and Energy

Unit 1

The reading on A_1 is 0.25 A. The reading on V is 5.0 V.
a) State the reading on A_2.
b) Calculate the resistance of R_2.

9 A circuit is set up as shown below to measure the resistance of an LDR at different light intensities.

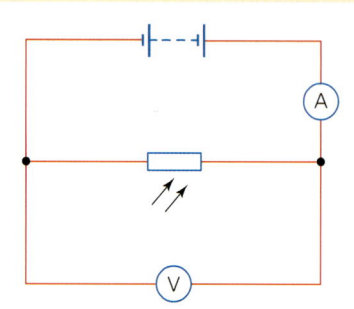

Figure E1.9

a) State whether the LDR is an input or an output device.
b) At one level of brightness the following readings were obtained:
Reading on A = 0.02 A
Reading on V = 4.0 V
Calculate the resistance of the LDR at this light level.
c) Lights of different brightness are shone on the LDR. The following results are obtained:

Level of brightness	Resistance of LDR (Ω)
very dim	1500
dim	560
daylight	?
bright light	25

The value of the resistance of the LDR in daylight is missing. Suggest a possible value for the resistance of the LDR in daylight.

10 a) An electronic system can be represented by a block diagram as shown below.

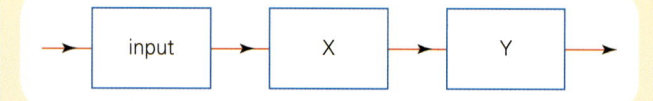

Figure E1.10

State the name given to:
(i) block X
(ii) block Y.
b) Part of an electronic system is shown below.

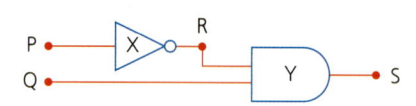

Figure E1.11

(i) State the names of logic gate X and logic gate Y.
(ii) The table shows the possible logic levels of inputs P and Q. Copy and complete the table to show the logic levels of R and S.

P	Q	R	S
0	0		
0	1		
1	0		
1	1		

11 The pressure at the bottom of a pool of water is greater than the pressure at the surface of the pool. A bubble of gas rises from the bottom of the pool. Explain what happens to the volume of the bubble as it rises.

12 The diagram shows a sample of gas contained in a cylinder.

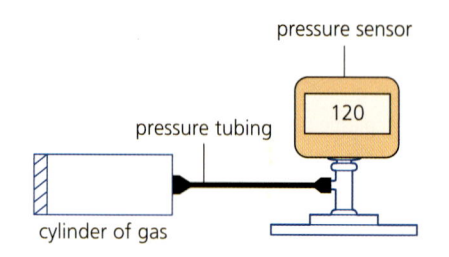

Figure E1.12

One end of the cylinder is connected to a pressure meter. The gas in the cylinder is heated. Use the kinetic theory of a gas to explain what happens to the reading on the pressure meter as the gas is heated.

Unit 2

Waves and Radiation

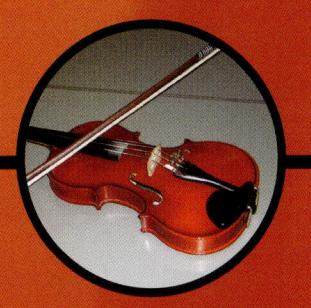

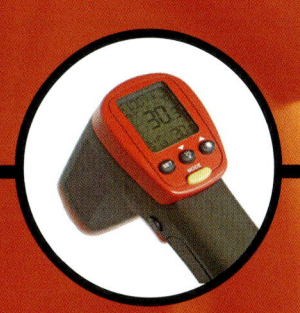

9 Wave characteristics

> **Learning outcomes**
>
> At the end of this chapter you should be able to:
> 1. State that a wave transfers energy.
> 2. State the difference between a transverse and a longitudinal wave.
> 3. State that the greater the amplitude of a wave, the more energy the wave transfers.
> 4. State that in a given medium, the speed of a wave is constant.
> 5. State that the frequency of a wave is the number of waves produced in one second.
> 6. Carry out calculations using:
>
> $$\text{frequency} = \frac{\text{number of waves}}{\text{time to produce waves}}$$
>
> 7. State that the frequency of a wave is determined by the source that produces the wave.
> 8. Use the following terms correctly in context: wave, crest, trough, frequency, wavelength, speed, amplitude.
> 9. Carry out calculations involving the relationship between distance, time and speed for waves.
> 10. Carry out calculations involving the relationship between speed, wavelength and frequency for waves.

What is a wave?

Imagine a piece of wood floating on the surface of a pond. When waves are produced and pass below the piece of wood, the wood bobs up and down. Since the piece of wood is now moving it must have 'gained' kinetic energy. This kinetic energy must have been transferred from the wave. This means that waves can transfer energy.

Types of wave

When a wave passes through a material (the material is often called the medium), the wave causes the particles of the material to vibrate.

> **Investigation**
>
> Attach a piece of tape to one of the coils near the centre of a slinky spring. Stretch the slinky between yourself and a partner. Produce a wave pulse in the slinky by moving your arm quickly at right-angles to the slinky. Watch what happens to the piece of tape.
>
> Now produce another wave pulse by quickly moving your arm back and forth in the same direction as the slinky. Watch what happens to the piece of tape.

When the particles of the medium vibrate at right-angles to the direction in which the wave is travelling, the wave is called a **transverse** wave.

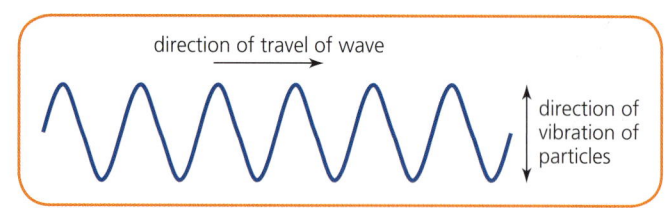

Figure 9.1 A transverse wave

When the particles of the medium vibrate parallel to the direction in which the wave is travelling, the wave is called a **longitudinal** wave.

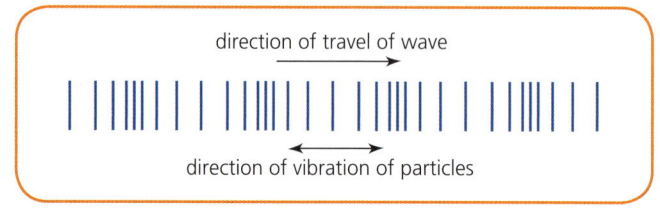

Figure 9.2 A longitudinal wave

Sound (and ultrasound) waves are longitudinal waves. All the other types of wave are transverse waves, for example light, microwaves and water waves.

Wave characteristics

Wave terms

The profile of a transverse wave is shown in Figure 9.3.

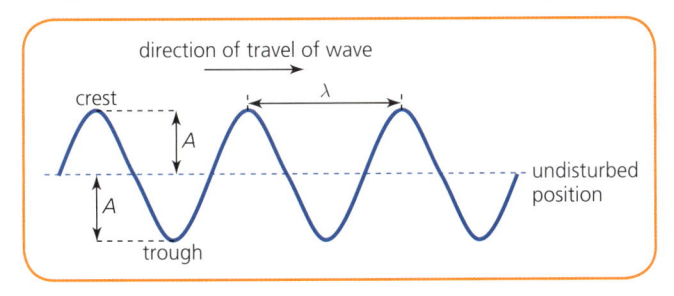

Figure 9.3 Wave terms

The following terms are used to describe a wave:

- Crest – the highest point or top of the wave.
- Trough – the lowest point or bottom of the wave.
- Amplitude (A) – half the height of the wave (from the top or bottom of a wave to the undisturbed position), measured in metres (m). The amplitude of a wave is a measure of how much energy a wave has – the bigger the amplitude, the more energy a wave has.
- Wavelength (λ – lambda) – the distance between two successive corresponding points (for example, from one crest to the next crest), measured in metres (m).
- Frequency (f) – the number of waves produced in one second, measured in hertz (Hz).

$$\text{Frequency} = \frac{\text{number of waves}}{\text{time to produce waves}}$$

The frequency of a wave is determined by the frequency produced by the source of the waves, i.e. if a source produces waves with a frequency of 20 hertz then this will always be the frequency of these waves. This means that 20 waves are produced in one second and 20 waves pass any point in one second.

- Speed of a wave (v) – the distance travelled by the wave in one second. Provided the material remains the same, then the speed of a wave is constant.

i.e. average speed of wave = speed of wave = $\dfrac{\text{distance}}{\text{time}}$

$$v = \frac{d}{t}$$

Wave speed

Consider the transverse wave shown in Figure 9.4.

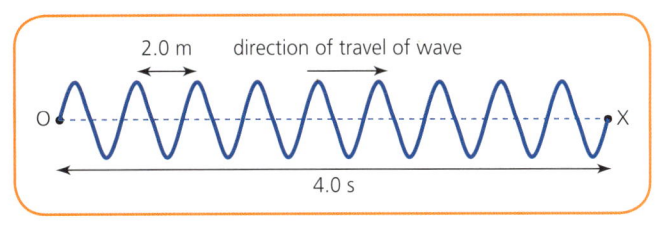

Figure 9.4

The wave takes 4.0 seconds to travel from O to X. Between O and X there are nine complete waves. Each wave has a wavelength of 2.0 metres (λ = 2 metres).

Therefore, the distance between O and X = 9 × 2 = 18 m

$$\text{Frequency of the waves} = \frac{\text{number of waves}}{\text{time}} = \frac{9}{4} \text{ hertz}$$

Since the medium does not change, then:

$$\text{average speed of wave} = \text{speed of wave} = \frac{\text{distance}}{\text{time}}$$

$$\text{speed of wave} = \frac{9 \times 2}{4} \text{ but frequency} = \frac{9}{4} \text{ and}$$

$$\text{wavelength} = 2 \text{ metres}$$

$$\text{speed of wave} = \text{frequency} \times \text{wavelength}$$

$$v = f\lambda$$

The speed of a wave in a given material (medium) can be found using:

$$\text{speed} = \frac{\text{distance}}{\text{time}} \text{ or speed} = \text{frequency} \times \text{wavelength}$$

$$v = \frac{d}{t} \quad \text{or} \quad v = f\lambda$$

where v = speed of wave, measured in metres per second (m/s)

d = distance, measured in metres (m)

t = time, measured in seconds (s)

f = frequency of wave, measured in hertz (Hz)

λ = wavelength of wave, measured in metres (m).

Waves and Radiation

Using the 'maths' triangle (see Rearranging physics equations on page 145) for the above equations gives:

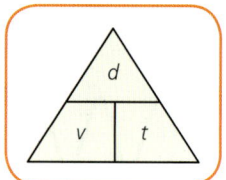

$$v = \frac{d}{t} \qquad d = v \times t \qquad t = \frac{d}{v}$$

and

$$v = f \times \lambda \qquad f = \frac{v}{\lambda} \qquad \lambda = \frac{v}{f}$$

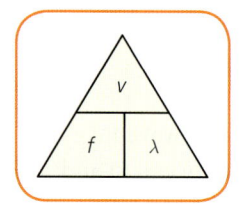

Worked examples

Example 1
A loudspeaker produces 13 600 sound waves in 10 seconds. The wavelength of the waves is 0.25 metres.
a) Calculate the frequency of the waves.
b) Calculate the speed of the waves.

Solution

a) Frequency = $\frac{\text{number of waves}}{\text{time to produce waves}}$

$= \frac{13\,600}{10} = 1360$ Hz

b) $v = f\lambda = 1360 \times 0.25 = 340$ metres per second

Example 2
A wave has a speed of 1500 metres per second. The frequency of the wave is 2.5 Hz. Calculate the wavelength of the wave.

Solution

$v = f\lambda$

$\lambda = \frac{v}{f} = \frac{1500}{2.5} = 600$ metres

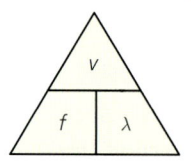

Example 3
The speed of water waves in a swimming pool is constant. At one end of the pool there is a wave-making machine. The length of the pool is 35 m. Waves take 25 s to travel the length of the pool. The waves have a wavelength of 2.0 m.
a) Calculate the speed of the waves.
b) Calculate the frequency of the waves.
c) The frequency of the wave-making machine is doubled. What effect does this have on the wavelength of the waves in the pool?

Solution

a) $v = \frac{d}{t} = \frac{35}{25} = 1.4$ m/s

b) $v = f\lambda$

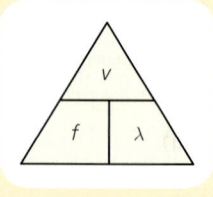

$f = \frac{v}{\lambda} = \frac{1.4}{2} = 0.7$ Hz

c) Since the speed of the waves is unchanged, when the frequency is doubled then the wavelength is halved (to keep the speed the same).

Key facts and physics equations: wave characteristics

- All waves transfer energy.
- When the particles of the medium vibrate at right-angles to the direction the wave is travelling in, the waves are called transverse waves.
- When the particles of the medium vibrate parallel to the direction the wave is travelling in, the waves are called longitudinal waves.

Wave characteristics

- The greater the amplitude of a wave, the more energy the wave transfers.
- The frequency of a wave is the number of waves produced in one second.
- Frequency = $\dfrac{\text{number of waves}}{\text{time to produce waves}}$
- The frequency of a wave is determined by the source that produces the wave.
- The speed of a wave is constant in a given medium.
- Speed of a wave = $\dfrac{\text{distance}}{\text{time}}$, i.e. $v = \dfrac{d}{t}$
- Speed of a wave = frequency of wave × wavelength of wave, i.e. $v = f\lambda$
- Speed is measured in metres per second (m/s), distance in metres (m), time in seconds (s), frequency in hertz (Hz), and wavelength in metres (m).

End-of-chapter questions

1 Two types of wave are shown in Figure 9.5.

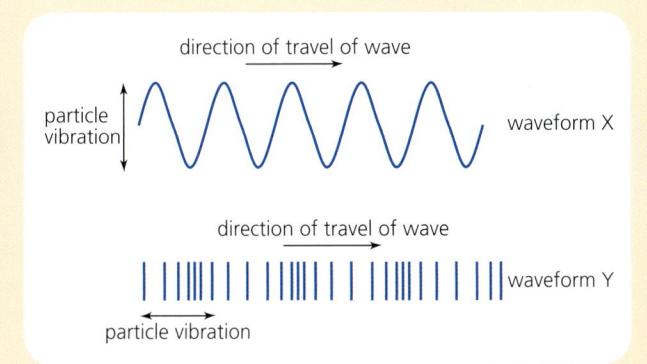

Figure 9.5

a) Which waveform, X or Y, represents a transverse wave?
b) Which waveform, X or Y, represents a longitudinal wave?

2 a) State what is meant by the frequency of a wave.
   b) State what is meant by the speed of a wave.

3 The names of a number of wave types are shown in the following list: light; microwaves; sound; water.
   a) Name one transverse wave from the above list.
   b) Name one longitudinal wave from the above list.

4 Figure 9.6 represents a wave.

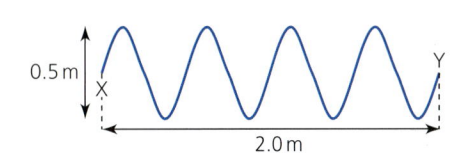

Figure 9.6

The wave travels from X to Y in 0.4 seconds. For this wave, calculate:
a) the amplitude
b) the frequency
c) the wavelength
d) the speed.

5 In the table shown, calculate the value of each missing quantity.

Speed (m/s)	Frequency (Hz)	Wavelength (m)
a)	50	1.2
b)	0.25	4.8
340	c)	0.25
270	d)	4.5
1500	5000	e)
340	200	f)

Waves and Radiation

6. The wavelength of a wave is 0.25 m. The frequency of the wave is 6000 Hz. Calculate the speed of the wave.
7. The speed of a wave is 270 m/s. The frequency of the wave is 500 Hz. Calculate the wavelength of the wave.
8. The speed of a wave is 1600 m/s. The wavelength of the wave is 0.32 m. Calculate the frequency of the wave.
9. Figure 9.7 represents a wave.

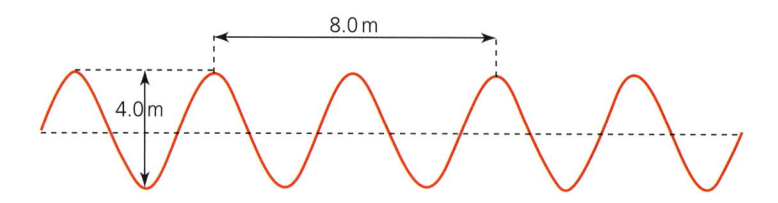

Figure 9.7

All the waves shown were produced in 2.5 s. For this wave, calculate:
   a) the amplitude
   b) the frequency
   c) the wavelength
   d) the speed.
10. The speed of water waves in a tank is 0.6 m/s. The wave generator produces 80 waves in 10 s.
   a) Calculate the frequency of the waves.
   b) Calculate the wavelength of the waves.

10 Sound

Learning outcomes

At the end of this chapter you should be able to:
1. State that for sound to be produced an object must vibrate.
2. State that sound is a wave that transfers energy.
3. State that the frequency of a sound is the number of waves produced in one second.
4. State that frequency is measured in hertz (Hz).
5. State that the higher the pitch of a sound, the greater the frequency.
6. State that the frequency produced by a vibrating string can be increased by shortening the length of the string or increasing the tightness of the string.
7. State that the frequency produced by a vibrating air column can be increased by shortening the length of the air column.
8. Identify from oscilloscope traces the signal that would produce:
    a) the loudest sound – greatest amplitude
    b) the highest frequency – largest number of waves.
9. Give an example that shows that the speed of sound in air is less than the speed of light in air.
10. Describe a method of measuring the speed of sound in air using the relationship between distance, time and speed.
11. Calculate the speed of sound using:
    $$speed = \frac{distance}{time}$$
12. State that sound can pass through solids, liquids and gases.
13. State that sound cannot pass through a vacuum.
14. State that the normal range of human hearing is from 20 hertz to 20 000 hertz.
15. State that high frequency sounds beyond the range of human hearing are called ultrasounds.
16. Give two applications of ultrasound.
17. State that sound levels are measured in decibels (dB).
18. Give two examples of noise pollution.
19. State that excessive noise can damage hearing.
20. State that noise cancellation technology can be used to reduce unwanted noise.

Sound

We are surrounded by sounds – but what is a sound?

Sound is a form of energy, just like heat and light. A sound is produced when something vibrates – moves backwards and forwards or shakes.

Figure 10.1 Instruments that make sound

A sound is produced when:

- the drum is struck with the drumstick – the skin of the drum vibrates
- the violin string is rubbed with the bow – the string vibrates
- air is blown into the trumpet – the air vibrates.

Energy from the vibrating source travels through the air as a sound wave. A sound wave is a longitudinal wave.

Waves and Radiation

Unit 2

The more rapid the vibrations, the more waves are produced in one second. The number of waves in one second is called the frequency. Frequency is measured in hertz (Hz).

> **Investigation**
>
> Clamp one end of a ruler to the edge of a table using your hand, as shown in Figure 10.2. Investigate how the frequency and loudness of a sound can be changed. 
>
> **Figure 10.2** Investigating sound using a ruler

Objects that vibrate slowly produce low frequency sounds – few waves per second.

Objects that vibrate quickly produce high frequency sounds – many waves per second.

The larger the vibration, the louder the sound.

> **Investigation**
>
> Use a sonometer or a stringed instrument to investigate how the frequency and loudness of a sound can be changed. 
>
> **Figure 10.3** Investigating sound using a sonometer

In stringed instruments, a short string produces a higher frequency or higher-pitched note than a long string. As a string is tightened, it produces a higher frequency or higher-pitched note.

> **Investigation**
>
> Fill a glass bottle with some water so that you have a column of air inside the bottle. Tap the bottle gently with a metal object and note the sound produced (Figure 10.4). Add more water to the bottle so that the air column is smaller and tap the bottle again. 
>
> **Figure 10.4** Investigating sound using a glass bottle
>
> Continue adding water to the bottle and tapping to find out how the length of the air column changes the frequency of the sound produced.

In wind instruments, such as a whistle, recorder, clarinet or trumpet, a short column of vibrating air produces a higher frequency or higher-pitched note than a long column of air.

'Seeing' sound waves on an oscilloscope

> **Investigation**
>
> Connect a microphone to an oscilloscope (Figure 10.5). 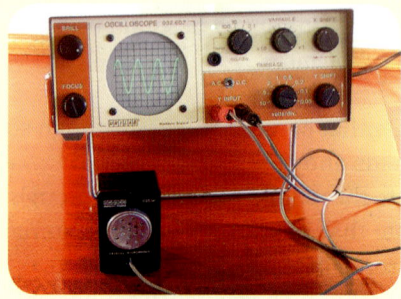
>
> **Figure 10.5** Investigating sound using a microphone and an oscilloscope
>
> Whistle notes of different frequencies (high pitched and low pitched) into the microphone. Look at the different traces displayed on the oscilloscope screen.
>
> Now whistle loud and quiet sounds into the microphone. Look at the different traces displayed on the oscilloscope screen.

The traces on an oscilloscope screen obtained from two sounds with the same loudness but different frequencies (pitch) are shown in Figure 10.6.

low frequency note   high frequency note

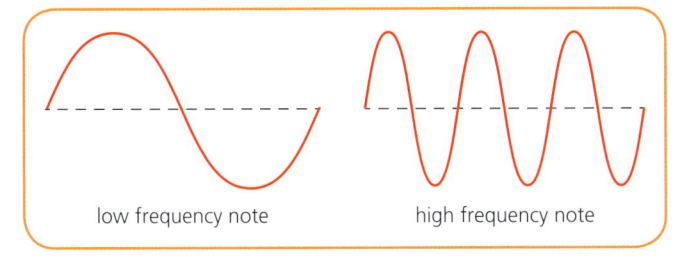

Figure 10.6

When the frequency of a sound changes, the number of waves displayed on an oscilloscope screen changes. The higher the frequency, the more waves are seen on the screen of the oscilloscope.

The traces on an oscilloscope screen obtained from two sounds with the same frequency (pitch) but different loudness are shown in Figure 10.7.

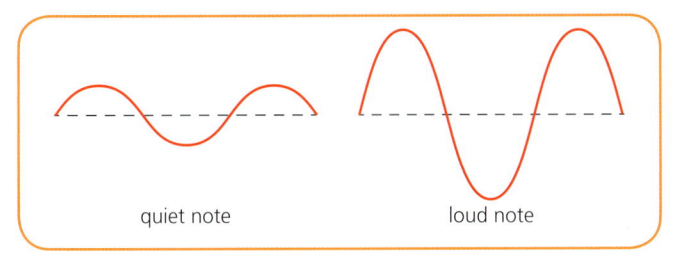

quiet note   loud note

Figure 10.7

When the loudness of a sound changes, the amplitude (height) of a trace on an oscilloscope screen changes. The louder the sound, the higher the amplitude seen on the oscilloscope screen.

The speed of sound

During a thunderstorm, the lightning and thunder are produced at the same time. However, when you are some distance from the storm, you see the lightning and then a short time later you hear the thunder. From this we can deduce that the speed of sound in air is less than the speed of light in air.

But what is speed? Speed is the distance travelled by an object in one second.

> ### Worked example
>
> ### Example
> Fiona runs from A to B. She covers a distance of 200 m in a time of 40 seconds.
>
> A ——— 200 m / 40 s ——— B
>
> Fiona travels 200 m in 40 seconds.
>
> Fiona travels $\frac{200}{40}$ metres in 1 second.
>
> Speed of Fiona = $\frac{200}{40}$ = 5 m/s
>
> This is Fiona's average speed – the steady speed she needs to cover 200 m in 40 seconds.

In the example, 200 m was the distance travelled and 40 seconds was the time taken.

$$\text{Average speed} = \frac{\text{distance}}{\text{time}}$$

$$\bar{v} = \frac{d}{t}$$

where $\bar{v}$ = average speed, measured in metres per second (m/s)

d = distance travelled, measured in metres (m)

t = time taken, measured in seconds (s).

Using the 'maths triangle' (see Rearranging physics equations on page 145) for the above equation gives:

$$\bar{v} = \frac{d}{t} \qquad d = \bar{v} \times t \qquad t = \frac{d}{\bar{v}}$$

For a sound wave travelling through a given material, the speed of the sound wave is constant. In this case the average speed of the sound wave is the same as the speed of the sound wave.

Waves and Radiation

Worked examples

Example 1
A sound wave takes 2.5 seconds to travel 3750 m through water. Calculate the speed of sound in water.

Solution

$$v = \frac{d}{t} = \frac{3750}{2.5} = 1500 \text{ m/s}$$

Example 2
During a storm you see a bolt of lightning and 5.0 seconds later you hear the thunder. The speed of sound in air is 340 m/s. Calculate how far the storm is away from you.

Solution

$$v = \frac{d}{t}$$

$d = vt = 340 \times 5 = 1700$ metres

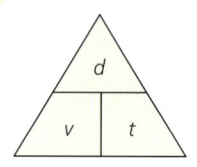

Example 3
A sound wave travels 187 m through air. The speed of sound in air is 340 m/s. Calculate the time taken for the sound to travel this distance.

Solution

$$v = \frac{d}{t}$$

$$t = \frac{d}{v} = \frac{187}{340} = 0.55 \text{ s}$$

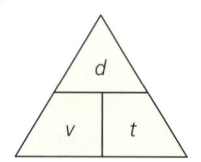

Measuring the speed of sound in air

Try to carry out the following three methods of measuring the speed of sound in air. Think about any improvements you could make.

Investigation

Method A
Apparatus needed: two pieces of wood, stopwatch and measuring tape

1. A person stands at one end of a field with two pieces of wood. When the pieces of wood are clapped together, a loud sound is produced.
2. At the other end of the field are some timekeepers with stopwatches.
3. When the timekeepers see the person clapping the pieces of wood together they start their stopwatches – this is the instant the sound is produced.
4. When the timekeepers hear the sound, the stopwatches are stopped and the times noted.
5. Measure the length of the field in metres using the measuring tape.
6. Calculate an average time for the sound to travel the length of the field.
7. Calculate the speed of sound in air using:

$$\text{speed of sound} = \frac{\text{distance}}{\text{time}}$$

Method B
Apparatus needed: two pieces of wood, stopwatch and measuring tape

1. The timekeepers and the person who is going to produce the sound stand side by side some distance from a tall building (Figure 10.8).

Figure 10.8 Measuring the speed of sound: method B

2. When the sound is produced the stopwatches are started. When the echo of the sound is heard, the stopwatches are stopped.
3. The distance between the timekeepers and the wall is measured in metres using the measuring tape. The distance travelled by the sound is the distance to the wall and back again. This is because the sound travels from the source of sound to the wall and then the same distance back again to the timekeepers.

4 Calculate the speed of sound in air using:

$$\text{speed of sound} = \frac{\text{distance}}{\text{time}}$$

Note: In the echo method the distance travelled is from you to the wall **and back again**.

What difficulties did you have in carrying out methods A and B? Why do you think these methods generally give an inaccurate measurement for the speed of sound in air?

Method C

Apparatus needed: two microphones, electronic timer

1 Place two microphones 1 m apart (see Figure 10.9).
2 Switch on the timer and make a sound in front of microphone X. When the sound reaches microphone X, the timer starts timing. When the sound reaches microphone Y, the timer stops timing.
3 Note the time for the sound to travel from microphone X to microphone Y.

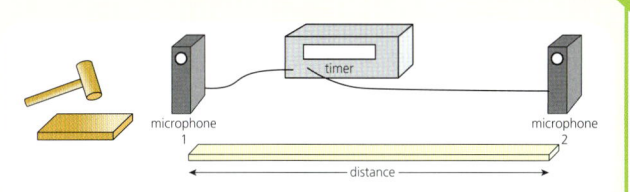

Figure 10.9 Measuring the speed of sound: method C

4 Calculate the speed of sound in air using:

$$\text{speed of sound} = \frac{\text{distance}}{\text{time}}$$

The speed of sound in air has an approximate value of 340 m/s.

Which of the three methods, A, B or C, was the most accurate?

Worked example

Example

A boy stands facing a high, wide wall. He shouts towards the wall. He hears the echo of his shout 1.2 seconds later. The speed of sound in air is 340 m/s. Calculate the distance he is away from the wall.

Solution

$$v = \frac{d}{t}$$

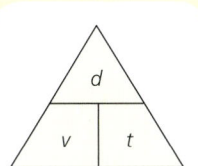

Note that d is the distance travelled by the sound, i.e. from boy to wall and back.

$$d = vt = 340 \times 1.2 = 408 \text{ m}$$

= distance to wall and back

$$\text{Distance of boy from wall} = \frac{408}{2} = 204 \text{ m}$$

Waves and Radiation

Unit 2

Using sound

> **Investigation**
>
> Design an experiment to show that a sound wave can travel through a) a solid and b) a liquid.
>
> Design an experiment to show that a sound wave cannot travel through a vacuum.

Before sound can be produced, an object must be made to vibrate. Solids, liquids and gases are made up of particles. A sound wave makes the particles vibrate and this allows the sound to pass through the solid, liquid or gas. Sound cannot pass through a vacuum as there are no particles in a vacuum to vibrate.

Worked example

Example

The table shows the speed of sound through a number of different materials.

Material	Speed of sound (m/s)	Material	Speed of sound (m/s)
air	340	water	1500
blood	1570	bone	4100
steel	6000	helium	970
oil	1400	carbon dioxide	260
concrete	3700		

Use the information in the table to answer the following questions.

a) In which **type** of substance does sound travel slowest?
b) In which **type** of substance does sound travel fastest?

Solution

a) Sound waves travel slowest in the gases listed – slowest in carbon dioxide, then air, then helium.
b) Sound waves travel fastest in the solids listed – fastest in steel, then concrete, and then bone.

Sound waves travel fastest in solids and slowest in gases.

The stethoscope

> **Investigation**
>
> Place the bell of a stethoscope on your partner's back and listen to their heartbeat. Count the number of heartbeats in one minute using the stethoscope.
>
> Place the bell of the stethoscope on the bench. Get your partner to scratch the bench lightly with a fingernail. How does the sound heard through the stethoscope compare with the sound heard without it?

A stethoscope is used to listen to sounds made inside the human body. It makes the sounds made inside the body much louder and easier to hear. This can help a doctor to identify certain illnesses.

Range of human hearing

> **Investigation**
>
> Connect a signal generator to a loudspeaker. Set the frequency control on the signal generator to about 25 000 Hz and switch on. Adjust the amplitude (volume) control to its maximum value. Now, slowly lower the frequency control on the signal generator. When you can first hear the sound from the loudspeaker, note the frequency. This frequency is your upper limit of hearing.

Most young people can hear sounds from a frequency as low as 20 Hz to as high as 20 000 Hz.

Humans are unable to hear sounds with a frequency above 20 000 Hz. High-frequency sounds above 20 000 Hz are called ultrasound.

Using ultrasound

Ultrasound can be used to safely take 'pictures' of the inside of the body. Figure 10.10 shows the image of a baby inside a mother's womb.

Sound

Figure 10.10 An ultrasound scan of an unborn baby

Ultrasound can also be used continuously to monitor movements within the body. A three-dimensional image can be obtained as the reflected signals take different times to return from objects at different distances from the ultrasound source.

Investigation

Dentists use ultrasound – ask your dentist the next time you visit how ultrasound is used.

Ultrasound is also used in industry to 'see' inside solid materials. Metal parts on an aircraft flex and bend during use. These metal components can have tiny cracks inside them. During flexing and bending these cracks can get larger and this can cause the component to break – this is known as metal fatigue. The metal components can be tested using ultrasound so that a 'picture' of the inside of the solid metal component can be obtained (Figure 10.11).

Figure 10.11 Metal being tested for cracks using ultrasound

Ships and fishing boats use sonar (SOund NAvigation and Ranging) to detect objects underneath the vessel, such as the sea-bed or a shoal of fish. Sound waves are sent out from a transmitter and travel down through the water until they reach an object. Some of the sound wave is reflected by the object as an echo back up to a receiver on the ship. The time taken for the sound waves to travel down from the transmitter and back up to the receiver is measured. Since the speed of sound in the water is known, the distance travelled by the sound waves and therefore the depth of the object below the vessel can be calculated.

Note that the distance travelled by the sound waves is from the transmitter to the object and back again.

Worked example

Example

A ship uses a depth finder to find the distance from the ship to the sea-bed.

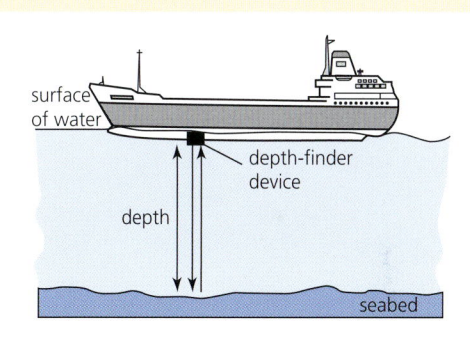

Figure 10.12

The depth finder emits sound waves. The sound waves travel at a speed of 1500 m/s in water. When the depth finder emits a sound, an echo is heard 2.2 seconds later. Calculate the depth of the sea at this point.

Solution

$$v = \frac{d}{t}$$

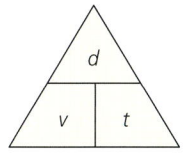

Note that d is the distance travelled by the sound, i.e. from ship to sea-bed and back.

$$d = vt = 1500 \times 2.2 = 3300 \text{ m}$$
$$= \text{distance to seabed and back}$$

$$\text{depth} = \frac{3300}{2} = 1650 \text{ m}$$

Waves and Radiation

Measuring sound level

The human ear is a sensitive detector of sound and can be damaged by very loud sounds. The loudness of sound is measured in **decibels** (dB) using a sound level meter.

> **Investigation**
>
> Use a sound level meter to measure the loudness of some sounds.
>
> Switch on the sound level meter and record the sound level readings for different sounds by pointing the detector at the source of the sound. Suggested sounds to record might include: a quiet area; a radio; a person talking quietly (1 m from the sound level meter); a person talking loudly (1 m from the sound level meter).
>
> Draw up a table of your results.

Noise pollution

> **Investigation**
>
> Make a list of four noises that are unpleasant to you.

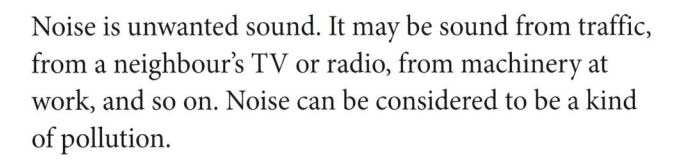

Noise is unwanted sound. It may be sound from traffic, from a neighbour's TV or radio, from machinery at work, and so on. Noise can be considered to be a kind of pollution.

Source of sound	Sound level (dB)
1 m from loudspeaker in a nightclub	120
pneumatic drill at 5 m	100
alarm clock 0.5 m from bedside	80
normal conversation at 1 m	60
residential area at night	40
quiet country lane	20
silence (hearing threshold)	0

Excessively loud noises are unpleasant and some can cause damage to the hearing. In factories or noisy workplaces (for example near pneumatic drills or aircraft or in heavy vehicles or tractors), the noise level can be over 100 dB. This level of noise can, over time, cause a serious loss of hearing ability. A 'ringing' sound heard after exposure to this level of sound is a warning sign that damage may have been done. Ear protection – such as earplugs, earmuffs or a helmet – can be used to reduce the level of noise heard by preventing most of the sound vibrations from reaching the ear.

Figure 10.13 Ear protection in use

During a normal day, you should not be exposed to a noise level above 90 dB unless you have some type of protection for your ears.

Noise cancellation

Noise cancellation is used in noisy situations such as a helicopter. A person wears a set of headphones. The headphones have a microphone that picks up the sounds to be cancelled and converts them into an electrical signal, as shown in Figure 10.14a). Electronics then invert this signal, as shown in Figure 10.14b). The inverted signal is fed to the headphones, where it is changed back into sound. This sound is in opposition to (cancels out) the sounds the person would otherwise hear.

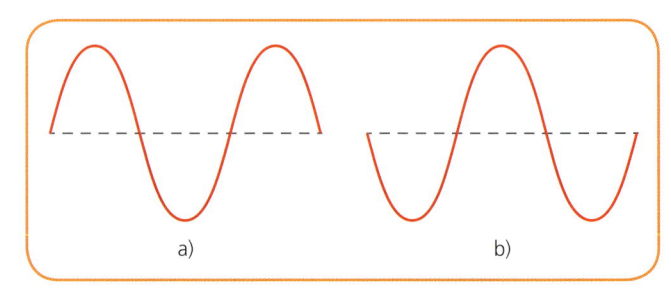

Figure 10.14 Noise cancellation: a) a sound wave and b) the sound wave inverted

Some hearing aids use noise cancellation circuitry to reduce unwanted background noises.

Sound

Sound reproduction technologies

Nowadays we have many different ways of reproducing sound, such as complex hi-fi systems, CD players, iPods, computers and tablets. They all use complex electronic systems which are able to give excellent sound reproduction. By using earphones, they allow the user to listen anywhere without disturbing other people. Technology has come a long way since the record player where the user had very little control over the reproduction of the sounds they were listening to. Today, modern technology allows the user to customise the sound reproduction to their own taste.

Key facts and physics equations: sound

- Frequency of a sound = number of waves in one second
- Frequency is measured in hertz (Hz).
- For a sound signal displayed on an oscilloscope screen: a) the more waves shown on the screen, the higher the frequency; b) the higher the trace (amplitude) shown on the screen, the louder the sound.
- The frequency of a sound is the same as the pitch – a high-pitched sound has a high frequency.
- A short string produces more waves per second than a long string, i.e. it produces a note of higher frequency (pitch) than a long string.
- Increasing the tightness of a string produces more waves per second and so a higher frequency.
- The shorter the length of the air column in a wind instrument, the more waves there are produced per second and the higher the frequency.
- The speed of light is faster than the speed of sound. This is why the flash from lightning is seen before the thunder is heard.
- Speed of sound = $\dfrac{\text{distance}}{\text{time}}$, i.e. $v = \dfrac{d}{t}$
- Sound can pass through solids, liquids and gases. Sound cannot pass through a vacuum.
- The normal range of human hearing is from 20 to 20 000 hertz (Hz).
- High-frequency sounds beyond the range of human hearing (above 20 000 Hz) are called ultrasounds.
- Ultrasound can be used to produce images of an unborn baby and of cracks inside a metal.
- The loudness of a sound is measured in decibels (dB).
- Sounds above 90 dB can cause damage to hearing.

End-of-chapter questions

1. In the following sentences the words represented by the letters A to F are missing.
   When an object ____A____, a sound is produced. Energy from the vibrating object travels out as a sound ____B____. The number of waves produced in ____C____ second by the vibrating object is called the ____D____. This is measured in ____E____. The frequency of a sound is often referred to as the ____F____ of the sound.
   Match each letter with the correct word below:
   frequency, hertz, one, pitch, vibrates, wave

2. A microphone is connected to an oscilloscope. When four different notes are played into the microphone, different traces are displayed on the oscilloscope screen, as shown in Figure 10.15.

   Which diagram:
   a) shows the loudest note?
   b) shows the quietest note?
   c) shows the note with the highest frequency?
   d) shows the note with the lowest frequency?

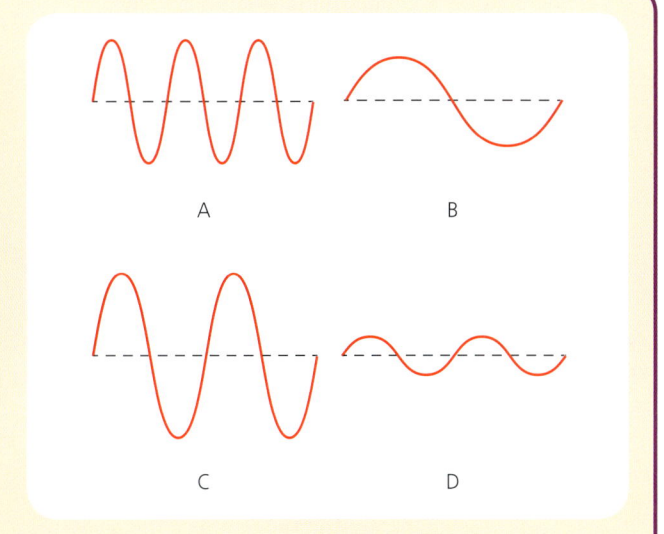

Figure 10.15

Waves and Radiation

3. A violin is being tuned. What will happen to the frequency of the note produced when the string being played is:
   a) increased in length
   b) tightened?

4. A small girl constructs a simple musical instrument. She half-fills a glass lemonade bottle with water and then taps it with a metal spoon (Figure 10.16). She hears a certain frequency of sound from her musical instrument.

Figure 10.16

The girl now adds more water to the bottle and taps it again. How does the frequency of the new sound compare with the frequency of the original sound?

5. A microphone is connected to an oscilloscope. A sound wave is played into the microphone. The trace displayed on the oscilloscope screen is shown in Figure 10.17a).

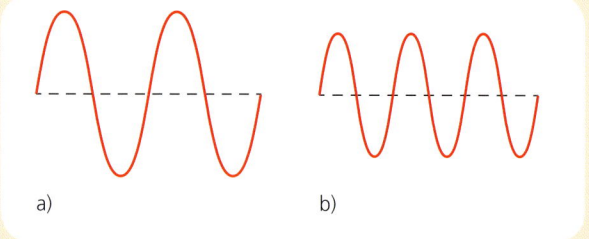

Figure 10.17

The controls on the oscilloscope are not changed. The sound is changed and the trace on the oscilloscope screen now appears as in Figure 10.17b).
What differences are there between the two sound waves played into the microphone?

6. John connects a microphone to an oscilloscope to look at the waveforms obtained from a music CD. He observes three different traces on the oscilloscope screen, as shown in Figure 10.18.

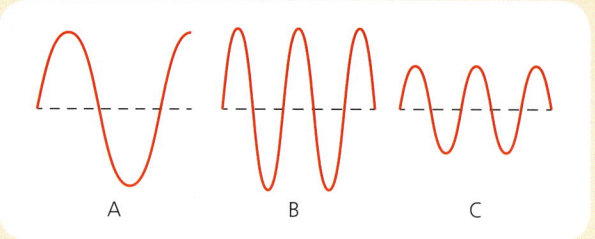

Figure 10.18

   a) Which note, A or B, has the higher pitch?
   b) Which note is louder, B or C?

7. The unit of frequency is:
   A seconds
   B metres
   C metres per second
   D hertz
   E decibels.

8. A musician finds that the frequency of vibration of a guitar string is too low. The frequency of vibration can be made higher by:
   A using a longer string
   B tightening the string
   C slackening the string
   D plucking the string harder
   E plucking the string more softly.

9. A microphone is connected to an oscilloscope. A sound of frequency 600 Hz is played into the microphone. The trace displayed on the oscilloscope screen is shown in Figure 10.19.

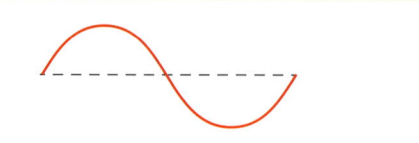

Figure 10.19

A sound of unknown frequency is now played into the microphone. The controls of the oscilloscope are not changed. The trace displayed on the oscilloscope screen is shown in Figure 10.20.

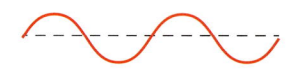

Figure 10.20

The frequency of the unknown signal is:
A   200 Hz
B   400 Hz
C   800 Hz
D   900 Hz
E   1200 Hz.

10 A student plays a musical note from a violin into a microphone. The microphone is connected to an oscilloscope. The student examines the pattern displayed on the oscilloscope screen. The pattern is shown in Figure 10.21.

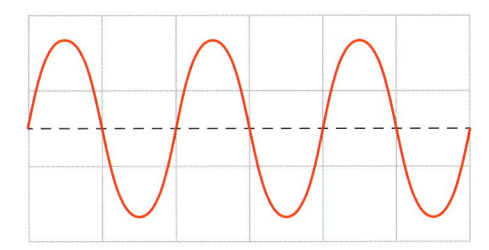

Figure 10.21

a) The student plays a second note into the microphone. The controls on the oscilloscope are unchanged. This note has the same loudness but a lower frequency than the first note.
Copy the diagram shown in Figure 10.22. Complete your diagram by drawing the pattern that would be produced on the oscilloscope screen by the second note.

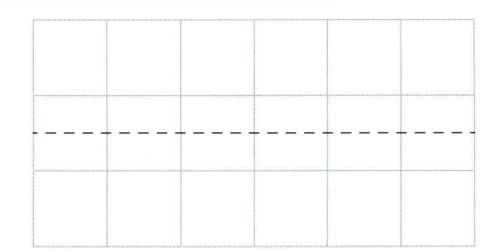

Figure 10.22

b) State one alteration the student could make to the violin string to produce a note with a lower frequency.

11 You tell a friend that the speed of sound in air is less than the speed of light in air. Give an example to support your statement.

12 In the table shown, calculate the value of each missing quantity.

Distance (m)	Time (s)	Speed (m/s)
24	6.0	a)
1000	40	b)
120	c)	1500
1700	d)	340
e)	2.5	270
f)	0.12	5200

13 In an experiment to measure the speed of sound in air, the following measurements were made:
Time taken for sound to travel from source to timekeeper = 1.4 seconds
Distance from source to timekeeper = 469 metres
Use this information to obtain a value for the speed of sound in air.

14 A man standing 2210 m away from a lightning strike hears the thunder 6.5 s after he sees the lightning. Calculate the speed of sound in air on this night.

15 A hammer hits one end of a metal pipe. The sound from the hammer blow takes 0.52 s to travel the length of the pipe. The speed of sound in the pipe is 1500 m/s. Calculate the length of the pipe.

16 A girl stands 255 m in front of a high, wide wall. She shouts and hears the echo 1.5 s later.
   a) What is the distance travelled by the sound in 1.5 seconds?
   b) Calculate the speed of sound on that day.

17 Two students stand some distance from each other. One student makes a loud sound by clapping two pieces of wood together. The other student starts a stopwatch on seeing the pieces of wood coming together and stops the stopwatch on hearing the sound. To calculate the speed of sound, what other measurement must be made?

18 a) A girl shouts into a canyon and a short time later she hears an echo. What causes this echo?
    b) The girl moves to a different point and again shouts into the canyon. She now hears two echoes. What is happening this time?

19 During a firework display the flash from a rocket exploding is seen. The sound of the explosion is heard 0.5 s later. The rocket exploded 170 m from the crowd. Calculate the speed of sound in air on the evening.

Waves and Radiation

20 Describe a method for measuring the speed of sound in air. Your answer should include:
   a) a labelled diagram
   b) a description of the measurements you would make
   c) details of how you would use these measurements to find the speed of sound in air.

21 In the following sentences the words represented by the letters A, B and C are missing.
   Sound waves from a vibrating object can travel through solids, liquids and ___A___. Solids, liquids and gases are made up of ___B___, which are made to vibrate by the sound waves. Sound cannot pass through a ___C___ since there are no particles to vibrate.
   Match each letter with the correct word below.
   vacuum, gases, particles

22 In the following sentences the words represented by the letters A to D are missing.
   Most humans can hear sounds with ___A___ from about 20 Hz to 20 000 Hz. Sounds with a frequency above 20 000 Hz are called ___B___. The loudness of sound is measured on the ___C___ scale. Sounds above 90 dB can cause long-term ___D___ to hearing.
   Match each letter with the correct word below.
   damage, frequencies, decibel, ultrasound

23 A dog owner cannot hear the sound from a whistle, although her dog can. Suggest a possible value for the frequency of the sound from this whistle.

24 The table shows the upper limit of hearing for a number of animals.

Animal	Frequency of upper limit of hearing (Hz)
cat	45 000
dog	30 000
human	20 000
whale	80 000

   a) Present the information in the table as a bar chart.
   b) Which of these animals would be able to hear a sound of frequency 35 000 Hz?

25 Ultrasound is important in both medical and industrial applications. Give **one** use of ultrasound in either medicine or industry.

26 Noise pollution can be a big problem to those people affected. Give **one** example of noise pollution.

27 What noise level, in decibels, can cause serious damage to human hearing if you are exposed to it over a long period of time?

28 What name is given to frequencies of sound above the range of human hearing?

29 Engineers working near aeroplane jet engines wear ear protectors. Explain why the ear protectors are needed.

30 A physicist uses sound waves to search for oil. An explosion is produced on the surface. The sound from the explosion travels through the rock and is reflected from the top of the oil, as shown in Figure 10.23.

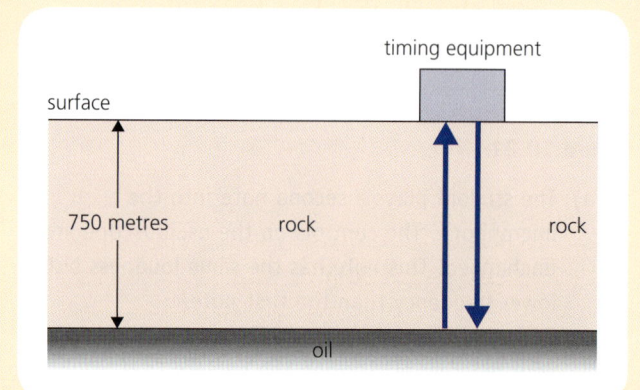

Figure 10.23

The top of the oil is 750 metres below the timing equipment. The time between the sound being produced and received is 0.3 seconds.
   a) How far does the sound wave travel through the rock in 0.3 seconds?
   b) Calculate the speed of sound in the rock.
   c) When the sound is produced the physicist has to wear ear protectors. Explain why the ear protectors are needed.

11 Electromagnetic spectrum

Learning outcomes

At the end of this chapter you should be able to:
1. State that a wave transfers energy.
2. State that all wave types in the electromagnetic spectrum are transverse waves.
3. State that all wave types in the electromagnetic spectrum are transmitted through a vacuum or air at a speed of 300 000 000 m/s.
4. State an application for each wave type in the electromagnetic spectrum.
5. State a hazard for two wave types in the electromagnetic spectrum.

The electromagnetic spectrum

Energy is transferred through space by a family of waves called the **electromagnetic spectrum**.

The electromagnetic spectrum consists of the waves shown in Figure 11.1.

These waves have the following properties:

- they are all transverse waves
- they all transfer energy
- they all travel at a speed of 300 000 000 m/s in a vacuum (and in air).

Some applications and hazards associated with each wave type in the electromagnetic spectrum are given below, and also details of how these radiations can be detected.

Radio and TV waves

Radio and TV waves are used for radio and television communication. They are detected using an aerial and a receiver. Long-wavelength radio signals can bend around hills and over the horizon and so have a very long range.

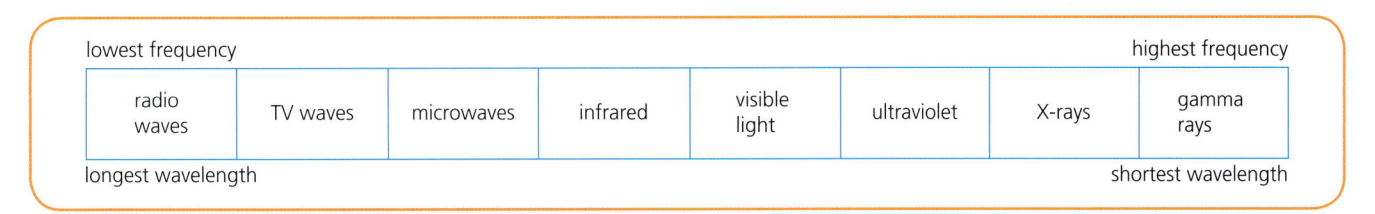

lowest frequency							highest frequency
radio waves	TV waves	microwaves	infrared	visible light	ultraviolet	X-rays	gamma rays
longest wavelength							shortest wavelength

Figure 11.1 Wave types in the electromagnetic spectrum

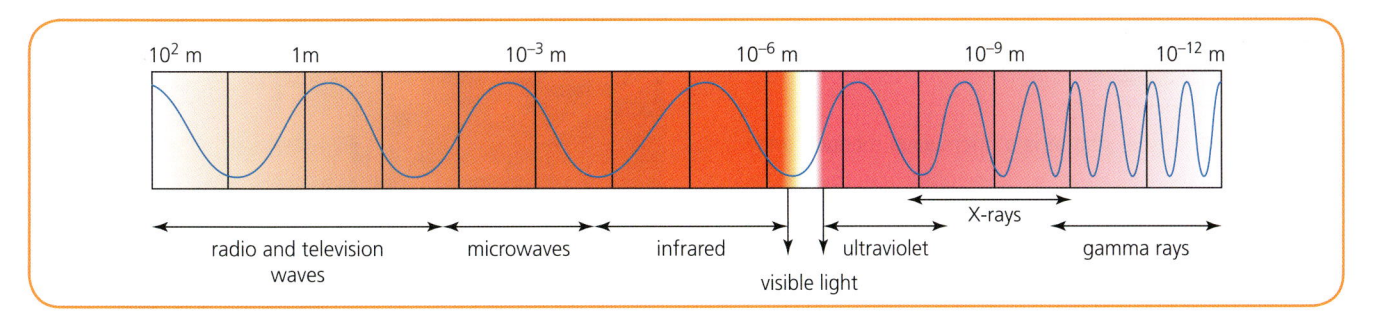

Figure 11.2 Wavelengths of the waves in the electromagnetic spectrum

87

Waves and Radiation

Unit 2

Figure 11.3 A television aerial

Microwaves

Microwaves are used in communication and in microwave ovens to heat food. Their very short wavelength means that they travel in straight lines. This makes microwaves ideal for line-of-sight satellite communication. They are detected by an aerial and a receiver.

Figure 11.4 A mobile phone is a microwave receiver and transmitter

Infrared

Infrared radiation is emitted by any hot object. It is invisible to the human eye but can be viewed using an infrared camera. Some cameras can produce colour photographs showing different temperatures. These pictures are called thermograms and can be useful in detecting unusually high temperatures in parts of the body.

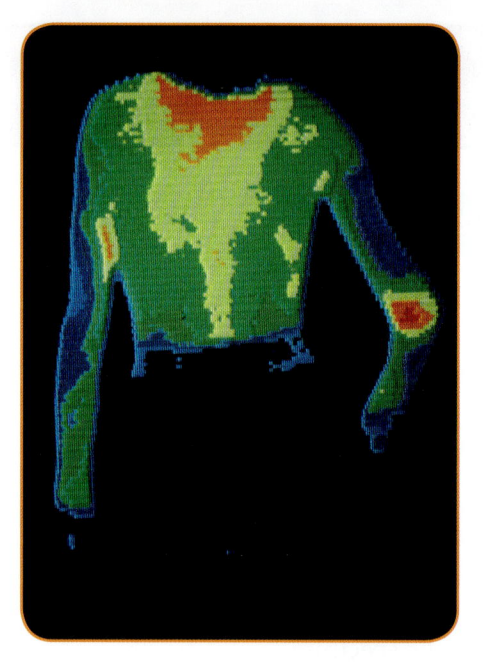

Figure 11.5 A thermogram of an arthritic elbow

Figure 11.5 shows a thermogram of an elbow joint. The orange/yellow colours show abnormally high temperatures, indicating inflammation of the elbow joint.

Physiotherapists use infrared radiation to penetrate the skin and heat damaged muscles. Heating causes an increased blood flow in the muscle, which then heals more quickly. Firefighters use special 'night vision' equipment to search for injured and unconscious people in damaged buildings. Infrared radiation is detected by special thermal-imaging cameras.

Figure 11.6 An infrared camera

Electromagnetic spectrum

Physics in action

Until recently, to measure your body temperature you would have to keep a mercury-in-glass thermometer in your mouth for a minute or two. These days, a plastic nozzle is pressed into your ear for a few seconds – this is a digital thermometer. This type of thermometer detects the infrared radiation given off by the eardrum. The amount of infrared radiation detected depends on the body temperature. The thermometer, although detecting infrared, is calibrated to give a reading of the body temperature.

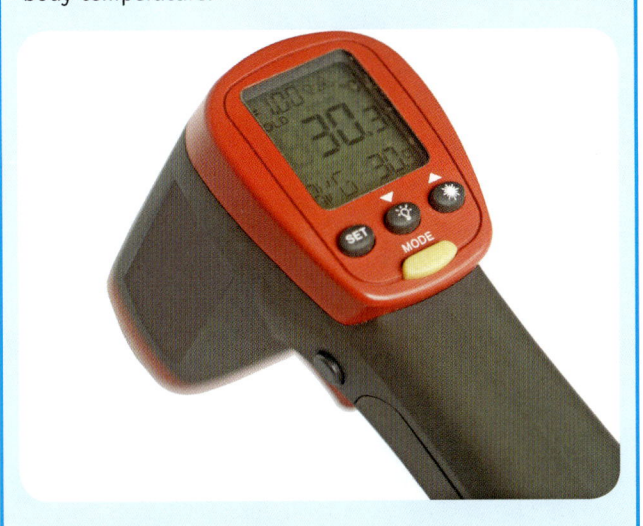

Figure 11.7 An infrared thermometer

Visible light

Visible light allows us to see things as it is detected by the human eye. It is also detected by photographic film and digital cameras.

Light waves undergo refraction. Refraction is the change in direction of the light when the light travels from one material into another material e.g. air into glass.

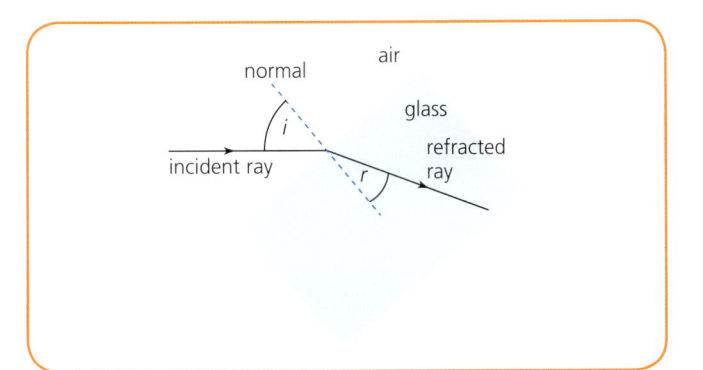

Figure 11.8

Physics in action

Opticians use convex and concave lenses to correct some sight defects.

Long sight

A long-sighted person can see distant objects clearly (this means the lens of the eye can be made thin enough). However, objects quite close to the eye appear blurred. This is because the eye lens cannot be made thick enough and light from a near object is focused beyond the retina. A converging (convex) lens is used to correct this defect. The convex lens increases the bending of the light rays before they enter the eye lens (Figure 11.9). This allows the eye lens to focus the rays of light onto the retina and so the near object is seen clearly.

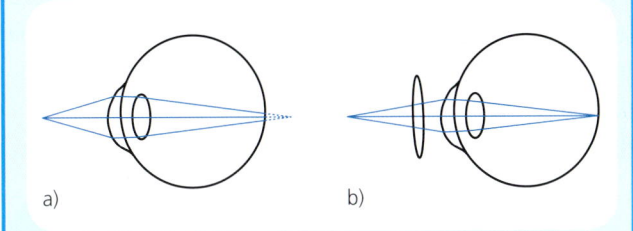

Figure 11.9

Short sight

A short-sighted person can see near objects clearly (this means the lens of the eye can be made thick enough). However, distant objects appear blurred. This is because the eye lens cannot be made thin enough and light from a distant object is focused in front of the retina. A diverging (concave) lens is used to correct this defect. The concave lens spreads the rays of light out more before they enter the eye lens (Figure 11.10). This allows the eye lens to focus the rays of light onto the retina and so the distant object is seen clearly.

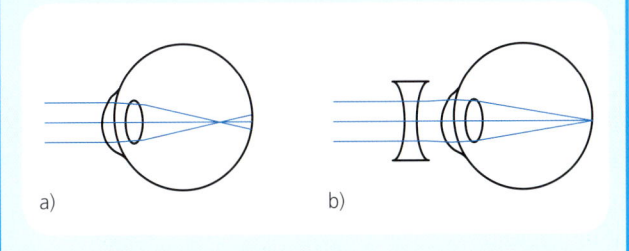

Figure 11.10

Waves and Radiation

Ultraviolet

Ultraviolet is emitted by stars such as our Sun and by certain lamps. Exposure to ultraviolet gives us a suntan and allows our bodies to make vitamin D. Vitamin D is important for good health, growth and strong bones. Ultraviolet is also used to treat some skin conditions such as acne. However, overexposure to ultraviolet causes sunburn and can lead to skin cancer. Sun creams, when used properly, absorb harmful ultraviolet rays and protect the skin.

Some materials glow or fluoresce when ultraviolet light is shone on them. Most banknotes have special security features that fluoresce when illuminated with ultraviolet. Forged banknotes do not fluoresce under ultraviolet (the forgers find it very difficult to produce these security features on their notes) and can therefore be detected. Special 'invisible' security pens are available to 'label' items in the home with 'invisible' security markings. These markings become visible when illuminated with ultraviolet light.

Figure 11.11 Security feature on a banknote fluoresces under ultraviolet light

X-rays

X-rays are detected by digital detectors or photographic film. X-rays are used to 'see' inside the human body (for example, an X-ray of a broken bone). Airport security uses X-ray machines to examine the contents of luggage.

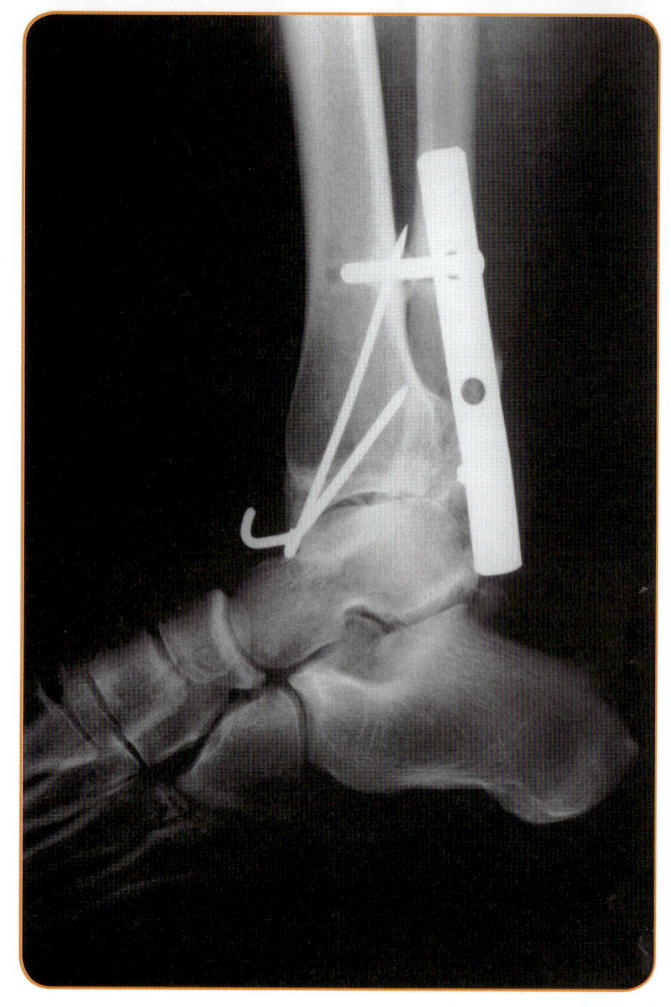

Figure 11.12 An X-ray

X-rays can be dangerous as they can damage healthy cells inside the body. For most people, this is not a problem as we rarely have an X-ray. However, people who operate the X-ray machines in hospitals (called radiographers) could be exposed to many X-rays. To prevent this, a radiographer wears a special lead-lined apron. The apron absorbs any X-rays before they reach the radiographer. Radiographers also wear a film badge that records the amount of radiation they receive over a period of time.

Electromagnetic spectrum

Physics in action

The film badge
A radiation film badge contains a small piece of photographic film behind thicknesses of different absorbers.

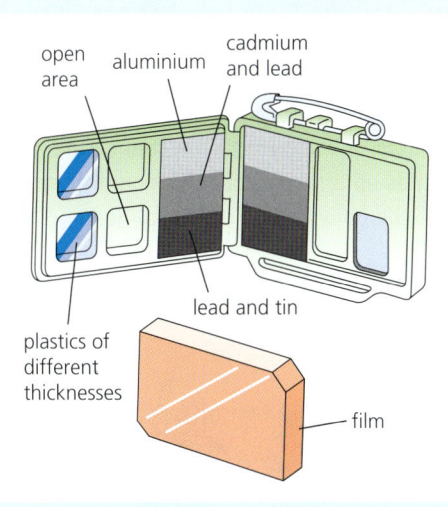

Figure 11.13 A film badge

When the film is developed, the amount of fogging (how black the film is) gives an indication of the amount and type of radiation exposure at the different parts of the badge. The blacker the film, the greater the exposure to radiation.

Airport security
Hand luggage at an airport is passed through an X-ray machine. The luggage is screened for possible weapons and materials that could make a bomb. The machine produces an image of the items inside the bag.

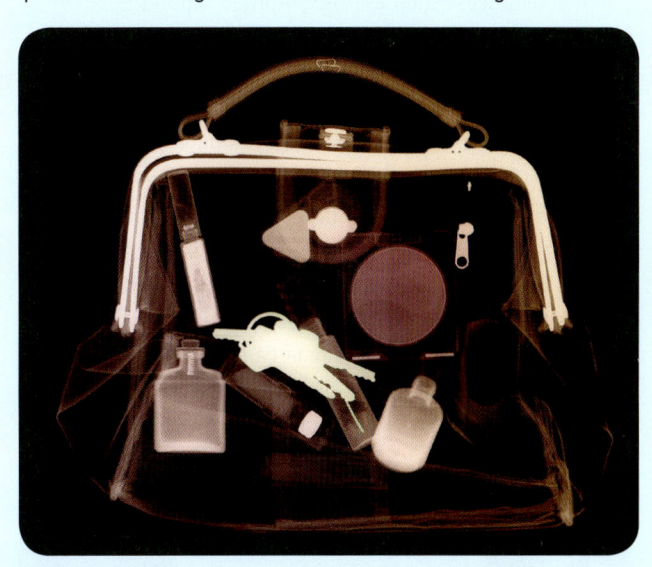

Figure 11.14 X-ray image of the contents of a bag

The machine is capable of displaying the items inside the bag in different colours according to their density and what they are made of. Paper and clothing are displayed in orange, while different metals are coloured blue or green.

Gamma rays

Gamma rays are emitted by radioactive nuclei. They are detected by a Geiger counter. Like X-rays, gamma rays are dangerous since they can damage healthy cells. They can be used in radiotherapy to kill cancerous cells inside the body (see Chapter 12).

Waves and Radiation

Physics in action

The gamma camera

Some substances, such as zinc sulphide, fluoresce when they absorb radiation, i.e. they are able to change the energy they absorb into tiny bursts of light. The flashes of light are called scintillations. Scintillations can be observed by the naked eye or they can be counted using a light detector and an electronic counting circuit.

A gamma camera is used to detect gamma radiation. Some patients are given drugs containing chemicals that emit gamma radiation (see radioactive tracers opposite). The gamma radiation emitted causes scintillations when it reaches the crystal in the gamma camera. These flashes of light are used to build up a picture of the organs inside the human body.

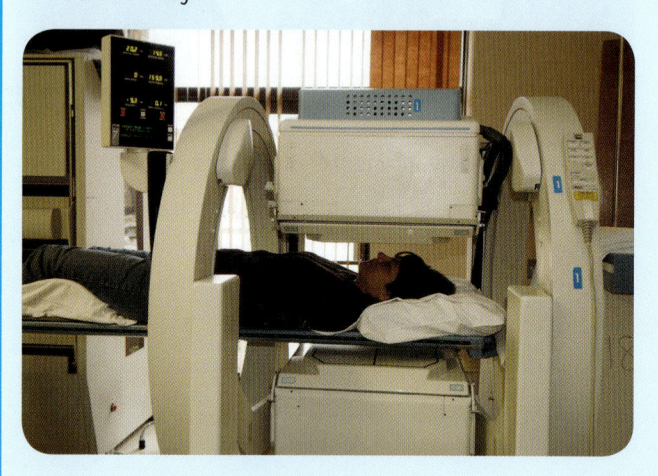

Figure 11.15 A gamma camera

Radioactive tracers

Doctors prefer to investigate a patient's body without the need for surgery. One way that this can be done is by injecting a small amount of radioactive material, called a tracer, into the bloodstream of the patient. This tracer travels round to all parts of the body. Gamma rays coming from the patient's body can then be detected using a gamma camera. A computer connected to the gamma camera builds up a picture of the amount of radiation in the part of the body that is being studied.

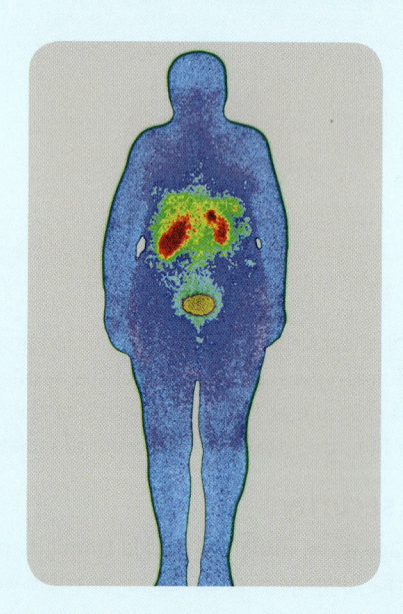

Figure 11.16 Gamma camera image of a patient

Energy and Frequency

Each member of the Electromagnetic Spectrum emits particles called photons. The higher the frequency, the greater the energy of the photon.

Key facts and physics equations: electromagnetic spectrum

- The members of the electromagnetic spectrum in order of decreasing wavelength are: radio, TV, microwaves, infrared, visible light, ultraviolet, X-rays and gamma rays.
- All members of the electromagnetic spectrum are transverse waves and are transmitted through a vacuum or air at a speed of 300 000 000 m/s.

End-of-chapter questions

1. A thermogram is used to detect heat radiation coming from a patient. What is the name given to the part of the electromagnetic spectrum that the thermogram detects?
2. During a hot, sunny day at the beach, a boy sunbathes. The boy's body receives more ultraviolet radiation than normal.
   a) Give a potential hazard associated with ultraviolet radiation.
   b) Suggest **one** way in which the boy could be protected from the ultraviolet radiation.
   c) State **one** medical use for ultraviolet radiation.
3. State **one** medical use for infrared radiation.
4. The diagram shows the members of the electromagnetic spectrum in order of wavelength.

| radio waves | TV waves | microwaves | P | visible light | ultraviolet | Q | gamma rays |

   a) Identify the radiations represented by P and Q.
   b) State **one** medical use for gamma rays.
   c) State **one** non-medical use for microwaves.
5. A radiographer is a person who operates the X-ray machine in a hospital. Radiographers are required to wear a lead apron when the X-ray machine is being used. Explain why a radiographer must wear a lead apron.
6. During a physics lesson on radiation, a teacher uses a gamma radiation source. The teacher tells the class that the source is giving off gamma rays. The students cannot see gamma rays coming from the source. Explain why they are unable to see the gamma rays.
7. Gamma rays are used in hospitals to treat cancerous tumours in a treatment called radiotherapy. During a radiotherapy treatment, what do the gamma rays do to the cancerous cells of the tumour?

Waves and Radiation

Unit 2

12 Nuclear radiation

Learning outcomes

At the end of this chapter you should be able to:
1. Describe a simple model of the atom that includes protons, neutrons and electrons.
2. State that nuclear radiation energy may be absorbed in the medium through which it passes.
3. State the range and absorption of alpha, beta and gamma radiation.
4. Explain the term 'ionisation'.
5. State that alpha particles are more ionising than beta particles or gamma rays.
6. Describe how one of the effects of nuclear radiation is used in a detector of the radiation.
7. State that nuclear radiation can kill or change the nature of living cells.
8. Describe the safety procedures necessary when handling radioactive substances.
9. Identify the radioactive hazard sign.
10. State that exposure to nuclear radiation is reduced by shielding, by limiting the time of exposure, or by increasing the distance from a source.
11. Describe one medical use of nuclear radiation based on the fact that nuclear radiation can destroy cells.
12. Describe one use of nuclear radiation based on the fact that the radiation is easy to detect.

Nuclear radiation

A simple model of the atom

All solids, liquids and gases are made up of atoms. An atom consists of a positively-charged centre or nucleus surrounded by a 'cloud' of rapidly revolving negative charges called electrons. The nucleus is made up of particles called protons (positively charged) and neutrons (uncharged). Compared to the overall size of the atom, the nucleus is very small.

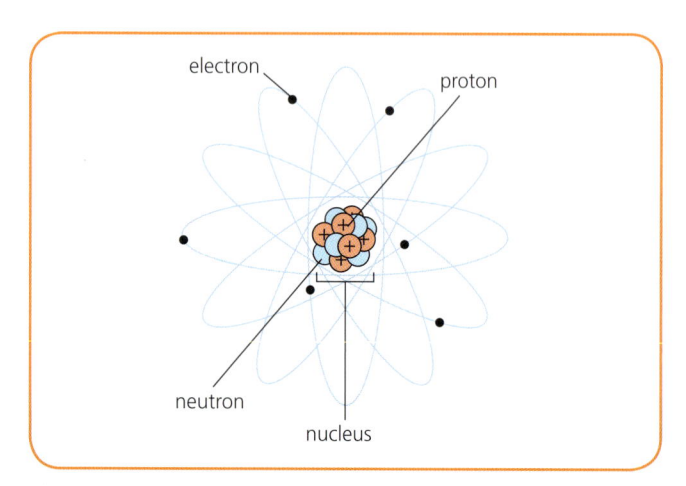

Figure 12.1 'Model' of the atom

In an uncharged atom the number of protons in the nucleus is equal to the number of electrons orbiting the nucleus.

Types of radiation

It is not a course requirement to know about alpha, beta and gamma radiations. However, the following information is provided to allow an understanding of how these radiations can be used to our advantage and to answer questions which may be set in an unfamiliar context.

The three types of nuclear radiation are:

- alpha particles, which have the symbol α
- beta particles, which have the symbol β
- gamma rays, which have the symbol γ. Gamma rays are part of the electromagnetic spectrum.

Most materials are made up of atoms in which the nuclei are stable. However, radioactive materials are made up of atoms that have unstable nuclei. These unstable nuclei may become stable when the nucleus disintegrates (or decays) by emitting alpha, beta or gamma radiation. When alpha, beta or gamma radiation is emitted from a nucleus, energy is transferred from the nucleus.

Nuclear radiation

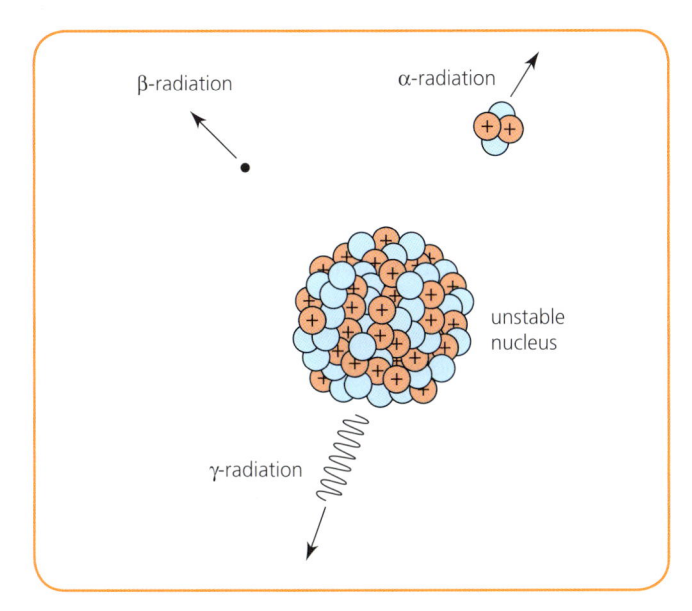

Figure 12.2 Types of radiation that can be emitted from an unstable nucleus

Beta particles are absorbed by a few metres of air or a few millimetres of aluminium.

Gamma rays require many kilometres of air or a few centimetres of lead (a very dense material) before they are absorbed.

The material that the radiation passes through absorbs the energy of the radiation. The amount of energy that is absorbed depends on the:

- type of radiation
- thickness of the absorbing material
- type of absorbing material.

Ionisation

When radiation passes through an absorbing material, electrons can be removed from the atoms or molecules in the material. This process is called ionisation. During ionisation, energy is transferred from the radiation to the absorber.

When an electron is removed from an atom, the atom becomes positively charged. The positively-charged atom and the 'free' electron are called ions. The charged atom is a positive ion and the electron is a negative ion.

Alpha radiation produces the most ionisation. The process of ionisation by an alpha particle is shown in Figure 12.4.

Absorbing alpha, beta and gamma radiation

When alpha particles, beta particles or gamma rays pass through a material, they transfer energy to the material due to interactions or collisions with the atoms making up the material. Eventually the radiations transfer so much energy due to these collisions that they can penetrate no further through the material and they are said to be absorbed.

Alpha particles are absorbed by a few centimetres of air or a thin sheet of paper.

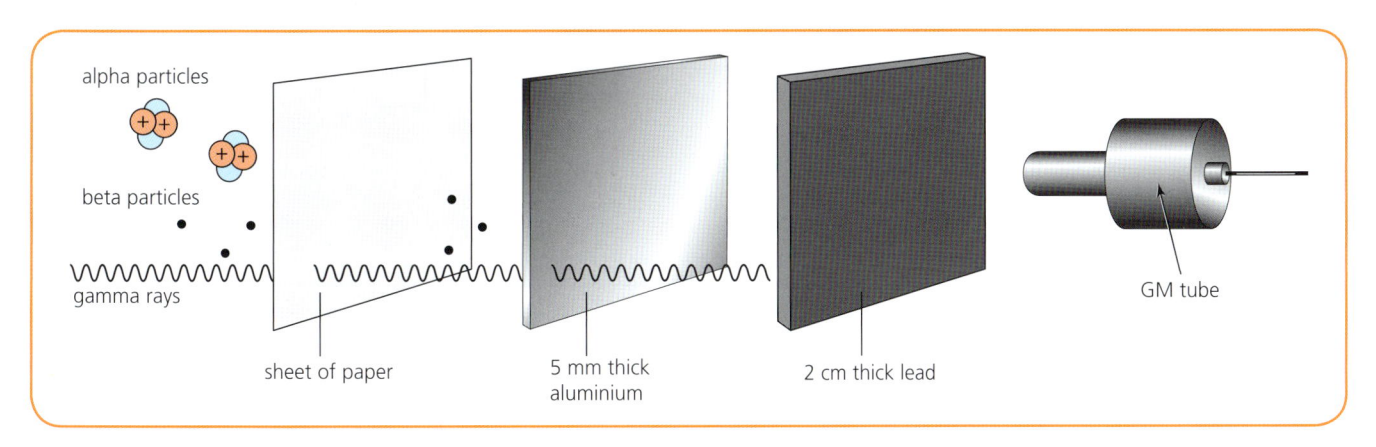

Figure 12.3 Absorption of alpha, beta and gamma radiations

95

Waves and Radiation

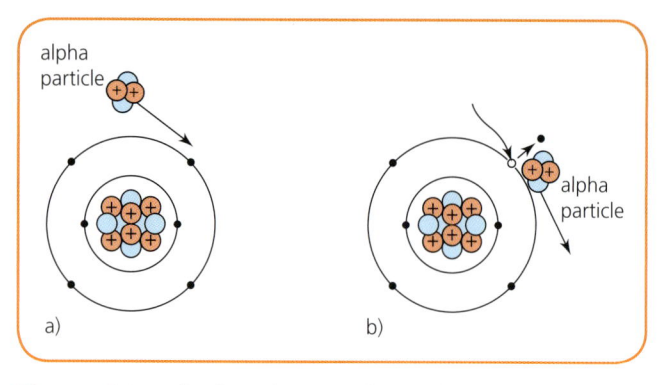

Figure 12.4 Ionisation of a neutral atom by an alpha particle: a) an alpha particle approaching the neutral atom; b) the alpha particle has passed by, having created an ion pair

Alpha, beta and gamma radiation are often called ionising radiations. Ionisation is the breaking up of a neutral atom into positive and negative pieces.

Detecting nuclear radiation

Three effects of radiation on non-living things are:

- radiation fogs (blackens) photographic film
- radiation causes ionisation
- radiation causes scintillations – light emitted from certain materials.

Physics in action

The Geiger counter

The Geiger-Müller tube (GM tube) or Geiger counter makes use of the ionising properties of alpha, beta and gamma radiations.

The GM tube is a hollow cylinder filled with a gas at low pressure. The tube has a thin window, made of a substance called mica, at one end. There is a central wire inside the tube. A voltage supply is connected across the casing of the tube and the central wire as shown in Figure 12.5.

When alpha, beta or gamma radiation enters the tube, the radiation produces ions in the gas. The ions created produce a current in the tube for a short time. This current produces a voltage pulse. The voltage pulses are counted and displayed on the counter screen. Each voltage pulse corresponds to one alpha particle, beta particle or gamma ray entering the GM tube.

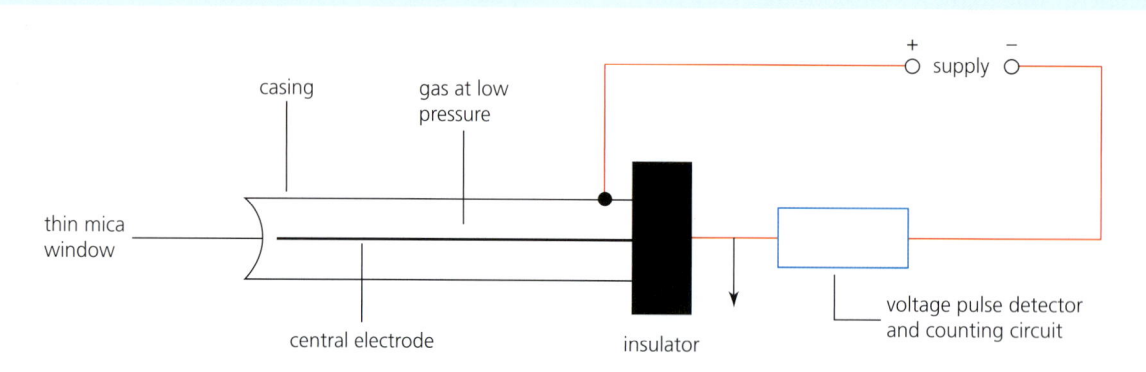

Figure 12.5 A Geiger-Müller tube and counter

Effect of nuclear radiation on living things

When living tissue absorbs alpha, beta or gamma radiation, ionisation takes place within the tissue. This can disturb the way the cells in the tissue operate and cause them to become cancerous.

Radiation may kill living cells or may change the nature of the living cell. This can cause great problems for the human body.

Alpha radiation

Alpha radiation produces a lot of ionisation within a short distance in body tissue. Alpha radiation outside the body is absorbed by the skin (it cannot penetrate the skin) and so no damage is done inside the body. However, a source of alpha radiation inside the body will produce a large amount of ionisation in the affected body tissue and this would be extremely dangerous.

Beta radiation

Beta radiation outside the body can penetrate the skin. It is absorbed by about 10 mm of body tissue and damage will be caused to that tissue. A source of beta radiation inside the body will cause internal organs to be damaged. Body tissue can be damaged whether the source of beta radiation is inside or outside the body.

Gamma radiation

Gamma radiation can pass straight through the body. Body tissue can be damaged whether the source of gamma radiation is inside or outside the body.

Background radiation

We are all exposed to both natural and manmade radiation all the time – this is called **background radiation**. If a Geiger counter is left switched on in a room, radiation will be recorded on the counter even though there is no radioactive source present.

By measuring the background counts over a period of time, the average number of counts recorded in a given time (usually a minute) can be calculated. This is called the **background count rate**.

> **Investigation**
>
> **Measuring background count rate**
>
> Make up a table to record ten measurements of background radiation.
>
> Switch on a Geiger counter. Note the number of counts recorded in one minute in your table.
>
> Reset the counter and repeat until the table is complete.
>
> Are all the values the same?
>
> Calculate the average background count rate in counts per minute.

The background count rate varies due to the random nature of radiation.

When a radioactive source is placed near the counter, the measured count rate will be equal to the source count rate and the background count rate added together. The **source count rate** is obtained by subtracting the background count rate from the measured count rate. This gives the **corrected count rate** – the count rate from the radioactive source alone.

$$\begin{matrix} \text{corrected count rate} \\ \text{(source count rate)} \end{matrix} = \text{total count rate} - \begin{matrix} \text{background} \\ \text{count rate} \end{matrix}$$

Sources of nuclear radiation

The pie chart in Figure 12.6 shows the main sources of radiation that we are exposed to on the Earth.

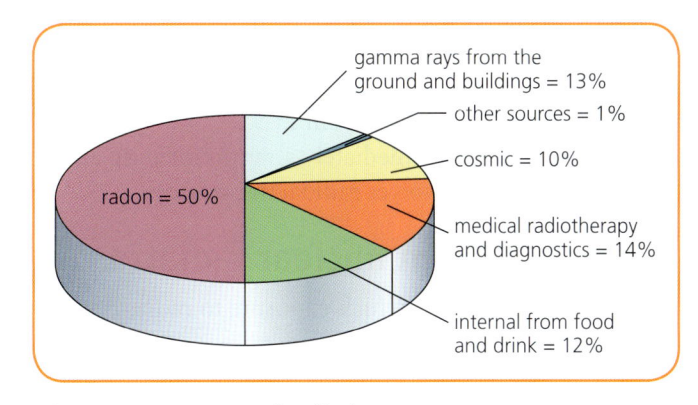

radon = 50%
gamma rays from the ground and buildings = 13%
other sources = 1%
cosmic = 10%
medical radiotherapy and diagnostics = 14%
internal from food and drink = 12%

Figure 12.6 Sources of radiation

We are exposed to natural background radiation due to the small amounts of the radioactive gas called radon that we breathe. The ground and buildings around us are also slightly radioactive. Our bodies contain some

Waves and Radiation

Unit 2

radioactivity from the food we eat, and we also absorb cosmic rays from outer space. These are called natural sources of radiation.

Our exposure to radiation is further increased by various processes, particularly in healthcare. We are exposed to radiation during medical examinations such as dental X-rays, the investigation of bone fractures, and other diagnostic procedures. These are called 'manmade' sources of radiation.

Handling radioactive sources

The radioactive warning sign is displayed wherever radioactive sources are stored or are in regular use.

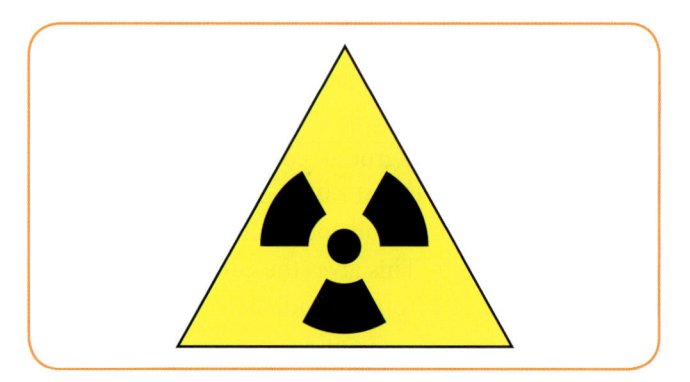

Figure 12.7 Radiation warning sign

When using radioactive sources, the following safety procedures should be followed:

- Always use tongs or wear special gloves when moving a source – never use bare hands.
- Arrange the source so that the radiation window points away from your body.
- Never point the source at your eyes.
- Wash your hands immediately after performing any experiment that involves radioactive sources.

Protection from nuclear radiation

There are three ways in which exposure to radiation can be reduced:

- Shielding – shield the source of radiation with an appropriate thickness of absorber.
- Limiting the time of exposure – radioactive sources should be moved and used as quickly as possible to reduce the radiation present.
- Distance from source – the further you are from the source, the less radiation you will receive.

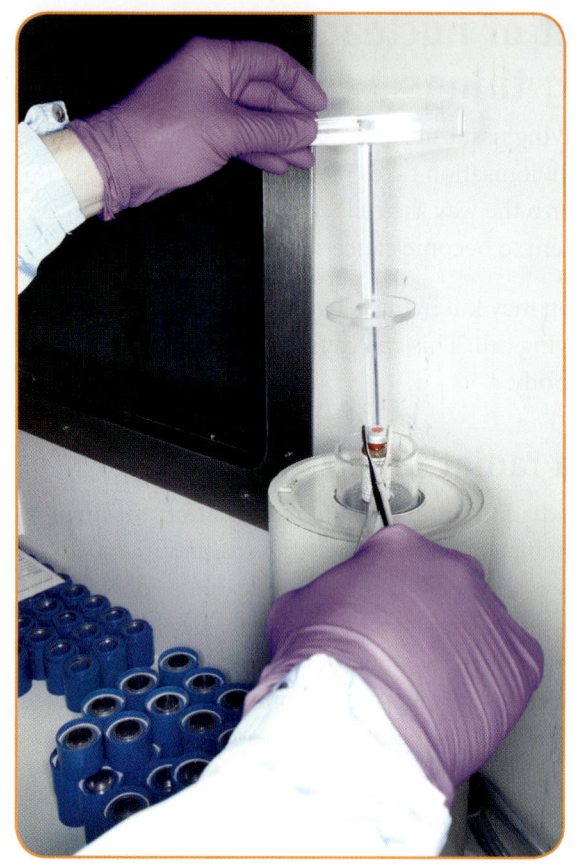

Figure 12.8 Using tongs to lift a radioactive source

Using nuclear radiation in medicine

Treating cancer: radiotherapy

A cancer is a bundle of cells that reproduce in an uncontrolled manner. The treatment of cancer by radiation is called radiotherapy. The purpose of radiotherapy is to damage the cancer cells and stop them reproducing. As a result the cancer or tumour will then shrink. However, during radiotherapy healthy cells will also be exposed to radiation and will be damaged. The damage to healthy tissue is minimised by carefully calculating the amount of radiation required to damage the cancer cells and by aiming the radiation very accurately at them.

To reach the tumour inside the body, gamma radiation is used. The gamma source is held safely in a thick metal container. A slit in the container allows a controlled narrow beam of gamma radiation to emerge. The radiation source is arranged so that it can rotate around the patient. Rotating the source of radiation means that the tumour receives a large dose of radiation while the healthy tissue receives a much smaller dose.

Radiotherapy is more effective when given as a series of small doses.

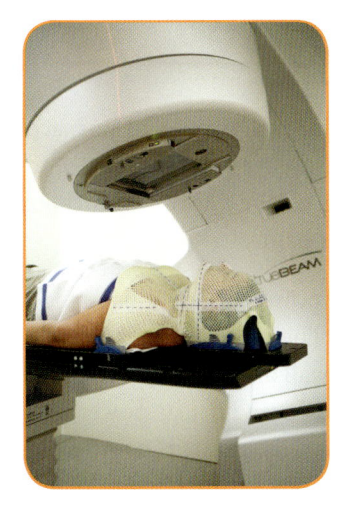

Figure 12.9 Radiotherapy treatment

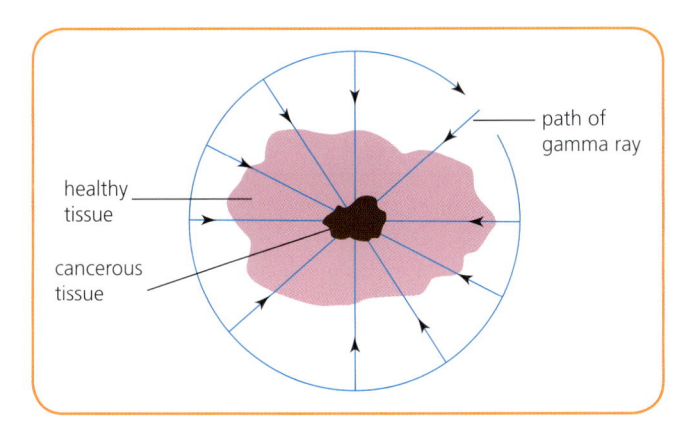

Figure 12.10 The gamma ray source is aimed at and rotates around the tumour

Sterilisation

Gamma radiation can be used to kill microorganisms present on medical items such as syringes (i.e. to sterilise them). The syringes are pre-packed and then exposed to an intense source of gamma radiation. This kills any microorganisms but does not make the syringe radioactive.

Radioactive tracers

Small amounts of radiation can easily be detected so the path of the radiation through an object can be followed. When the radioactive substance is used like this, it is called a tracer.

In medicine

The radioactive tracer is either injected into the patient or the patient drinks it. The substances used are chosen so that they:

- concentrate in the organ that is to be examined
- lose their radioactivity quickly
- emit gamma radiation, which can be detected outside the body (alpha and beta radiation would be absorbed inside the body).

A gamma camera can be used to detect the gamma radiation.

In industry

A leaking underground pipe can be detected by adding a radioactive tracer to the liquid in the pipe. Some of the liquid and tracer will leak into the soil surrounding the pipe. More gamma radiation will be detected at the surface at this point, indicating the position of the leak.

Power stations

Electrical energy is mainly generated in large, central power stations fuelled by coal, gas or nuclear fuel. These power stations operate in similar ways:

- Water is heated to form steam, which turns a turbine.
- The turbine drives a generator to produce electrical energy.
- The exhaust steam from the turbine is condensed to water and returned to the boiler or reactor to be reheated.

Normally fossil fuels (coal and gas) are burned to release the heat needed to boil the water. However, the burning of fossil fuels has a number of important disadvantages:

- There is a finite amount of fossil fuels available – they will eventually run out.
- When they are burned they cause air pollution.
- Carbon dioxide is produced (a greenhouse gas).

Nuclear power: advantages and disadvantages

The main advantages of using nuclear energy to produce electricity are:

- no carbon dioxide (a greenhouse gas) is produced
- no gases that cause air pollution are produced
- the same mass of nuclear fuel produces much more energy than the fossil fuels.

Waves and Radiation

The main disadvantages of using nuclear fuel are:

- the nuclear waste produced is difficult to dispose of safely
- the possibility of an accident – a nuclear explosion
- there is a finite amount of nuclear fuel available – it will eventually run out.

Nuclear waste

One of the major problems with using nuclear energy is the radioactive waste produced. The three categories of waste product are:

- low-level radioactive solid waste
- medium-level radioactive waste
- high-level radioactive waste.

Describing waste as 'low-level' or 'medium-level' radioactive waste does not mean that it is not dangerous. It means that the radioactivity is less concentrated but the waste has still to be stored carefully.

High-level radioactive waste is mainly spent nuclear fuel. The materials left in the fuel rods are highly radioactive. This type of waste has to be stored for a very long time in a suitable environment before the radiation reaches a safe level. Initially the spent fuel rods are stored in cooling ponds. The water removes some of the heat and also absorbs the radiation. The fuel rods are then removed and sealed in drums, and the drums are stored in vaults.

Nuclear accidents

Despite very strict safety precautions, accidents involving nuclear energy are possible and have happened. This can be due to technical breakdowns, human error or natural events.

In 2011, a very powerful earthquake took place off the coast of Japan. The resulting tsunami overwhelmed the protecting sea wall and damaged the reactor cooling systems at Fukushima nuclear power plant. Without adequate cooling, the reactors overheated and several explosions took place, which led to major releases of radioactivity. People living within a 30 km radius had to be evacuated for their own safety. It is not known when they will be able to return to their homes.

Key facts and physics equations: nuclear radiation

- A simple model of the atom includes protons, neutrons and electrons.
- The energy from radiation is absorbed by the medium through which it passes.
- An alpha particle is absorbed by a thin sheet of paper.
- A beta particle is absorbed by a few millimetres of aluminium.
- A gamma ray is absorbed by a few centimetres of lead.
- Ionisation is the breaking up of a neutral atom into positive and negative pieces.
- Alpha particles are more ionising than beta particles or gamma rays.
- When handling radioactive sources, always use tongs and point the source window away from your body. Never point the source at your eyes and always wash your hands immediately after using radioactive sources.

Nuclear radiation

End-of-chapter questions

1. A simple model of the atom contains protons, neutrons and electrons.
   Draw a diagram of the atom. Label each of the particles and state the nature of their charges.

2. Nuclear radiation causes ionisation.
   a) What is meant by the term 'ionisation'?
   b) Alpha, beta and gamma radiations are absorbed in a body tissue.
      (i) Which of the above radiations is most likely to produce the greatest amount of ionisation?
      (ii) Which of the above radiations has the greatest range in air?

3. A technician working with nuclear radiation wears a film badge to monitor the amount of radiation she is exposed to. The film is contained in a plastic holder with windows of different materials as shown in Figure 12.11. No light can reach the film.

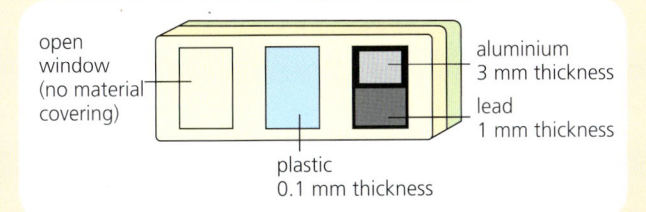

   open window (no material covering)
   plastic 0.1 mm thickness
   aluminium 3 mm thickness
   lead 1 mm thickness

   Figure 12.11

   a) Why does the technician's level of exposure to radiation have to be carefully monitored?
   b) The technician is exposed to beta radiation. Which window or windows on the film badge will be affected by the beta radiation? Give a reason for your choice.

4. A hospital uses a radioactive tracer to investigate the blood flow in a patient's kidney. The radiation from the tracer is detected outside the patient's body. Sources of alpha, beta or gamma radiation are available to use as the tracer.
   Which source of radiation would be suitable to use as the tracer in this investigation? Explain your answer.

5. A technician is asked to check whether alpha, beta or gamma radiation is emitted from three different sources of nuclear radiation. Each of the sources emits only one type of radiation, alpha, beta or gamma. The technician has the following absorber materials: a thin sheet of paper; 5-mm-thick aluminium; 20 mm of lead.
   Describe how the technician would identify the radiation emitted by each of the three sources.

6. Three types of box of the same shape and size are available to store a gamma source in: a wooden box, an aluminium box, and a lead-lined wooden box. The gamma source is kept in a lead-lined wooden box. Explain why the other two boxes are not suitable to store the gamma source.

7. Four radiations are described in the following list: cosmic rays coming from outer space; gamma rays in a radiotherapy treatment; radon gas coming from the ground; an X-ray of a bone fracture.
   a) From the above list, name a natural source of radiation.
   b) From the above list, name a source of 'manmade' radiation.

8. a) State **one** advantage of using nuclear fuel instead of fossil fuel to generate electrical energy.
   b) State **one** disadvantage of using nuclear fuel to generate electrical energy.

9. Describe what happens to high-level nuclear waste so that it does not pose a danger to the environment.

Waves and Radiation

Unit 2 exam practice

1. Water waves are transverse waves. Water waves are produced in a pool using a wave machine. The depth of water in the pool does not change. The waves travel 30 m in a time of 7.5 s. The wave machine produces 5.0 waves every second.
   a) Explain what is meant by a *transverse wave*.
   b) State the frequency of the waves produced by the wave machine.
   c) Calculate the wavelength of the waves produced by the machine.

2. The profile of a wave is shown below.

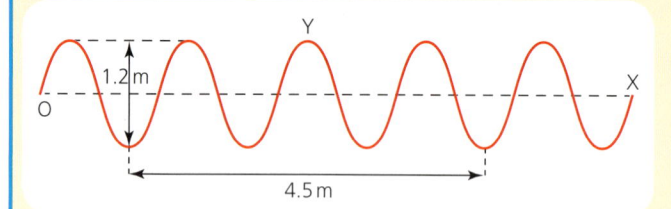

Figure E2.1

The waves take 2.5 s to travel from O to X.
   a) What name is given to point Y on the wave?
   b) State the amplitude of the waves.
   c) Calculate the frequency of the waves.
   d) Calculate the wavelength of the waves.
   e) Calculate the speed of the waves.

3. A microphone is connected to an oscilloscope as shown.

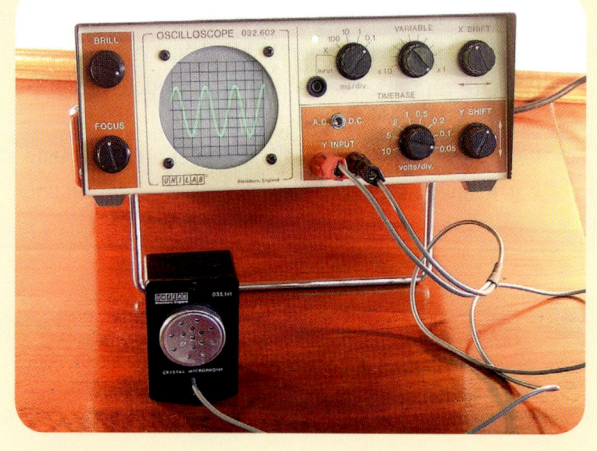

Figure E2.2

A note of frequency 1020 Hz from a violin is played into the microphone. The following trace is seen on the oscilloscope.

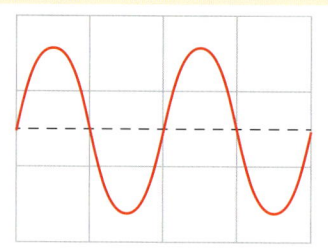

Figure E2.3

   a) How many sound waves does the string of the violin produce in one second?
   b) Copy Figure E2.3. On the diagram show the trace obtained when a quieter note of frequency 510 Hz is played into the microphone. The controls of the oscilloscope remain unchanged.

4. A student connects two sound-operated switches to a timer as shown below.

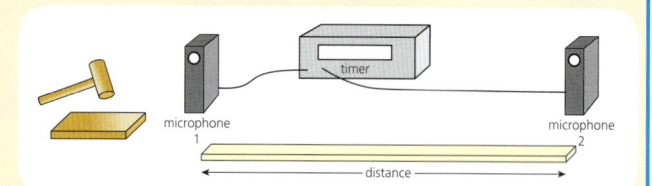

Figure E2.4

A sound is produced. When the sound wave reaches microphone 1, the timer starts timing. When the sound wave reaches microphone 2, the timer stops timing. The student records the following measurements.

Distance (m)	0.5	1.0	1.5	2.0	2.5
Time on timer (s)	0.0015	0.0030	0.0044	0.0059	0.0074

   a) Present the information in the table as a line graph.
   b) Calculate the speed of sound in air when the time taken for the sound to travel between the microphones was 0.0059 seconds.

Nuclear radiation

5. The sound detected by headphones is shown below.

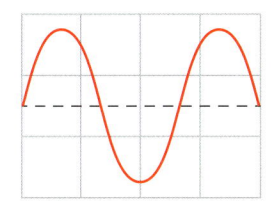

Figure E2.5

a) The speed of sound in air is 340 m/s. The wavelength of the sound in air is 0.2 m. Calculate the frequency of the sound wave.

b) Copy the diagram of the sound wave shown above. On the diagram, use a dotted line to show the signal that would need to be fed into the headphones to cancel out the sound being heard.

6. The chart shows the members of the electromagnetic spectrum.

a) Which end of the chart, P or Q, has the waves with the longest wavelength?

b) State the name of the radiation represented by the letter R.

c) (i) Describe **one** use of infrared radiation in medicine.
   (ii) State **one** use of gamma rays.

7. a) On holiday, your luggage passes through a scanner as part of a security check. Which kind of radiation is used by the scanner to check your luggage?

b) While on holiday, you decide to sunbathe for a short time each day in order to get a suntan.
   (i) Which kind of radiation provides a suntan?
   (ii) If you receive more of this type of radiation than you should, what kind of health problem might it cause?

8. The table below provides some information about members of the electromagnetic spectrum.

a) State a possible value for the wavelength of microwaves.

b) State a possible source for gamma radiation.

c) State a possible use for infrared radiation.

d) State a possible detector for visible light.

e) State two sources of electromagnetic radiation that can be used in communications.

P							Q
radio waves	TV waves	microwaves	infrared	visible light	R	X-rays	gamma rays

Electromagnetic wave	Example of sources of waves	Approximate wavelength	Examples of detectors	Some uses
radio and TV	transmitters; outer space	1 kilometre to 1 metre	aerial and electronic circuit	communications; radio; television; astronomy
microwaves	transmitters; outer space	a few centimetres	aerial and electronic circuit	communications; satellites; ovens
infrared	electronic devices; warm objects; the Sun	a fraction of a millimetre	special film; thermo-couple; thermistor	security systems; remote control for television
visible light	stars and the Sun; lamps; LED	a fraction of a millionth of a metre	eye; photographic film; LDR	sight; photography
ultraviolet	fluorescent tubes; very hot objects; the Sun	a hundredth of a millionth of a metre	film; fluorescent material	suntan lamps; production of vitamin D
X-rays	X-ray machines; outer space	a thousandth of a millionth of a metre	film; electronic sensor	checking for defects in metals; airport luggage checks; medical diagnosis
gamma rays	radioactive materials; the Sun	a millionth of a millionth of a metre	film; Geiger-Müller tube and counter	medical tracers; killing bacteria

Waves and Radiation

Unit 2

9. The diagram below shows how far two nuclear radiations, X and Y, travel when different absorbers are placed in front of a radioactive source.

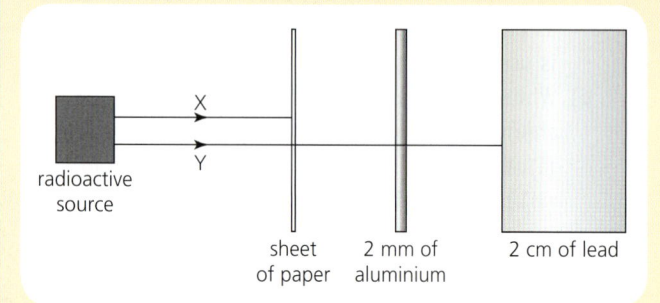

Figure E2.6

a) (i) State the name of radiation X.
   (ii) State the name of radiation Y.
b) Alpha-emitting radioactive material is never injected into the body in order to provide images of parts of the body. State two reasons why alpha-emitting radioactive material is not suitable for this procedure.

10. The pie chart shows the main sources of radiation that we are exposed to on the Earth.

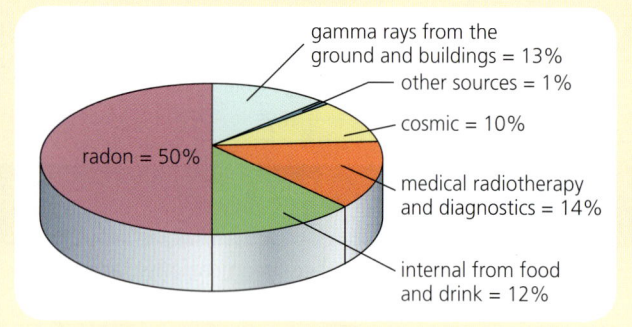

(radon = 50%, gamma rays from the ground and buildings = 13%, other sources = 1%, cosmic = 10%, medical radiotherapy and diagnostics = 14%, internal from food and drink = 12%)

Figure E2.7

a) State:
   (i) **one** source of natural radiation
   (ii) **one** source of manmade radiation.
b) What percentage of the radiation that we receive comes from:
   (i) cosmic radiation
   (ii) food and drink?

11. a) State one advantage of using nuclear energy to generate electricity.
b) One of the disadvantages of using nuclear energy to generate electricity is the nuclear waste produced. Two sites, X and Y, have been proposed for the storage of nuclear waste.
   Site X: in the countryside, close to some hills and near the sea.
   Site Y: close to a large city and situated on marsh ground.
   (i) State one reason why site X might be suitable for storing the nuclear waste.
   (ii) State one reason why site Y might not be suitable for storing the nuclear waste.

Unit 3

Dynamics and Space

Dynamics and Space

Unit 3

13 Speed and acceleration

Learning outcomes

At the end of this chapter you should be able to:
1. Describe how to measure average speed.
2. Carry out calculations involving distance, time and average speed.
3. Describe how to measure instantaneous speed.
4. Identify situations where average speed and instantaneous speed are different.
5. Explain the terms 'speed' and 'acceleration'.
6. State that acceleration is the change in speed in one second.
7. Describe how to measure acceleration.
8. Carry out calculations involving the relationship between initial speed, final speed, time and constant acceleration.
9. Draw speed–time graphs for constant acceleration.
10. Describe the motion represented by a speed–time graph.
11. Calculate distance and acceleration from speed–time graphs for constant acceleration.

Speed

Speed is the distance travelled by an object in one second. The unit of speed is metres per second (m/s).

Average speed

Consider David running a race between points A and B, as shown in Figure 13.1.

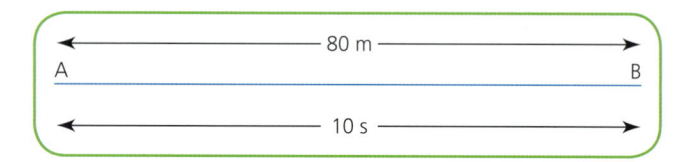

Figure 13.1 Measuring average speed

Points A and B are 80 m apart. David takes 10 s to run from A to B.

This means that David would on average travel 8 m every second – an average speed of 8 metres per second (8 m/s).

The average speed is the steady or constant speed that David would need to travel at, all of the time, to cover 80 metres in a time of 10 seconds.

Measuring average speed requires the measurement of the distance travelled and the time taken to travel this distance.

$$\text{Average speed} = \frac{\text{distance}}{\text{time}}$$

$$\bar{v} = \frac{d}{t}$$

where $\bar{v}$ = average speed, measured in metres per second (m/s)

d = distance travelled, measured in metres (m)

t = time taken, measured in seconds (s).

Using the 'maths triangle' (see Rearranging physics equations on page 145) for the above equation gives:

$$\bar{v} = \frac{d}{t} \qquad d = \bar{v} \times t \qquad t = \frac{d}{\bar{v}}$$

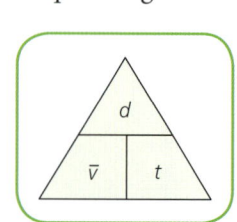

Speed and acceleration

Worked examples

Example 1
A bus takes 250 seconds to travel a distance of 2000 metres. Calculate the average speed of the bus.

Solution

$$\bar{v} = \frac{d}{t} = \frac{2000}{250} = 8 \text{ m/s}$$

Example 2
During a journey, a car travels at an average speed of 15 m/s. The car takes 450 s to make the journey. Calculate the distance travelled by the car.

Solution

$$\bar{v} = \frac{d}{t}$$

$$d = \bar{v} \times t = 15 \times 450 = 6750 \text{ m}$$

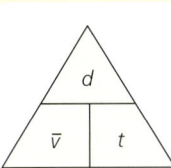

Example 3
A boy runs a 400 m race. The average speed of the boy during the race is 3.2 m/s. Calculate the time taken for the boy to run 400 m.

Solution

$$\bar{v} = \frac{d}{t}$$

$$t = \frac{d}{\bar{v}} = \frac{400}{3.2} = 125 \text{ s}$$

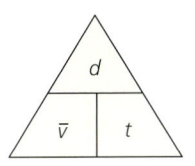

Investigation: Measuring average speed using a stopwatch

Measure out two points on the ground 20 metres apart.

Record in a table the time for one member of your group to cover the 20 metres for the following motions:

- walking between the two points
- sprinting from rest between the two points
- sprinting when already moving between the two points.

Calculate the average speed for each of the three motions using the equation:

$$\text{average speed} = \frac{\text{distance}}{\text{time}} = \frac{20}{\text{time on timer}}$$

Explain why the average speeds are not the same.

When using a stopwatch it can be very difficult to start the timer at the correct 'instant' and stop it at the correct 'instant'. A more accurate way of starting and stopping the timer is to use an electronic switch called a light gate. When the light beam of the light gate is complete, the switch is open. When a card (sometimes called a mask) 'breaks' the light beam of the light gate, the switch is closed. The light gate switch can therefore be used to start and stop a timer.

Investigation: Measuring average speed using a light gate, card and timer (computer)

Set up a runway so that it is sloping slightly (Figure 13.2). Attach the card to the trolley. Position the two light gates 0.5 m apart at points X and Y and connect them to the timer (computer).

Set the timer (computer) to start timing when the card on the trolley breaks the light beam at X.

Set the timer (computer) to stop timing when the card on the trolley breaks the light beam at Y.

Release the trolley, from rest, at the top of the slope. Calculate the average speed using:

$$\text{average speed} = \frac{\text{distance between X and Y}}{\text{time to travel from X to Y}}$$

107

Dynamics and Space

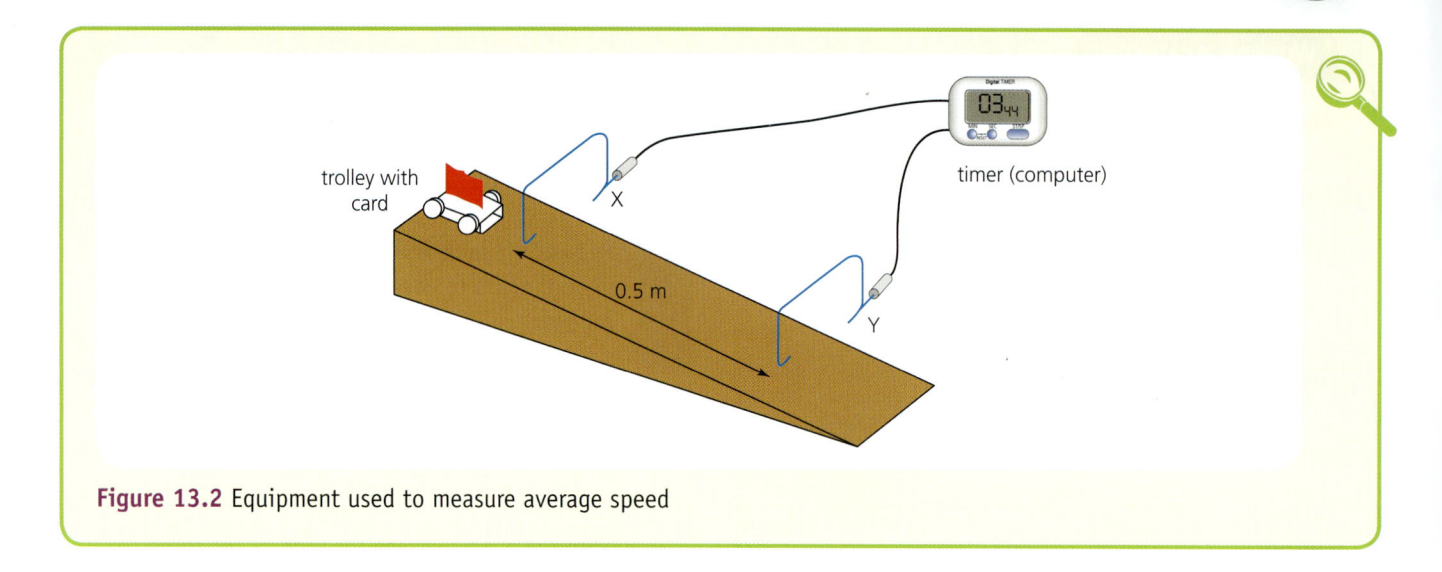

Figure 13.2 Equipment used to measure average speed

Average speed and instantaneous speed

During David's 80-metre race, his speed was not actually constant at 8 m/s but changed over time. At the start of the race he was stationary and so his speed was zero. When he started, his speed rapidly increased until he reached his maximum speed. Towards the end of the race, as David began to tire, his speed decreased slightly. This means that the average speed and the speed at any particular time – the instantaneous speed – during the race are unlikely to be the same.

Instantaneous speed is the speed of an object at a particular time (or instant).

What if we wish to measure David's speed at, say, point X during the race?

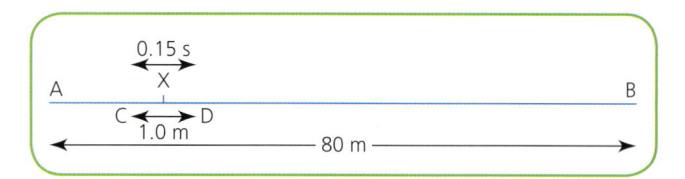

Figure 13.3 Measuring instantaneous speed

Since the time interval between A and B is large, David's speed at X is unlikely to be the same as the average speed for the whole race. However, by measuring the time taken for David to travel from point C (just before X) to point D (just after X) gives:

distance CD = 1.0 m

time to travel from C to D = 0.15 s

average speed between C and D = $\frac{1.0}{0.15}$ = 6.7 m/s

This is a much better estimate of the speed at X because the time interval involved is very small. This means that any change in speed as David moves between C and D will be very small.

The instantaneous speed of an object is approximately the same as the average speed of the object as long as the time used in the equation for average speed is very small.

Measuring instantaneous speed

To measure short time intervals requires the use of a light gate connected to an electronic timer. When a card mounted on the trolley breaks the light beam of the light gate, the timer starts timing. When the card has passed through the light gate, the light beam is restored and the timer stops timing. The time taken for the card to pass through the light gate is recorded on the timer.

$$\text{instantaneous speed} = \frac{\text{length of card}}{\text{time on timer}}$$

Speed and acceleration

Worked example

Example

A card of length 0.10 m is attached to a vehicle. The vehicle is released from point X and runs down a slope.

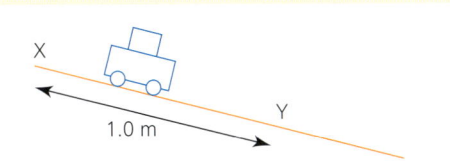

Figure 13.4

The card passes through a light gate positioned at point Y.
Distance from X to Y = 1.0 m

Length of card that passes through light gate = 0.10 m
Time for trolley to travel from X to Y = 2.50 s
Time for card to pass through light gate = 0.125 s

a) Calculate the average speed of the trolley between X and Y.
b) Calculate the instantaneous speed of the trolley at Y.

Solution

a) $\bar{v} = \dfrac{d}{t} = \dfrac{1.0}{2.5} = 0.4$ m/s

b) Instantaneous speed at Y = $\dfrac{d}{t} = \dfrac{0.10}{0.125} = 0.8$ m/s

The speed at Y is approximately the instantaneous speed, as the time for the card to pass through the light gate is very small.

Investigation

Measuring instantaneous speed

Once you have set up the runway for method A, do not alter the slope for methods B and C.

Method A: using a stopwatch

Arrange a runway so that it is sloping slightly (Figure 13.5). Make a mark, X, near the bottom of the slope. Release the trolley, from rest, at the top of the slope.

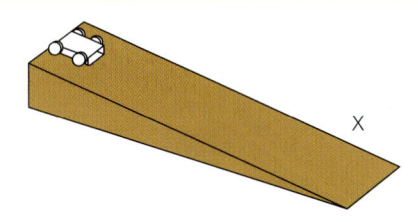

Figure 13.5 Measuring instantaneous speed: method A

When the front of the trolley passes X, start the stopwatch. When the rear of the trolley passes X, stop the stopwatch. Measure the length of the trolley. Calculate the instantaneous speed using:

$$\text{instantaneous speed} = \dfrac{\text{length of trolley}}{\text{time on stopwatch}}$$

Why was method A difficult to do?

Method B: using a light gate, 10 cm card and timer (computer)

Use the same sloping runway as in method A (Figure 13.6). Attach the card to the trolley.

Set up a light gate at point X on the runway. Connect the light gate to the timer (computer). Set the timer (computer) to start timing when the card on the trolley breaks the light beam. Set the timer (computer) to stop timing when the light beam is restored, i.e. the timer (computer) records the time taken for the card to pass through the light beam.

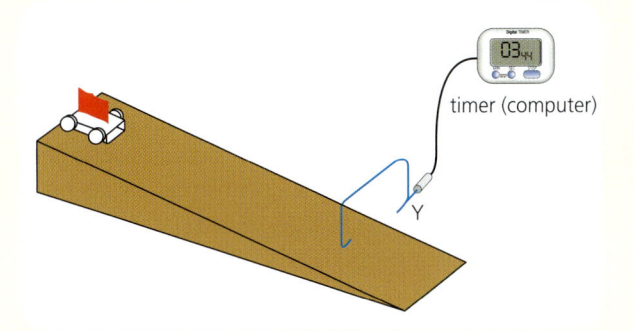

Figure 13.6 Measuring instantaneous speed: method B
Release the trolley, from rest, at the top of the slope.

Dynamics and Space

Unit 3

Calculate the instantaneous speed using:

$$\text{instantaneous speed} = \frac{\text{length of card}}{\text{time on timer}}$$

Why is method B better than method A?

Method C: using a light gate, 10 cm card and timer (computer) set to measure speed

Use the same set-up as in method B but set the timer (computer) to measure 'Speed' and program it with the length of the card (10 cm).

When the card on the trolley breaks the light beam, the timer (computer) starts timing. When the light beam is restored, the timer (computer) stops timing, i.e. the timer (computer) records the time taken for the card to pass through the light beam.

The timer (computer) then calculates the instantaneous speed using:

$$\text{instantaneous speed} = \frac{\text{length of card}}{\text{time on timer}}$$

Release the trolley, from rest, at the top of the slope. Note the instantaneous speed from the timer (computer).

Compare your answers from methods A, B and C.

Why is method C better than method B?

Physics in action

Speed cameras

Figure 13.7 A speed camera

A sensor in the speed camera measures the speed of a passing vehicle. If the vehicle is travelling above the speed limit for the area then two photographs are taken a known time apart. A powerful flash is used to show the registration plate and the white lines marked on the road. The speed of the vehicle can then be calculated using the formula:

$$\text{average speed} = \frac{\text{distance}}{\text{time}}$$

This is the speed of the vehicle, since the time is short.

The problem with speed cameras is that a speeding motorist can see the speed camera or the lines marked on the road and simply slow down for the camera and then speed up again shortly after.

Average speed cameras

Figure 13.8 Average speed cameras

When a car enters the area controlled by the average speed cameras, a camera records the registration plate and the time, t_1, at which the vehicle passes the camera. A few miles down the road another camera records the registration plate and the time, t_2, that the vehicle passes this camera. The distance between the two cameras is known, so the average speed can be calculated:

$$\text{average speed} = \frac{\text{distance between cameras}}{t_2 - t_1}$$

The cameras work day and night as they use infrared light (see Chapter 11) to read the registration plate of the vehicle.

Acceleration

When the speed of an object changes, the object is said to accelerate. Acceleration gives some idea of how quickly the speed of the object is changing.

acceleration = change in speed in one second

$$\text{acceleration} = \frac{\text{change in speed}}{\text{time taken for the speed to change}}$$

$$\text{acceleration} = \frac{\text{final speed} - \text{initial speed}}{\text{time taken for the speed to change}}$$

$$a = \frac{v - u}{t}$$

where a = acceleration of the object, measured in metres per second squared (m/s^2)

v = final speed of object, measured in metres per second (m/s)

u = initial speed of object, measured in metres per second (m/s)

t = time taken for the speed to change, measured in seconds (s).

Using the 'maths triangle' (see Rearranging physics equations on page 145) for the above equation gives:

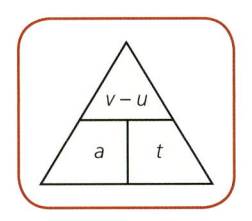

$$a = \frac{v - u}{t} \qquad v - u = at \qquad t = \frac{v - u}{a}$$

When the acceleration of an object does not change, the object is said to have a constant or uniform acceleration.

An acceleration of 5 m/s^2 means that the speed of the object is increasing by 5 m/s every second.

If the object starts from rest ($u = 0$) then after 1 s the speed of the object will be 5 m/s, after 2 s the speed of the object will be 10 m/s, after 3 s the speed of the object will be 15 m/s, and after 10 s the speed of the object will be 50 m/s.

If the object has an initial speed of 3 m/s ($u = 3$ m/s) then after 1 s the speed of the object will be 8 m/s, after 2 s the speed of the object will be 13 m/s, after 3 s the speed of the object will be 18 m/s, and after 10 s the speed of the object will be 53 m/s.

When an object slows down the final speed will be less than the initial speed and so the change in speed will be negative. This means that the object has a **negative acceleration** (sometimes called a deceleration).

An acceleration of –2 m/s^2 means that the speed of the object is decreasing by 2 m/s every second.

Dynamics and Space

Unit 3

Worked examples

Example 1
A car starts from rest and travels in a straight line. The car accelerates uniformly for a time of 12 seconds. The speed of the car is now 24 m/s. Calculate the acceleration of the car.

Solution

$$a = \frac{v - u}{t} = \frac{24 - 0}{12} = \frac{24}{12} = 2 \text{ m/s}^2$$

Example 2
A lorry is travelling in a straight line. The lorry slows down from 20 m/s to 5.0 m/s. The time taken for this is 10 s. Calculate the acceleration of the lorry.

Solution

Note that final speed $v = 5$ m/s; initial speed $u = 20$ m/s

$$a = \frac{v - u}{t} = \frac{5 - 20}{10} = \frac{-15}{10} = -1.5 \text{ m/s}^2$$

Example 3
When taking off from a runway an aeroplane travels in a straight line. The plane accelerates uniformly from rest with an acceleration of 2.4 m/s². The plane reaches a speed of 60 m/s. Find the time taken to reach this speed.

Solution

$$a = \frac{v - u}{t}$$

$$t = \frac{v - u}{a} = \frac{60 - 0}{2.4} = \frac{60}{2.4} = 25 \text{ s}$$

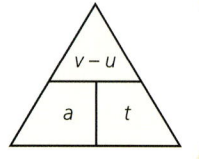

Example 4
A motorcyclist is initially at rest. The motorcyclist then accelerates uniformly at 1.5 m/s² for 6.0 s. Calculate the final speed of the motorcyclist.

Solution

$$a = \frac{v - u}{t}$$

$$v - u = a \times t$$

$$v - 0 = 1.5 \times 6$$

$$v = 9 \text{ m/s}$$

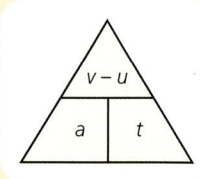

Example 5
A train is travelling in a straight line at a constant speed. The train now brakes uniformly to rest in a time of 100 s. The acceleration of the train is −0.2 m/s². Calculate the initial speed of the train.

Solution

$$a = \frac{v - u}{t}$$

$$v - u = a \times t$$

$$0 - u = -0.2 \times 100$$

$$-u = -20$$

$$u = 20 \text{ m/s}$$

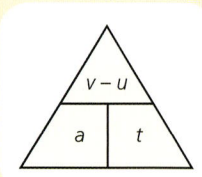

Measuring acceleration

To measure the acceleration of a vehicle travelling in a straight line down a slope requires the measurement of the initial and final speeds of the object and the time taken for the speed to change.

Investigation

Measuring acceleration

Once you have set up the runway for method A, do not alter the slope for method B.

Method A

Using two light gates, stopwatch, 10-cm card and timer (computer) set to measure two speeds

Arrange a runway so that it is sloping slightly (Figure 13.9).

Attach a 10-cm card to the trolley. Position the two light gates 0.5 m apart and connect them to the timer (computer). Set the timer (computer) to measure two 'Speeds' and program it with the length of the card (10 cm).

Speed and acceleration

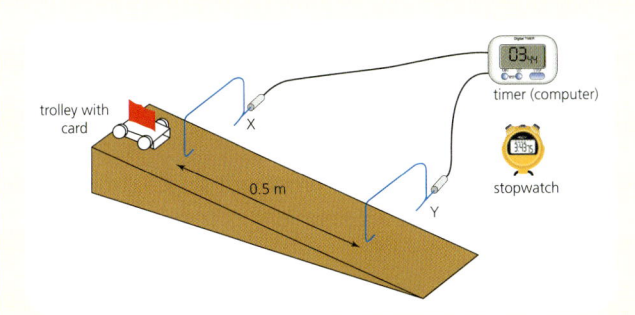

Figure 13.9 Measuring acceleration

Release the trolley, from rest, at the top of the slope. When the card reaches the first light gate, start a stopwatch. When the card reaches the second light gate, stop the stopwatch. The time recorded on the stopwatch is taken as the time taken for the change in speed to occur.

When the card breaks the first light beam, the timer (computer) calculates:

$$\text{initial speed} = \frac{\text{length of card}}{\text{time to pass through 1}^{st}\text{ light beam}}$$

When the card breaks the second light beam, the timer (computer) calculates:

$$\text{final speed} = \frac{\text{length of card}}{\text{time to pass through 2}^{nd}\text{ light beam}}$$

Note the initial speed, final speed and time on stopwatch (time taken for the speed to change).
Calculate the acceleration of the trolley using:

$$\text{acceleration} = \frac{\text{final speed} - \text{initial speed}}{\text{time on stopwatch}}$$

Method B

Using light gate, special card and timer (computer) set to measure acceleration

Use the same set-up as in method A but only one light gate (Y) is required. You should also replace the length of card with the special card shown in Figure 13.10.

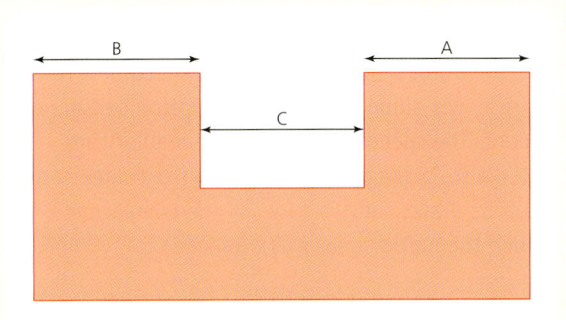

Figure 13.10 Special card for measuring acceleration

For the special card, length of A = length of B. Set the timer (computer) to measure 'acceleration' and program it with the length of A.

Release the trolley, from rest, at the top of the slope.

When length A of the card passes through the light beam, the timer (computer) times how long it takes for length A to pass through the light beam. The timer (computer) calculates the initial speed of the trolley from:

$$\text{initial speed, } u = \frac{\text{length of A}}{\text{time to pass through light beam}}$$

When length B of the card passes through the light beam, the timer (computer) times how long it takes for length B to pass through the light beam. The computer calculates the final speed of the trolley from:

$$\text{final speed, } v = \frac{\text{length of B}}{\text{time to pass through light beam}}$$

The timer (computer) also measures the time taken for gap C to pass through the light beam. The time taken for the speed to change (t) is calculated by the timer (computer).

The timer (computer) then calculates the acceleration of the trolley using:

$$a = \frac{v - u}{t}$$

Compare the accelerations calculated using methods A and B.

Dynamics and Space

Unit 3

Speed–time graphs

Investigation

Use a motion sensor to record the speed of a trolley as it moves along a runway (the motion sensor records the speed of the trolley at regular time intervals – a speed-time graph for the trolley can then be drawn, in this case, by the computer to which the motion sensor is attached).

Obtain speed-time graphs for the trolley when:

- the runway is level – trolley moves along the runway at constant speed
- the runway has a gentle downward slope – trolley speeds up (accelerates) as it moves down the slope
- the runway has a steeper downward slope – trolley speeds up (greater acceleration) as it moves down the slope
- the runway has a gentle upward slope – trolley slows down (a negative acceleration) as it moves up the slope.

In physics, a graph showing how the speed of an object varies with time is called a speed–time graph.

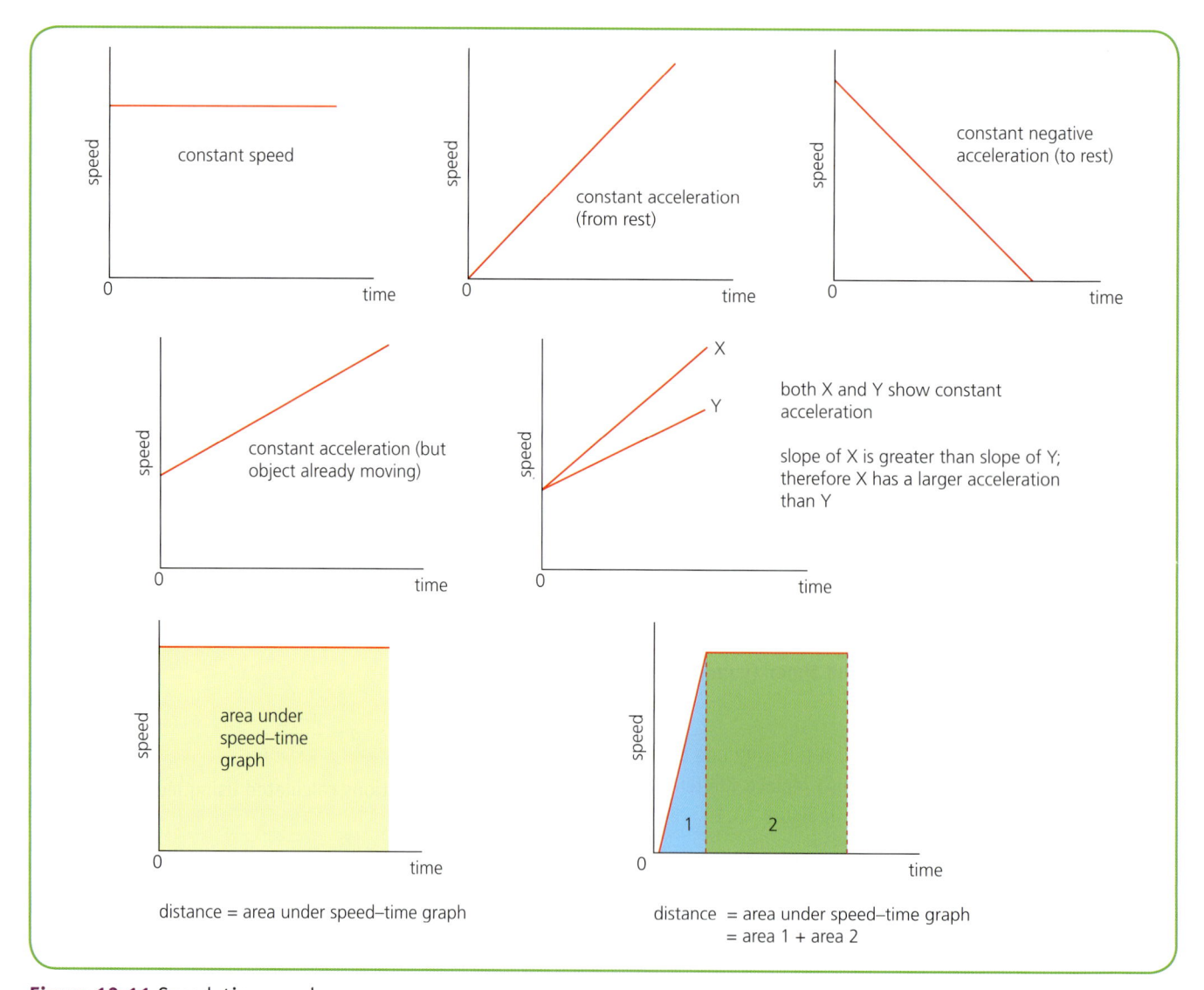

Figure 13.11 Speed-time graphs

- The slope or gradient of a speed–time graph gives the acceleration of the object.
- The area under a speed–time graph is equal to the distance travelled by the object.

Speed and acceleration

Worked examples

Example 1
An object is moving in a straight line. The graph shows how the speed of the object varies with time.

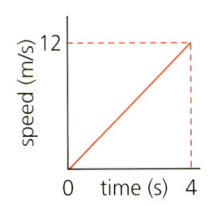

Figure 13.12

a) Describe the motion of the object.
b) Calculate the acceleration of the object.
c) Calculate the distance travelled by the object.
d) Calculate the average speed of the object.

Solution
a) constant acceleration from rest for 4 s
b) $a = \dfrac{v - u}{t} = \dfrac{12 - 0}{4} = \dfrac{12}{4} = 3 \text{ m/s}^2$
c) distance = area under speed–time graph
   = area of triangle
   = ½ × 4 × 12
   = 24 m
d) $\bar{v} = \dfrac{d}{t} = \dfrac{24}{4} = 6 \text{ m/s}$

Example 2
A car accelerates uniformly from rest along a straight road. The speed of the car after 4.0 s is 12 m/s. The car then travels at this speed for a further 6.0 s.
a) Sketch a graph to show how the speed of the car varies with time.
b) Show that the average speed of the car is 9.6 m/s.

Solution
a)

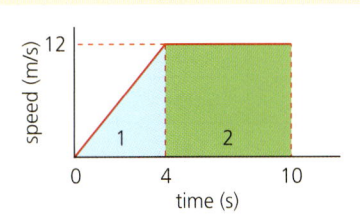

Figure 13.13

b) distance travelled = area under speed–time graph
   = area 1 + area 2
   = (½ × 4 × 12) + (6 × 12)
   = 24 + 72 = 96 m
$\bar{v} = \dfrac{d}{t} = \dfrac{96}{10} = 9.6 \text{ m/s}$

Key facts and physics equations: speed and acceleration

- Average speed = $\dfrac{\text{distance}}{\text{time}}$

  i.e. $\bar{v} = \dfrac{d}{t}$

- Average speed is measured in metres per second (m/s), distance travelled in metres (m) and time taken in seconds (s).
- Acceleration is the change in speed of an object in one second.
- Acceleration = $\dfrac{\text{change in speed}}{\text{time taken for the speed to change}}$

- Acceleration = $\dfrac{\text{final speed} - \text{initial speed}}{\text{time taken for the speed to change}}$

  i.e. $a = \dfrac{v - u}{t}$

- Acceleration is measured in metres per second squared (m/s^2), change in speed in metres per second (m/s) and time in seconds (s).
- An acceleration of 10 m/s^2 means that the speed of the object increases by 10 m/s every second.
- An acceleration of –5 m/s^2 means that the speed of the object decreases by 5 m/s every second.
- The slope of a speed–time graph gives the acceleration.
- The area under a speed–time graph gives the distance travelled.

Dynamics and Space

End-of-chapter questions

1. You are about to make a journey in a car. You wish to measure the average speed of the journey. Describe how you would measure the average speed of your journey, indicating what measurements you would make and how you would use the measurements to calculate the average speed.

2. Calculate the value of each missing quantity in the table shown.

Distance (m)	Time (s)	Average speed (m/s)
25	10	a)
3200	400	b)
1000	c)	4.0
1.6	d)	0.2
e)	50	3.5
f)	1500	2.4

3. A ball is rolled across a floor. It comes to rest after 4.5 seconds. The ball covers a distance of 1.8 metres in this time. Calculate the average speed of the ball.

4. A man takes 800 seconds to make a nonstop journey from his house to a shop. During the journey, the average speed of the man is 0.8 m/s. Calculate the distance travelled by the man.

5. A girl runs a 100 m race at an average speed of 8.0 m/s. Calculate the time taken for the girl to run the race.

6. Describe how you could measure the instantaneous speed of a bicycle. You are given a tape measure and a stopwatch.

7. A car, starting from rest, uniformly accelerates along a straight road for 12 s. The car reaches a speed of 15 m/s. Calculate the acceleration of the car.

8. A sledge, starting from rest, accelerates uniformly in a straight line down a slope. After 5.0 s, the speed of the sledge is 4.0 m/s. Calculate the acceleration of the sledge.

9. A car is travelling in a straight line at a speed of 30 m/s. The car now brakes and slows down uniformly at -1.5 m/s^2. Calculate the time taken for the car to come to rest after the brakes are applied.

10. A van is accelerating at 2.5 m/s^2 along a straight road. How long does it take for the speed of the van to increase from 2.0 m/s to 9.5 m/s?

11. An object is travelling in a straight line. The graph shows how the speed of the object varies with time.

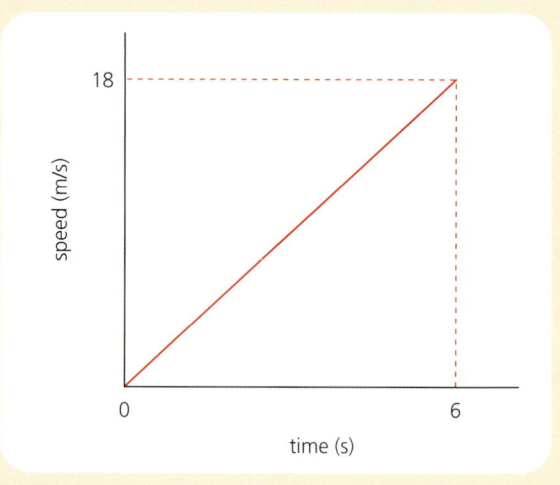

Figure 13.14

a) Calculate the acceleration of the object.
b) Show that the distance travelled by the object is 54 m.
c) Calculate the average speed of the object.

12. A vehicle is travelling in a straight line. The graph shows how the speed of the vehicle varies with time.

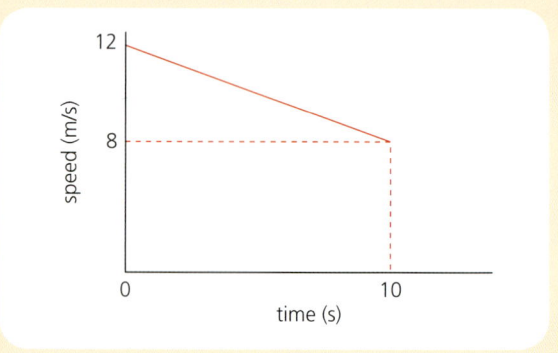

Figure 13.15

a) Describe the motion of the vehicle.
b) Calculate the acceleration of the vehicle.
c) Show that the average speed of the vehicle for this journey is 10 m/s.

13 A vehicle accelerates uniformly from rest in a straight line. The speed of the vehicle after 4.0 s is 5.0 m/s. The vehicle then brakes uniformly for 3.0 s. The speed of the vehicle is now 2.0 m/s.
   a) Draw a graph to show how the speed of the vehicle varies with time.
   b) Calculate the acceleration of the vehicle during the first 4 seconds.

14 The graph shows how the speed of a vehicle varies with time.

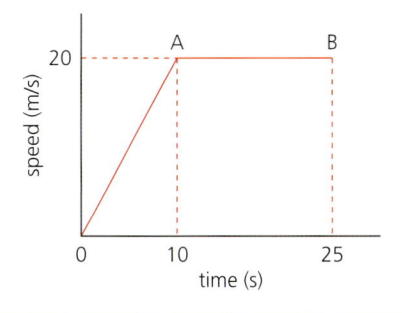

Figure 13.16

a) Describe the motion of the vehicle between:
   (i) OA
   (ii) AB
b) Calculate the acceleration of the vehicle between:
   (i) OA
   (ii) AB
c) Calculate the distance travelled by the vehicle.
d) Calculate the average speed of the vehicle.

Dynamics and Space

Unit 3

14 Relationship between forces, motion and energy

Learning outcomes

At the end of this chapter you should be able to:
1. Describe the effects of forces in terms of their ability to change the shape, speed and direction of travel of an object.
2. Describe the use of a Newton balance to measure force.
3. State that forces that are equal in size but act in opposite directions on an object are called balanced forces and are equivalent to no force at all.
4. State what is meant by an unbalanced force.
5. State that the force of friction can oppose the motion of an object.
6. Describe and explain situations in which attempts are made to increase or decrease the force of friction.
7. Explain the movement of objects in terms of Newton's first law.
8. Describe the qualitative effects of change of mass or of an unbalanced force on the acceleration of an object.
9. Carry out calculations using the relationship between acceleration, unbalanced force and mass.
10. Define the newton.
11. Distinguish between mass and weight.
12. State that weight is a force and is the pull of a planet on an object.
13. State that the weight of an object on the Moon or on different planets is different from its weight on Earth.
14. State that the gravitational field strength on a planet is the force exerted by the planet on a 1.0 kg mass.
15. Carry out calculations involving the relationship between weight, mass and gravitational field strength, including situations where g is not equal to 9.8 N/kg.
16. State that an effect of friction is the transformation of kinetic energy into heat.
17. State one risk and one benefit associated with space exploration.

What can forces do?

When an object is pushed or pulled, a force is exerted on the object. A force can change the:

- motion of an object, i.e. speed it up or slow it down (accelerate the object)
- direction of a moving object
- shape of an object (Figure 14.1).

These changes depend upon how large a force is applied to the object.

Measuring force

A spring can be used to measure force:

- A spring stretches evenly when acted on by a force. Doubling the force doubles the size of the stretch, i.e. the force is directly proportional to the stretch.
- A spring returns to its original length when the force is removed.

A Newton (or spring) balance uses a spring to measure force.

Figure 14.1 The force from the golf club changes the shape of the golf ball

Relationship between forces, motion and energy

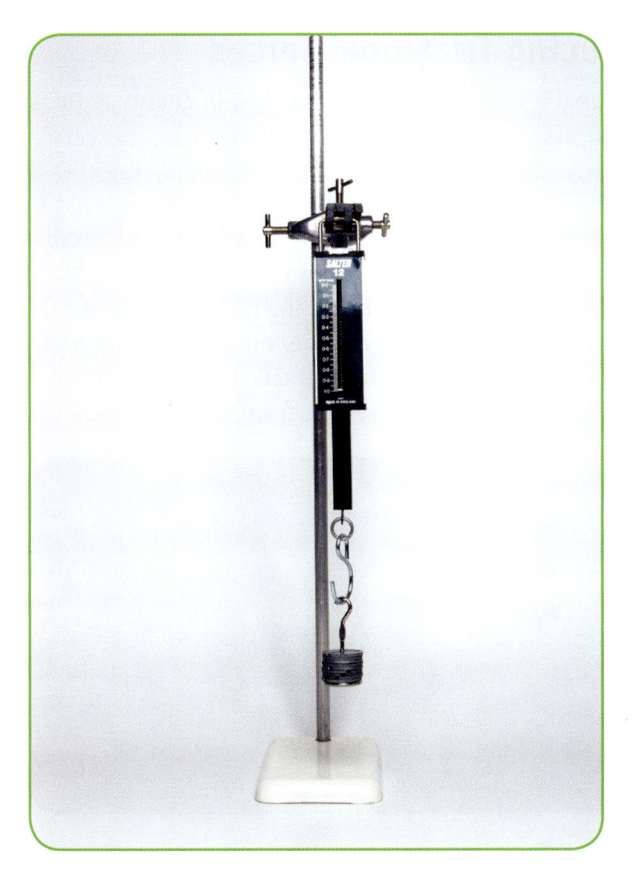

Figure 14.2 A Newton balance

Forces are measured using a Newton balance and the unit of force is the newton (N).

Balanced forces

Figure 14.3 shows two forces acting on an object X.

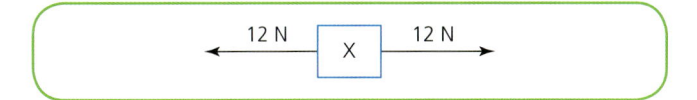

```
   12 N  ← [ X ] → 12 N
```

Figure 14.3 Forces acting on object X

The two forces are equal in size but act in opposite directions. The forces cancel each other out. This is the same as no force acting on the object. The forces are said to be **balanced**.

Balanced forces:
- have the same size
- act in opposite directions
- act on the same object.

Figure 14.4 Tug-of-war

Figure 14.4 shows two teams involved in a tug-of-war contest. When the two teams pull with the same size of force in opposite directions, the forces are balanced. When either team pulls with a force that is greater than that of the opposing team, the forces will no longer be balanced.

Unbalanced force

An unbalanced force is a single force acting on an object. It may be the result of a number of forces acting on the same object.

Figure 14.5 shows two forces acting on objects P and Q.

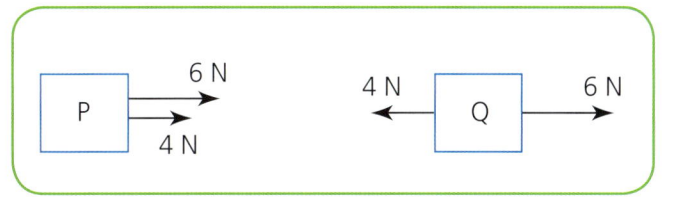

```
        6 N                  4 N            6 N
  [ P ] →              ←  [ Q ]  →
        4 N
```

Figure 14.5 Forces acting on objects P and Q

For object P, the two forces are not equal in size but do act in the same direction.

Unbalanced force acting on P = 6 + 4 = 10 newtons (to the right).

For object Q, the two forces are not equal in size and act in opposite directions – they partly cancel out.

Unbalanced force acting on Q = 6 − 4 = 2 newtons (to the right).

119

Dynamics and Space

Worked example

Example

Two forces act on an object as shown in Figure 14.6. What is the unbalanced force acting on the object?

6 N ← □ → 18 N

Figure 14.6

Solution

Unbalanced force = 18 − 6 = 12 N (to the right)

Frictional forces

Investigation

Push a bag across the bench so that it moves at a constant speed.

Stop pushing the bag – what does the bag do? What must have acted on the bag?

When the particles that make up one object slide over the particles that make up another object, there is a force present called the 'force of friction' or 'frictional force'. The force of friction, as far as we are concerned, is a force that always acts to oppose the motion of an object, i.e. to stop the object from moving. If an object is moving to the right, the force of friction will act towards the left.

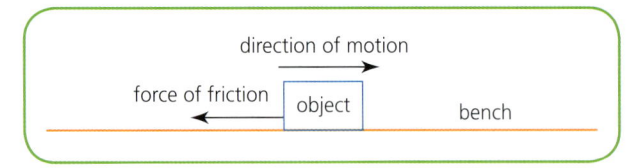

Figure 14.7 An object moving along a bench

Reducing frictional forces

Frictional forces can cause a great deal of energy to be wasted when an object is moving. In this case it is very useful to reduce frictional forces. This can be done by:

- lubrication – this involves putting a fluid (a liquid or gas) between the two surfaces that slide across each other. Oil is used to lubricate the moving parts of a car engine, because the oil does not evaporate at high temperatures. In a linear air track, a thin layer of air is used to separate the vehicle from the track.

Figure 14.8 A linear air track

- streamlining the shape of an object so that the object offers as little resistance to the air as possible. This is particularly important in vehicles that are required to move at high speeds.

Figure 14.9 A Formula 1 car is streamlined

Relationship between forces, motion and energy

Increasing frictional forces

When a moving object has to be slowed down, the force of friction on the object must be increased. In a bicycle brake this is done by squeezing rubber blocks against the metal wheel rim, so increasing the frictional force. In a car, applying the brakes causes a pad to rub against a disc on each of the wheels, increasing the force of friction.

Figure 14.10 Bicycle brakes

Figure 14.11 Car brakes

Newton's first law

> **Investigation**
>
> Set up a linear air track. Make sure that the track is perfectly level.
>
> Place a vehicle, at rest, on the linear air track. Does the vehicle start moving? Are there any horizontal forces acting on the vehicle?
>
> Now, give the vehicle a short, gentle push. Is the speed of the vehicle constant at different positions along the track? After you stopped pushing the vehicle, were there any horizontal forces acting on the vehicle?

An object will remain at rest or move at constant speed in a straight line unless acted on by an unbalanced force. This means that if an object is at rest or is moving at a constant speed in a straight line, then there is either no force acting on the object or the forces acting on the object are balanced.

Worked example

Example

A speedboat on a loch is travelling in a straight line at a constant speed. Draw and name the forces acting horizontally on the speedboat.

Solution

Since the speedboat is travelling at a constant speed in a straight line, then Newton's first law applies – either there are no forces acting on the speedboat, or the forces acting on the speedboat are balanced. However, a speedboat will only travel at a constant speed when the engine provides a force to balance out the resistive forces acting on the speedboat.

```
                    constant speed
                         →
    resistive forces  ┌──────────┐  engine force
         ←────────────│ speedboat│────────────→
                      └──────────┘
```

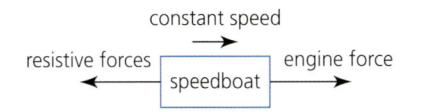

Figure 14.12

Newton's second law

Figure 14.13 shows a vehicle on a level linear air track. A card of known length is attached to the vehicle. As the vehicle moves along the track, the card passes through a number of light gates. The light gates are connected to electronic timers. These timers calculate the acceleration of the vehicle as it moves along the track. A mass at one end of the linear air track is attached to the vehicle by a light string and a pulley.

Dynamics and Space

Figure 14.13 Measuring the acceleration of a vehicle on a linear air track

Investigation

Set up a linear air track. Make sure that the track is perfectly level.

Place a vehicle, at rest, on the linear air track. Apply a constant unbalanced force to the vehicle (via a mass at one end of the linear air track attached to the vehicle by a light string and a pulley). Release the vehicle. What effect does an unbalanced force have on the vehicle?

Acceleration (*a*) and unbalanced force (F_{un})

Apply different constant unbalanced forces to the same mass of linear air track vehicle and measure the acceleration of the vehicle. Construct a table of your results.

What happens to the acceleration of the vehicle as the unbalanced force increases?

Acceleration (*a*) and mass (*m*)

Apply the same unbalanced force to different masses of air track vehicle and measure the acceleration of the vehicle. Construct a table of your results.

What happens to the acceleration of the vehicle as the mass of the vehicle increases?

When a constant unbalanced force is applied to an object, the acceleration of the object is found to be constant and in the same direction as the unbalanced force.

The acceleration, *a*, of the object doubles as the unbalanced force, F_{un}, on the object doubles.

The acceleration, *a*, of the object halves as the mass, *m*, of the object doubles.

From the above it can be seen that:

unbalanced force = mass of × acceleration
on object   object   of object

$$F_{un} = ma$$

where F_{un} = unbalanced force on object, measured in newtons (N)

m = mass of object, measured in kilograms (kg)

a = acceleration of object, measured in metres per second squared (m/s^2).

Using the 'maths triangle' (see Rearranging physics equations on page 145) for Newton's second law gives:

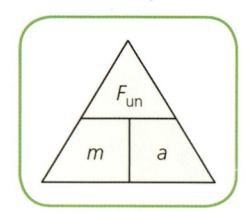

$$F_{un} = ma \qquad m = \frac{F_{un}}{a} \qquad a = \frac{F_{un}}{m}$$

1.0 newton is the constant unbalanced force that gives a 1.0 kilogram mass a constant acceleration of 1.0 m/s^2. This is the definition of the newton.

The acceleration of an object can only be changed by:

- changing the size of the unbalanced force on the object (increasing F_{un} increases *a*)
- changing the mass of the object (increasing *m* decreases *a*).

Relationship between forces, motion and energy

Worked examples

Example 1
The acceleration of an object is 0.5 m/s². The mass of the object is 1.2 kg. Calculate the unbalanced force acting on the object.

Solution

$F_{un} = ma = 1.2 \times 0.5 = 0.6$ N

Example 2
The mass of an object is 2.0 kg. The unbalanced force acting on the object is 120 N. Calculate the acceleration of the object.

Solution

$F_{un} = ma$

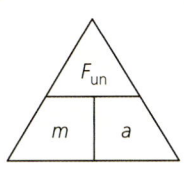

$a = \dfrac{F_{un}}{m} = \dfrac{120}{2} = 60$ m/s²

Example 3
An unbalanced force of 5.4 N is applied to a vehicle. The acceleration of the vehicle is 0.15 m/s². Calculate the mass of the vehicle.

Solution

$F_{un} = ma$

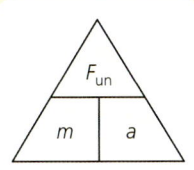

$m = \dfrac{F_{un}}{a} = \dfrac{5.4}{0.15} = 36$ kg

Physics in action

Seat belts
When a moving car brakes suddenly, any unrestrained object will continue to move at the car's original speed (Newton's first law) until, most likely, it collides with some part of the interior. This will probably cause damage to the object (or injury to a person).

A seat belt applies a force in the opposite direction to the car's motion, which rapidly decelerates the wearer. The webbing straps are designed to have a certain amount of 'give' so that this increases the time taken to bring the person to rest. This means that there is a smaller unbalanced force acting on the wearer.

Air bags
Air bags are designed to provide a cushion between you and the dashboard or steering wheel of a car. This increases the time taken to bring you to rest. This means that the negative acceleration (deceleration) is smaller and so you experience a smaller unbalanced force, which means you are less likely to be injured.

Head restraints
Head restraints are designed to reduce neck injuries. They are most useful when a car is hit from behind. As the car is pushed forward, the back of your seat pushes you forward. Without a head restraint, your head will tend to remain where it is, while the rest of your body moves forward. This can cause a 'whiplash' injury.

Crumple zones
In a collision, the crumple zones in a car allow the car to come to rest over a longer time. The size of the negative acceleration (deceleration) of the car is reduced. There means that there is a smaller unbalanced force acting on the car and its occupants.

Mass
Mass is the quantity of matter forming an object. It depends on the number and type of particles that make up the object. Mass is measured in kilograms (kg). Provided the number and type of particles making up the object do not change, the mass of the object will remain the same no matter where it is.

123

Dynamics and Space

A hammer has a mass of 0.5 kg on the Earth. Since the hammer is made up of a certain number and type of particles, the same hammer on the Moon will still have a mass of 0.5 kg. Taking the same hammer into outer space will again not change the number or type of particles and so it will still have a mass of 0.5 kg there.

Force of gravity

The force of gravity can be defined in the following ways:

- force of gravity = downward pull of a planet on an object
- force of gravity = force (or pull) exerted by a planet on an object
- force of gravity = gravitational force on an object
- force of gravity = weight of an object

Weight

The weight of an object depends on:

- its mass – the number and type of particles that make up the object
- the location – for most situations this will be the surface of the Earth. However, a 0.5-kg hammer has a smaller weight on the surface of the Moon than it does on the Earth.

Since **weight** is a **force**, it is measured in newtons (N).

Investigation

Use a Newton balance to measure the weight of a 0.1 kg mass.

Repeat for masses of 0.2, 0.3, 0.4 … up to a 1.0 kg mass. Construct a table of your results. Calculate the weight ÷ mass for each one – what do you notice about each of these values?

Gravitational field strength

For any object on a planet:

$$\frac{\text{weight of object}}{\text{mass of object}} = \frac{W}{m} = \text{gravitational field strength}$$

(symbol g)

Gravitational field strength (g) is the force exerted by a planet on a 1.0 kg mass.

Gravitational field strength is measured in newtons per kilogram (N/kg).

This is normally written as:

weight of object = mass of object × gravitational field strength

$$W = mg$$

where W = weight of object, measured in newtons (N)

m = mass of object, measured in kilograms (kg)

g = gravitational field strength, measured in newtons per kilogram (N/kg).

Using the 'maths triangle' (see Rearranging physics equations on page 145) on the above equation gives:

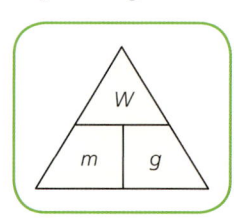

$$W = mg \qquad m = \frac{W}{g} \qquad g = \frac{W}{m}$$

The gravitational field strength for the Earth is 9.8 N/kg (9.8 newtons for every kilogram of mass). This means that on Earth, a 1.0 kg mass has a weight of 9.8 N and a 10 kg mass has a weight of 98 N.

A table of gravitational field strengths is given on the Data sheet on page 146.

Worked examples

Example 1

The mass of a hammer is 0.5 kg. Calculate the weight of the hammer on the surface of:
a) the Earth
b) the Moon
c) Jupiter.

Solution

a) On the Earth, $W = mg = 0.5 \times 9.8 = 4.9$ N
   (Note g for Earth from Data sheet on page 146)
b) On the Moon, $W = mg = 0.5 \times 1.6 = 0.8$ N
   (Note g for the Moon from Data sheet on page 146)
c) On Jupiter, $W = mg = 0.5 \times 23 = 11.5$ N
   (Note g for Jupiter from Data sheet on page 146)

Relationship between forces, motion and energy

Example 2
The mass of an object is 80 kg. The weight of the object on the surface of Mars is 296 N. Calculate the gravitational field strength on the surface of Mars.

Solution
$W = mg$
$g = \dfrac{W}{m} = \dfrac{296}{80} = 3.7$ N/kg

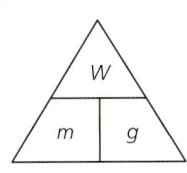

Example 3
The weight of an object on the surface of Neptune is 1320 N. Calculate the mass of the object. Use the Data sheet on page 146 to help you.

Solution
$W = mg$
$m = \dfrac{W}{m} = \dfrac{1320}{11} = 120$ kg

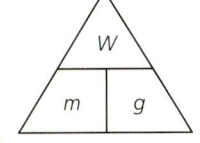

Example 4
On a windless day a hot air balloon is moving upwards at a constant speed. Draw and name the forces acting vertically on the balloon.

Solution
Since the balloon is moving upwards at a constant speed, then Newton's first law applies – either there are no forces acting on the balloon or the forces acting on the balloon are balanced. However, a balloon will only move upwards at a constant speed when the balloon provides an upwards force to balance out the weight of the balloon and any resistive forces.

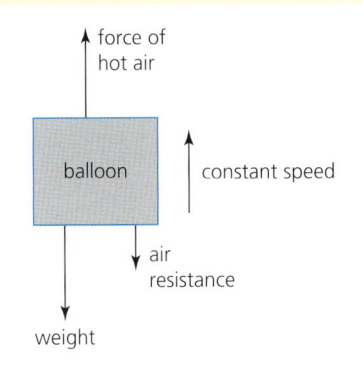

Figure 14.14

Benefits of space exploration
Space exploration has greatly increased our knowledge of the universe. New materials have had to be developed to allow space vehicles to explore space. This is particularly important when spacecraft have to return safely to Earth.

Re-entry
When a spacecraft re-enters the Earth's atmosphere, it is travelling at high speed. As it collides with the air particles making up the atmosphere, a large resistive force acts on the spacecraft (a resistive force is a force that opposes the movement of an object). The work done by this resistive force changes most of the kinetic energy of the spacecraft into heat. A large amount of this heat is 'lost' to the surroundings but some is absorbed by the spacecraft. Without special protection from this heat, the spacecraft would be destroyed.

The Apollo space capsules used a heat shield made mainly from stainless steel. Most of the heat shield was vaporised by the intense heat generated during re-entry, but this protected the capsule and the astronauts inside. After entering the atmosphere, parachutes would be deployed to further slow the capsule down and allow it to make a gentle 'splashdown' in the sea.

Figure 14.15 Apollo spacecraft after re-entering the Earth's atmosphere

Dynamics and Space

Since the heat shield was largely destroyed during re-entry and could not be replaced on the capsule, Apollo space capsules could not be re-used.

The Apollo missions allowed 12 men to walk on the surface of the Moon. The first Apollo spacecraft to land on the Moon, Apollo 11, landed in July 1969. The last mission was Apollo 17, which took place in December 1972.

The Space Shuttle was a reusable 'plane' that made an unpowered glide through the atmosphere and would land on a runway using its wheels just like an ordinary aircraft. It used special tiles, made from a silica compound, to protect it from the intense heat of re-entry. The tiles were able to transfer heat away very quickly.

Figure 14.16 A Space Shuttle coming in to land

Space disasters

You may have watched the film *Apollo 13*. This film depicts the events that took place aboard Apollo 13 during its intended mission to the Moon in April 1970. On its way to the Moon, an explosion on board the spacecraft put the safety of the three crew members in doubt. Only due to the training of the astronauts and the skills of the scientists and engineers on the ground was it possible for the spacecraft and its crew to come back to Earth safely.

Not all space missions have ended happily. Many astronauts, both American and Russian, have died during space missions. Two of the most recent disasters involved the Space Shuttles Challenger and Columbia. The Challenger (1986) disaster occurred 73 seconds after lift-off as a result of a failure of a component on one of the external solid rocket boosters. All seven crew members, one of whom was a school teacher, died. The Columbia (2003) disintegrated during re-entry into the Earth's atmosphere as a result of damage to the thermal tiles on the left wing. Again, all seven crew members were killed.

Key facts and physics equations: forces and motion

- A force can change the speed, direction of travel and shape of an object.
- A Newton balance is used to measure force in newtons (N).
- Forces that are equal in size but act in opposite directions on an object are called balanced forces and are equivalent to no force acting on the object.
- Newton's first law: an object will remain at rest or move at constant speed in a straight line unless acted on by an unbalanced force.
- Newton's second law: unbalanced force = mass × acceleration, i.e. $F_{un} = ma$
- Unbalanced force is measured in newtons (N), mass in kilograms (kg) and acceleration in metres per second squared (m/s^2).
- Mass is the quantity of matter making up an object. It always remains the same.
- Weight is a force and is the planet's pull on an object.
- Weight = mass × gravitational field strength, i.e. $W = mg$.
- Weight is measured in newtons (N), mass in kilograms (kg) and gravitational field strength in newtons per kilogram (N/kg).
- Gravitational field strength on a planet is the weight of a 1.0 kg mass and is constant for that planet.

Relationship between forces, motion and energy

End-of-chapter questions

If further information is required in order to answer the following questions, this can be found on the Data sheet on page 146.

1. The mass of a car is 800 kg. The engine of the car applies a forward force to the car. The car is moving at a constant speed in a straight line.
   Explain in terms of forces why the car is travelling at a constant speed.

2. Two forces act on a crate as shown in Figure 14.17.

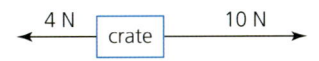

   4 N ← crate → 10 N

   Figure 14.17

   Calculate the unbalanced force produced by these two forces.

3. A car is travelling in a straight line along a road. The engine force and the resistive force are the only forces acting horizontally on the car.
   a) Draw a labelled diagram showing the forces acting horizontally on the car.
   b) How do these forces compare when the car:
      (i) is travelling at a constant speed
      (ii) is speeding up?

4. Figure 14.18 shows the four forces acting on a flying aircraft.

   a) Match each of the letters A to D with the correct force from this list: weight; air resistance; engine force; lift force (from wings).
   b) The aircraft is flying at a constant speed in a straight line and at a constant height above the ground. State how the following pairs of forces compare in size and direction:
      (i) A and C
      (ii) B and D.

5. The mass of a bus is 5000 kg. The bus has an acceleration of 0.12 m/s^2. Calculate the unbalanced force acting on the bus.

6. An unbalanced force of 0.2 N acts on a linear air track vehicle. The mass of the vehicle is 0.40 kg. Calculate the acceleration of the vehicle.

7. An unbalanced force of 5400 N acts on a light plane. The acceleration of the plane is 2.7 m/s^2. Calculate the mass of the plane.

8. A woman is holding a glass. The glass has a mass of 0.20 kg. Calculate the weight of the glass.

9. A space probe is sent from Earth and lands on Mars. On Earth the mass of the probe is 150 kg.
   a) What is the mass of the probe on Mars?
   b) Calculate the weight of the probe on the surface of:
      (i) the Earth
      (ii) Mars.

10. A lampshade has a weight of 4.9 N. Calculate the mass of the lampshade.

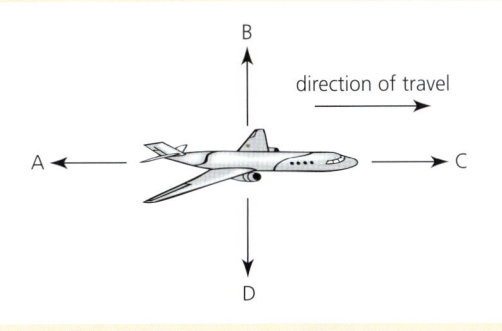

Figure 14.18

127

Dynamics and Space

Unit 3

15 Satellites

Learning outcomes

At the end of this chapter you should be able to:
1. Give examples of the uses made of satellites.
2. State that the period of satellite orbit depends on its height above the Earth.
3. State that a geostationary satellite has a period of 24 hours.
4. State that a geostationary satellite appears to stay above the same point on the Earth's surface.
5. Describe how satellites are used in communications.
6. State that curved reflectors (dishes) can make the received signal stronger.
7. Explain how curved reflectors (dishes) and receivers make the signal stronger.
8. Explain the action of curved reflectors on certain transmitters.
9. Carry out calculations involving the relationship between distance, time and speed in problems on satellite communication.

Satellites

A satellite is an object that revolves around a large object, usually a planet. As the Moon revolves around the Earth, the Moon is a satellite of the Earth.

In 1957, the first artificial satellite, called Sputnik 1, was placed into orbit above the Earth. Since then many more (artificial) satellites have been placed into orbit above the Earth. These satellites have many different uses:

- communications – 'instant' round the world audio (sound) and visual (picture) communication
- weather – allowing better weather prediction
- positioning – global positioning satellites (GPS) 'tell us' where we are
- environmental – vegetation monitoring, geological mapping and mineral prospecting, atmospheric chemistry, water vapour content, ocean and land surface temperatures
- scientific – furthering our understanding of the global impact of human actions on the Earth and increasing our understanding of the Solar System and the universe.

Figure 15.1 A communications satellite orbiting the Earth

Figure 15.2 A weather satellite image of a snow-covered Britain

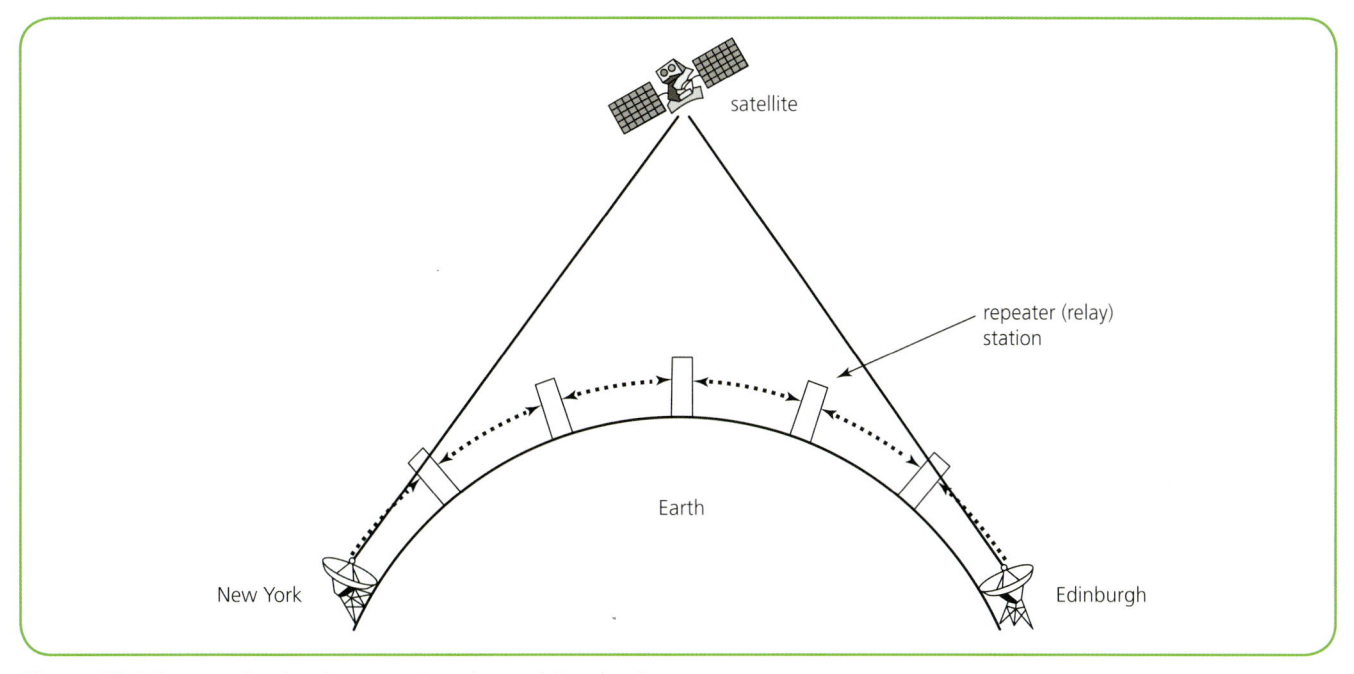

Figure 15.3 Communication between America and Scotland

Satellite communication

The signals used for communication normally travel in straight lines. This means that the transmitter and receiver must be able to 'see' each other. This is called 'line of sight' communication. However, the Earth is curved, so to achieve line of sight communication over reasonable distances the transmitter and receiver are located on high buildings or towers. Even on high towers, the maximum distance for line of sight communication between the transmitter and receiver is limited to about 40 km.

Sending a communication signal between America and Scotland using surface-based line of sight would require a very large number of transmitter and receiver stations (called repeater stations). This would be very difficult as many of these repeater stations would have to be in the Atlantic Ocean. However, using line of sight with a satellite makes it 'easier' to send a signal between America and Scotland.

Signals are transmitted from the Earth to the satellite. The satellite receives the signal and then transmits the signal back to Earth. To make signal communication as simple as possible, the satellite should always appear in the same place above the surface of the Earth – then you always know where it is and it is easier to direct signals towards it. This type of satellite is called a geostationary satellite.

Geostationary satellites

The time taken for a satellite to make one complete orbit is called the period. The period of a satellite depends on its height above the Earth's surface.

Height of satellite above surface of Earth (km)	Period of satellite (hours)
200	1.5
2000	2.0
20 000	12
36 000	24

The further the satellite is from the Earth's surface, the slower it appears to move and the longer the period:

- A satellite at a height of 200 km above the Earth's surface has a period of about 90 minutes. Earth observation satellites and spy satellites use these

Dynamics and Space

orbits, as the satellites are able to 'see' the surface of the Earth more clearly.
- A satellite at a height of 20 000 km above the Earth's surface has a period of about 12 hours. Navigation satellites, like the ones used for a car's GPS system, use these orbits.
- A satellite at a height of 36 000 km above the Earth's surface has a period of 24 hours. This orbit is used mainly for communications and weather satellites.

The Earth takes 24 hours to complete one rotation and a satellite in orbit 36 000 km above the equator completes one orbit in the same time of 24 hours. The satellite will therefore appear to stay above the same spot on the Earth's surface. The satellite is said to be in a geostationary orbit. Geostationary satellites have a period of 24 hours and are about 36 000 km above the Earth's equator – they are in equatorial orbit.

Curved reflectors – dish aerials

You may have noticed curved dishes on some houses and other buildings. These dishes are used to pick up satellite TV and communication signals. Satellites in space use the same kind of dishes.

Figure 15.4 A satellite dish

Receiving dishes

> **Investigation**
>
> Set up a ray box to give three parallel rays of light. Shine the rays onto a curved mirror (Figure 15.5). Where is the reflected light brightest? The point where the light is brightest is called the focus of the dish. 
>
> **Figure 15.5** A ray box and a curved mirror
>
> Where should an aerial be placed for a receiving dish to receive the strongest signal?

As the distance from the Earth to the geostationary satellite is very great, the signal that reaches the satellite from the Earth is very weak. Figure 15.6 shows that the aerial on the satellite would receive very little of the signal – a very weak signal. Figure 15.7 shows that a much stronger signal is received as a result of the dish reflecting some of the transmitted signal back to the focus of the dish. The aerial is placed at the focus in order to receive the strongest signal. Figure 15.8 shows that a dish with a larger diameter reflects even more of the transmitted signal back to the focus and the aerial receives an even stronger signal.

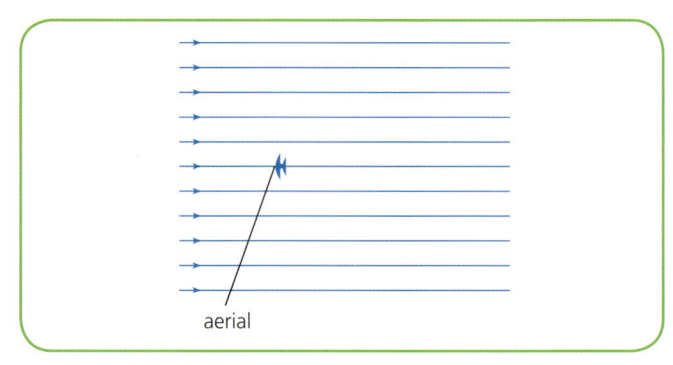

Figure 15.6 A receiving aerial picks up a very weak signal

Satellites

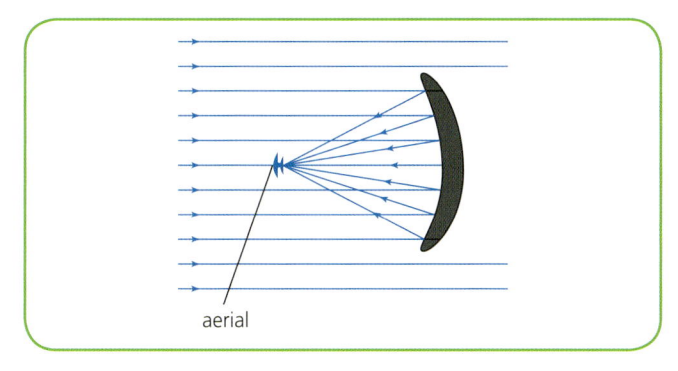

aerial

Figure 15.7 A receiving aerial picks up a strong signal

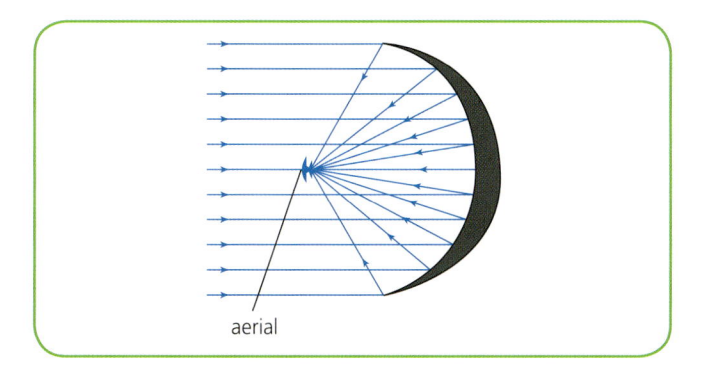

aerial

Figure 15.8 A receiving aerial picks up a stronger signal

Transmitting dishes

These act in the opposite way to receiving dishes – the rays are reversible. An aerial placed at the focus of the dish sends waves towards the dish. At the dish the waves are reflected to form a narrow parallel beam (Figure 15.9). In this way a concentrated signal can be transmitted over a long distance.

transmitting aerial

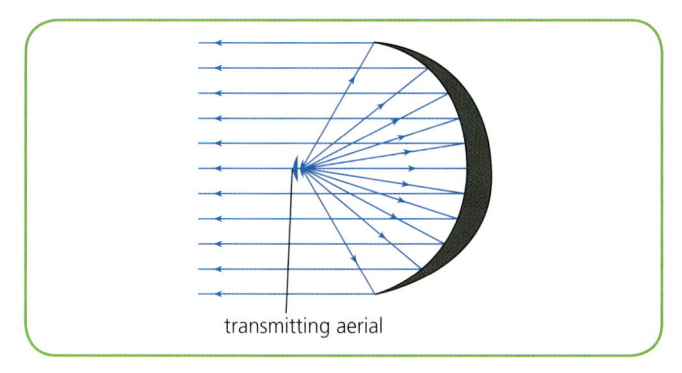

Figure 15.9 A transmitting dish aerial

A satellite uses a receiving dish aerial to pick up signals sent to it from one part of the Earth. These signals can then be sent from a transmitting dish aerial to another satellite or point on the Earth.

Physics in action

Round the world communication can be achieved using only three satellites (repeater stations in the sky). The satellites, positioned above the equator, are equally spaced 120° apart. Using their transmitting and receiving dishes to communicate with each other and with ground stations means that a communication from one side of the world can be sent to the opposite side using only these satellites.

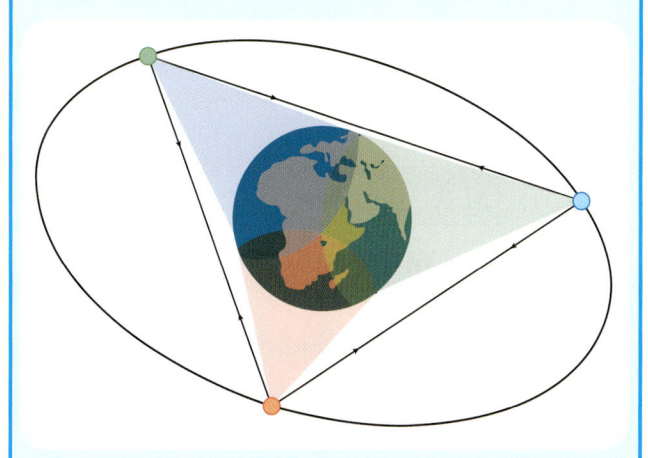

Figure 15.10 Round the world communication

Worked example

Example

A TV news report is sent from the USA to Scotland via a satellite. The distance from the USA to the satellite is 36 300 km. This is the same as the distance from the satellite to Scotland. The speed of the signal is 300 000 000 m/s. Calculate the minimum time taken for the signal to be sent from the USA to Scotland.

Solution

Note 36 300 km = 36 300 000 m

d = distance from USA + distance from satellite
      to satellite   to Scotland

$= 36\,300\,000 + 36\,300\,000$

$= 72\,600\,000$ m

$v = \dfrac{d}{t}$

$t = \dfrac{d}{v} = \dfrac{72\,600\,000}{300\,000\,000} = 0.242$ s

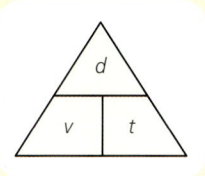

Dynamics and Space

Unit 3

Investigation

Spotting a satellite

The best time to spot a satellite is just after sunset or just before sunrise, when it is dark at ground level but the Sun's rays can reflect off the satellite. Scan slowly across the sky – be patient. You will see a point of light moving steadily against the stationary background stars. A satellite takes about four minutes to travel from horizon to horizon.

Key facts and physics equations: satellites

- The period of a satellite's orbit depends on its height above the Earth – the higher the orbit, the longer the period.
- A geostationary satellite has a period of 24 hours and appears to stay above the same point on the Earth's surface.
- Curved reflectors (dishes) make the received signal stronger by reflecting the rays to the focus of the dish.
- Satellites are used in many ways, such as communication, global positioning systems (GPS), weather monitoring and environmental monitoring.

Physics in action

Laboratories in space – International Space Station (ISS)

Construction of the International Space Station (ISS) started in 1998. A partnership of 16 countries worked to create the largest spaceship ever built. ISS has a multi-module design and it orbits at a height of about 400 km above the surface of the Earth.

The permanent crew of the ISS work in laboratories. They carry out experiments in areas including investigating materials, life sciences and medical research. These experiments could be carried out on Earth. However, scientists hope that the environment on the ISS will allow them to produce materials and medicines with far greater purity than is possible on Earth.

Global Positioning System (GPS)

A network of satellites orbit about 20 000 km above the Earth's surface. The satellites continually transmit radio time signals.

A computer in a car or a handset picks up these time signals. The computer calculates the time taken for a satellite signal to reach it. By taking readings from four satellites, the computer can quickly calculate its position on the Earth.

Figure 15.11 The International Space Station

Satellites

End-of-chapter questions

1. The height of satellite X above the Earth's surface is 200 km. The height above the Earth's surface of an identical satellite Y is 400 km.
   Which satellite, X or Y, has a longer period?

2. a) What is meant by the term *geostationary satellite*?
   b) Give an advantage of using a geostationary satellite for communications.

3. Satellites are used in some telecommunication systems. Four satellites, P, Q, R and S, orbit at different heights above the surface of the Earth. Information about the orbits of these satellites is shown in the table.

Satellite	Height above surface of Earth (km)	Time to orbit Earth (hours)
P	2000	2
Q	36 000	24
R	?	9
S	42 000	?

   a) Which satellite would appear to stay above the same point on the Earth's surface?
   b) (i) Suggest a possible value for the height of satellite R above the surface of the Earth.
      (ii) Suggest a possible value for the time it takes satellite S to orbit the Earth.

4. A satellite uses a curved dish reflector to receive signals from a transmitter on the Earth.
   Figure 15.12 shows three rays coming from a transmitter towards the curved dish reflector.
   a) Copy and complete Figure 15.12 to show what happens to the rays after they reflect from the reflector.
   b) Mark on your diagram where a signal detector should be placed to detect the strongest signal.
   c) What is the name given to the point where the strongest signal is detected?

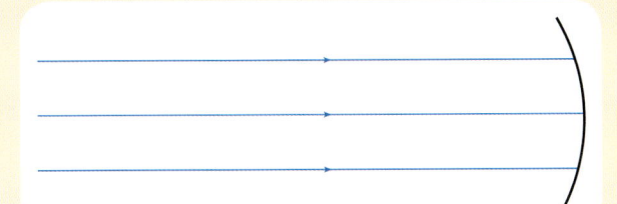

   Figure 15.12

5. Figure 15.13 shows a dish that is used to receive signals on a satellite. It consists of a curved dish with the signal detector fixed a short distance in front of it.

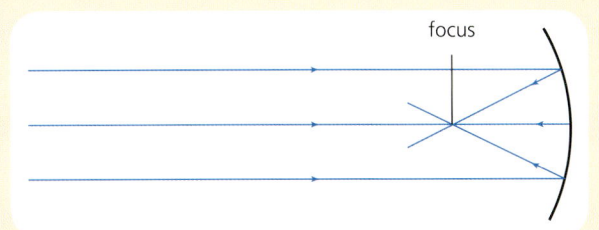

   Figure 15.13

   a) Where should the signal detector be positioned to detect the strongest possible signal?
   b) A dish with a larger diameter is now used. The signal detector is again placed so as to detect the strongest possible signal. Would the signal detected be weaker than, the same as, or stronger than the signal detected in a)? Explain your answer.

6. A radio signal is broadcast from the Earth to the Moon. The distance between the Earth and the Moon is 345 000 km. The radio signal travels at 300 000 000 m/s. Calculate the time taken for the signal to reach the Moon.

7. A satellite is in orbit 180 km above the surface of the Earth. The satellite sends a signal to a receiving station on the Earth when it is directly above the station. The signal travels at a speed of 300 000 000 m/s. Calculate the time taken for the signal to travel from the satellite to the receiving station.

8. A communications satellite is in orbit above the equator. A transmitting station, X, sends a signal up to the satellite. The satellite retransmits the signal to a receiving station Y. The time taken for the signal to travel from X to Y is 0.24 s. The speed of the signal is 300 000 000 m/s.
   a) Calculate the height of the satellite above the surface of the Earth.
   b) What is the orbital period of the satellite?

133

Dynamics and Space

Unit 3

9 The graph in Figure 15.14 shows how the time it takes a satellite to go round the Earth varies with its height above the equator.

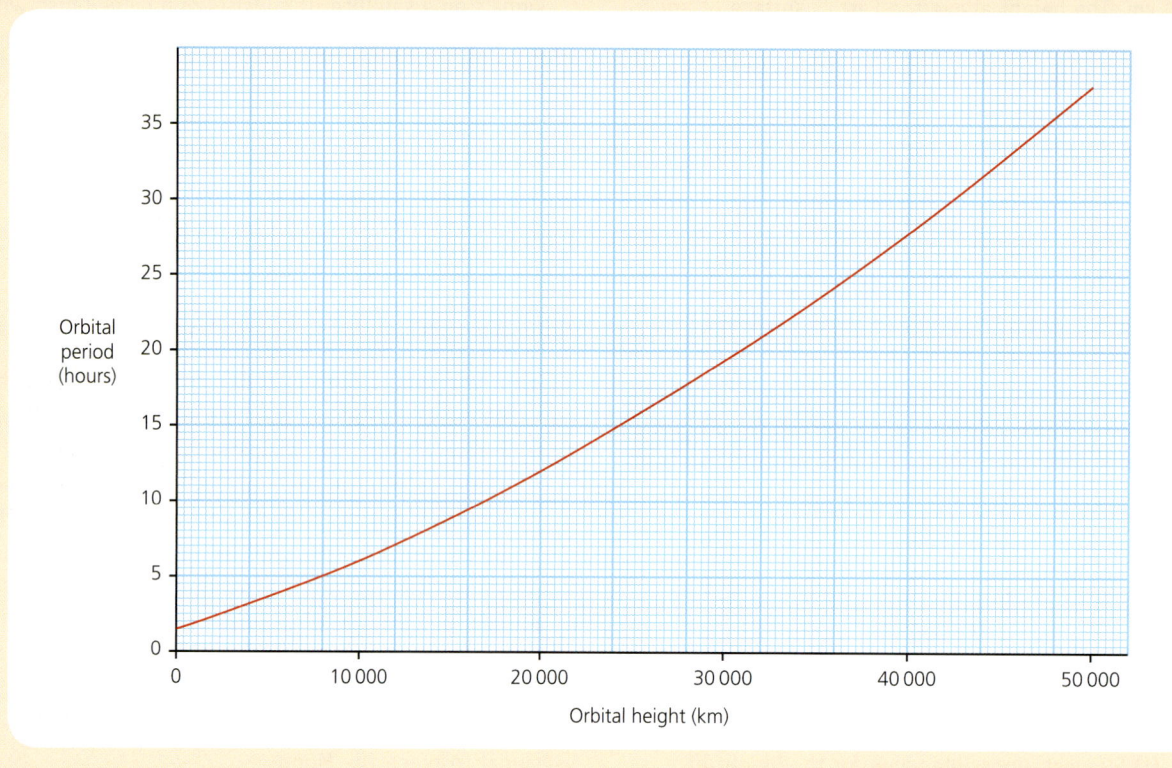

Figure 15.14

a) Use the graph to find the height of a geostationary satellite.
b) A weather satellite orbits the Earth twice each day. Use the graph to find the height of the weather satellite.

16 Cosmology

Learning outcomes

At the end of this chapter you should be able to:
1. Use correctly in context the following terms: moon, planet, Sun, star, Solar System, galaxy, universe, exoplanet, light year.
2. Convert between light years and metres.
3. State that liquid water is required to sustain life.

Cosmology is the study of the universe. Useful terms in cosmology include:

- planet – an object that orbits a star
- moon – an object that orbits a planet
- star – a ball of very hot gas produced by nuclear reactions
- galaxy – an immense system of stars, dust and gas
- universe – the whole of space, everything!

Figure 16.1 The night sky

We live on a planet called **Earth**. The Earth is the third of eight planets that orbit around the Sun. The Sun is a star that glows, giving off both heat and light.

Figure 16.2 The Earth from space

The eight planets circle around the Sun and form our **Solar System**. The Solar System is a very small part of the thousands of millions of stars that form part of a **galaxy** called the **Milky Way**. There are millions more galaxies besides our own, all of which together form the **universe**.

Figure 16.3 Relative sizes and distances of the Sun and its planets

135

Dynamics and Space

Planet	Diameter (km)	Distance from Sun (million km)	Time to orbit the Sun (days)	Time for one complete spin (hours)
Mercury	4900	58	88	4200
Venus	12 100	108	224	2800
Earth	12 800	150	365	24
Mars	7000	228	687	25
Jupiter	143 000	779	4300	10
Saturn	121 000	1434	11 000	11
Uranus	51 100	2873	31 000	17
Neptune	50 000	4495	60 000	16

Table 16.1 The eight planets in our Solar System

Figure 16.4 Our galaxy – the Milky Way

Stars outside our Solar System also have planets circling them, like our Sun does. Because these planets are so far away from us, we are unable to see them. They are called exoplanets.

The universe is thought to have begun at a single point in space with an explosion or 'big bang'. All the material that was thrown out, in all directions, from this 'big bang' has been expanding ever since. The 'big bang' is thought to have occurred about 15 000 million years (15 billion years) ago.

Table 16.1 gives data on the eight planets in our Solar System.

The light year

Everything connected with space is on a truly vast scale. For instance, the distance between the Earth and Proxima Centauri (our nearest star after our Sun) is 4.0×10^{16} m! (4 with 16 zeros after it). This is a truly enormous distance, but Proxima Centauri is a star that is very, very close to the Earth compared with most stars in our galaxy. To cope with such large distances requires a 'new unit' for distance, the **light year**. A light year is the distance in metres travelled by light in air or a vacuum in one year:

Speed of light = 3×10^8 m/s = 300 000 000 m/s

Distance travelled by light in 1 second = 3×10^8 m

Distance travelled by light in 1 year = $3 \times 10^8 \times$ number of seconds in 1 year

1 year = 365 days
= (365 × 24) hours
= (365 × 24 × 60) minutes
= (365 × 24 × 60 × 60) s

Distance travelled by light in 1 year = $3 \times 10^8 \times (365 \times 24 \times 60 \times 60)$

= 9.5×10^{15} m

1 light year = 9.5×10^{15} m

Cosmology

Source of light	Time taken for light to travel to Earth	Distance travelled (m)	Number of light years
Sun	8 minutes	1.5×10^{11}	1.6×10^{-5}
Proxima Centauri – nearest star after the Sun	4.2 years	4.0×10^{16}	4.2
Other side of our galaxy, the Milky Way	100 000 years	9.5×10^{20}	100 000
Andromeda galaxy	2 500 000 years	2.4×10^{22}	2 500 000

Table 16.2 Light from distant parts of space

The light year is required as a unit for measuring distance because the distances involved in space are so very, very large.

Table 16.2 shows the time taken for light to travel to the Earth from distant parts of space, the distance travelled in that time, and the number of light years it represents.

Space exploration

Space exploration is the ongoing discovery and investigation of the physical conditions in outer space. This is ongoing due to evolving space technology. The study of space is mostly carried out by astronomers using telescopes. The actual exploration of space is carried out by unmanned probes and manned spaceflight.

We explore space to find out more about the Earth, our Solar System, how stars evolve, and how the universe was formed. The following is a short list of the milestones in space exploration:

- 1957 – first manmade satellite (Sputnik 1) orbits the Earth
- 1961 – first human spaceflight – Yuri Gagarin in Vostock 1
- 1965 – first spacewalk – Alexei Leonov
- 1967 – first (unmanned) landing on the Moon
- 1969 – first manned landing on the Moon by the crew of the Apollo 11 spacecraft
- 1971 – launch of the first space station – Salyut 1
- 1990+ – launch of the space shuttle programme and the International Space Station (ISS).

Space probes

Most of space exploration, in the early days, was directed at the Earth and the Moon. The focus has since shifted to the other members of our Solar System. Space probes allow us to investigate their temperature, atmosphere, the nature of their surface, and the presence or absence of water, for example.

Figure 16.5 Rosetta space probe and lander performing a detailed study of a comet

Space observatories

Many space observatories, like the Hubble Space Telescope, have been launched in order to examine the distant universe. They have sent back amazing pictures taken in visible light. The observatories can also observe stars and galaxies at wavelengths that are invisible to the human eye – radio, infrared, ultraviolet, X-rays and gamma rays. The information obtained and the discoveries made have changed the way we look at the universe.

Dynamics and Space

Unit 3

Figure 16.6 The Hubble Space Telescope

The future

Due to the very high cost of putting spacecraft into space, astronomers have to fight hard to obtain funding. This is likely to become even more difficult, because probes and satellites designed to find out more about distant parts of the universe have no obvious positive contribution to make to the economy, unlike telecommunications and weather satellites, for example.

It is likely that space tourism will be an addition to space travel in the future.

Figure 16.7 Space tourism

Is there life out there?

The Earth is the only planet in our Solar System that has intelligent life. What makes the Earth so special?

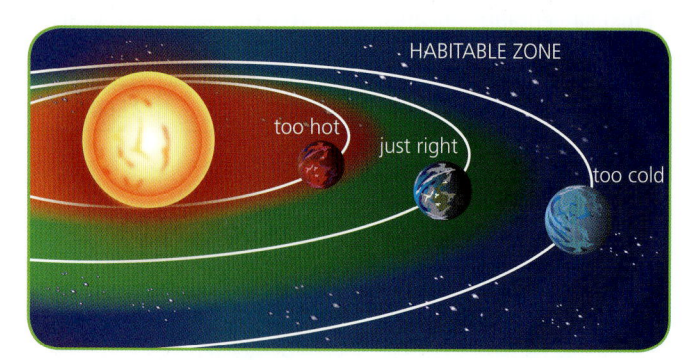

Figure 16.8 The habitable zone – where liquid water can exist on the surface of a planet

Scientists believe that the most important requirement for life is that liquid water should be present. This means that the planet cannot be too cold (the water would then be in the form of ice) or too hot (the water would be in the form of steam). Mercury is very close to the Sun. As a result, it absorbs a lot of heat and its surface is extremely hot – if there was water on Mercury, it would be in the form of steam. Neptune is a very great distance away from the Sun. As a result, it absorbs only a little heat from the Sun and is very cold – if there was water on Neptune, it would be in the form of ice.

Venus, Earth and Mars are all about the right distance from the Sun for water, if present, to be in the form of a liquid. This area of space is called the 'habitable zone'. The atmosphere surrounding the Earth helps to regulate the temperature during the day (keeping it from getting too hot) and at night (stopping it getting too cold).

Key facts and physics equations: cosmology

- A light year is the distance travelled by light in 1 year.
- Liquid water is required to sustain life.

Cosmology

End-of-chapter questions

1. In the following sentences the words represented by the letters A to H are missing.
   The ___A___ is the nearest star to the Earth.
   ___B___ move around a star. There are eight in orbit around the Sun, the nearest to the Sun being Mercury and the most distant Neptune.
   A ___C___ is an object that orbits a more massive object in space. ___D___ are natural satellites of the planets. Jupiter has 63 natural satellites. The Earth has one natural and many manmade satellites.
   ___E___ are massive objects in space, consisting mainly of very hot gases and producing vast amounts of energy.
   The ___F___ is the Sun and the eight planets, including the Earth, which orbit it. A ___G___ is a star system, containing millions of stars. The ___H___ is the whole of space.
   Match each letter with the correct word below.
   galaxy; moons; planets; satellite; Solar System; stars; Sun; universe

2. The Sun is 1.5×10^{11} m from the Earth. Light from the Sun travels at a speed of 300 000 000 m/s. Calculate the time taken, in minutes, for light to travel from the Sun to the Earth.

3. During the early Moon landings a reflector was placed on the Moon's surface. A powerful light beam was sent from the Earth to the Moon and reflected back off the reflector to Earth. The beam took 2.3 seconds to return to the Earth after being transmitted.
   a) How long does it take light to travel from the Earth to the Moon?
   b) The light beam travels at a speed of 300 000 000 m/s. Calculate the distance of the Moon from the Earth.

4. Sirius is 8.6 light years from the Earth. The speed of light is 300 000 000 m/s.
   a) Show that 1 light year is 9.5×10^{15} m.
   b) Calculate the distance, in metres, of Sirius from the Earth.

5. Many exoplanets have been discovered in galaxies close to our own.
   a) What is meant by the term 'exoplanet'?
   b) State **one** condition required for life to be found on an exoplanet.

Unit 3 exam practice

1. A trolley accelerates down a slope from X to Y as shown.

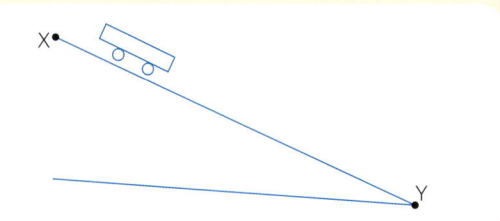

   Figure E3.1

   a) Describe how the average speed of the trolley between X and Y can be found. You should state:
   (i) the measuring instruments you would use
   (ii) the measurements you would make
   (iii) how you would use the measurements to find the average speed.
   b) Explain why the speed of the trolley at Y is not the same as the average speed of the trolley.

2. The graph shows how the speed of an object varies with time for part of a journey.

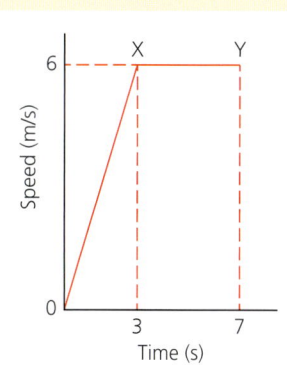

   Figure E3.2

   a) Describe the motion of the object between:
   (i) O and X
   (ii) X and Y.

Dynamics and Space

Unit 3

b) Calculate the acceleration of the object between:
   (i) 0 and X
   (ii) X and Y.
c) Show that the distance travelled by the object during the 7.0 s is 33 m.
d) Calculate the average speed of the object for this part of the journey.

3 The table provides some information about three cars.

Name of car	Maximum speed (miles per hour)	Time to go from 0 to 60 miles per hour (seconds)
Whizbang	102	7.2
Rocketry	98	6.3
Stellar	121	8.1

a) On a test track, while travelling at maximum speed, which car would travel 2 miles in the shortest time?
b) (i) Which car has the greatest acceleration?
   (ii) Explain your answer to (b) (i).

4 The horizontal forces acting on an object are shown below.

Figure E3.3

The mass of the object is 3.0 kg. The object is accelerating horizontally at 2.0 m/s².
a) Calculate the unbalanced force acting on the object horizontally.
b) State the value of force X.
c) As the object continues to accelerate, the size of force X increases.
   (i) Explain what will happen to the acceleration of the object as the size of force X increases.
   (ii) The size of force X reaches 18 N. Describe the motion of the object at this time and explain your answer.

5 A car is travelling along a straight, flat road. The car reaches a certain speed. It cannot go any faster now, even if the accelerator pedal is pushed further down.
a) (i) Name the horizontal forces acting on the car at this time.
   (ii) Are these forces balanced or unbalanced at the car's top speed?
b) One way of increasing the maximum speed of a car is to make it more streamlined.
   (i) Name the force that streamlining the car will help to reduce.
   (ii) Describe one way of streamlining the car.

6 Satellites orbiting the Earth can be used in communications. Satellites orbit the Earth at different heights.
a) Satellite X takes a shorter time to orbit the Earth once compared to satellite Y. Which satellite, X or Y, is at a greater height above the Earth?
b) (i) What name is given to a satellite that appears to stay above the same point on the Earth?
   (ii) State the speed at which radio signals are sent from the Earth to any satellite.
   (iii) A satellite is 36 000 km above the surface of the Earth. Calculate the time taken for a radio signal to travel from the surface of the Earth to the satellite.

7 A simplified version of the receiving dish on a satellite is shown below.

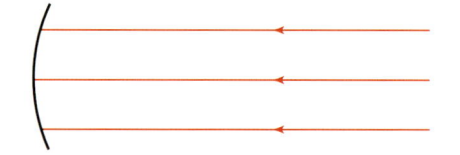

Figure E3.4

a) Explain why a receiving dish is attached to the satellite.
b) (i) Copy and complete the diagram to show what happens to the incoming signal when it reaches the receiving dish.
   (ii) Mark with an X the point where the receiving aerial should be placed. Justify your answer.

Name of planet	Distance from Hodgib (millions of km)	Gravitational field strength (N/kg)	Time to orbit Hodgib once (years)	Time for planet to spin on its axis once
Jonmit	62	4.0	1.2	24
Rodgl	127	16	2.7	72
Sceeb	269	7.6	3.9	10
Glahi	408	8.9	5.2	30

8 In a science fiction film, four planets orbit a star called Hodgib. The table above provides some information about the four planets.

   a) The mass of a robot is 12 kg. Calculate the weight of the robot on Sceeb.
   b) As the distance of a planet from Hodgib increases, what happens to the time taken for the planet to orbit Hodgib once?
   c) Which planet has the longest day?

9 Read the following passage.
   Galaxies may be spiral – like our own galaxy, the Milky Way – or ellipse-shaped. Galaxies are grouped in clusters. Though they vary in size, galaxies typically contain around 100 billion stars. The fact that the stars that make up galaxies are not falling towards the centre of the galaxy suggests that the stars are rotating around the centre of the galaxy. Evidence from radio signals from within our own galaxy confirms this view. Stars that are nearer to the centre of the galaxy than our Solar System appear to move in the opposite direction to those that are further away than our Solar System. This indicates that it is not the galaxy that is rotating – the stars orbit the centre of the galaxy in the same way as the planets orbit our Sun.

   Use information from the passage to answer the following questions.
   a) What is the name of our galaxy?
   b) What name is given to a group of galaxies?
   c) Which type of shape is our galaxy?
   d) How many stars does a typical galaxy contain?
   e) Which type of electromagnetic radiation confirmed the view that the stars orbit the centre of a galaxy?
   f) What evidence indicates that it is not that the galaxy is rotating but that the stars are orbiting the centre of the galaxy?

10 a) State what is meant by an exoplanet.
   b) State the main condition needed for a planet to sustain life.

National 4 Added Value Unit

Below are some suggestions for topics to investigate.

Practical electrical and electronic circuits
- how resistance of a thermistor varies with temperature
- how resistance of a light-dependent resistor (LDR) varies with brightness
- how resistance of a wire varies with length/thickness/material/cost/impact
- car headlamps – compare LED and filament lamp 'efficiency'/cost/lifetime/impact on 'safety'.

Generation of electricity
- wind turbines – how output power or voltage varies with number of blades/angle of blades/shape of blades; impact on generation
- energy sources – source and how long available; importance of replacing fossil fuels; impact of renewable sources and nuclear.

Electrical power
- power stations – input/output power, all types of generators; efficiency; cost; impact on environment of 'building' stations.

Nuclear radiation
- disposal of nuclear waste – absorbers/lifetime; impact on society.

Sound
- hearing – hearing response and frequency; high frequency deafness; hearing aids
- noise pollution – loudness and absorbing material; impact of noise pollution and hearing
- ultrasound – ultrasound against nuclear radiation in medicine; pros/cons of effect on patient.

Electromagnetic spectrum
- sunglasses – different factors of sunglass material and effect on absorption of UV/IR; impact on safety of user
- suntan protection – different factors and effect on UV; safety of wearer
- transfer of information – compare 'efficiency' of methods: wires; fibre optics; microwaves; satellite; impact on communication
- use of electromagnetic spectrum in medicine.

Relationship between forces, motion and energy
- braking distance – variation with speed/road surface/tyres; impact on road safety
- resistive forces – effect of shape on time to cover a certain distance; impact on moving objects in, for example, cycling/swimming/skiing/car shape.

Satellites
- satellites – height and period; importance when period = 24 hours; impact on communication.

Physics Assignment for National 4 Physics

For your Assignment you have to choose a relevant, topical issue in physics to investigate. This must relate to a Unit of the National 4 Physics course and must have an impact on the environment and/or society. The list of topics on this page may help you to choose an appropriate topic. An example of how you might then carry out the Assignment is shown below.

National 4 Added Value Unit

Issue to be investigated
How the resistance of a thermistor varies with temperature.

Relevance of issue
Thermistors are used in cars to measure the temperature of the oil and coolant. The electronic circuit containing the thermistor sends this information to instruments on the dashboard. The thermistor is being used as a data-gathering tool. Thermistors are also used in room thermostats to accurately sense room temperature.

Sources of information
Data for source 1 came from an experiment.

Title of experiment: Investigating how the resistance of a thermistor varies with temperature

Aim of experiment: To find out how the resistance of a thermistor varies with temperature

Source 2: Data Sheet for 502AT thermistor, Rapid Electronics, 2007

Procedure
The thermistor used in this experiment was a 502AT. The circuit shown below was set up.

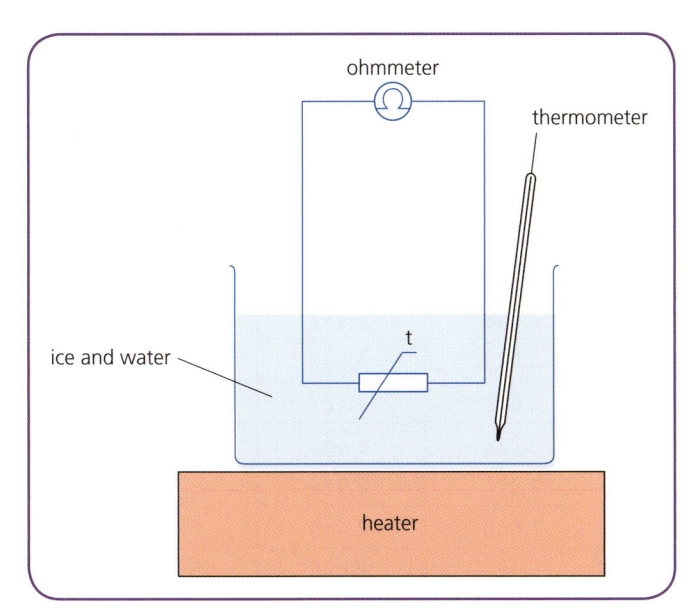

The reading on the ohmmeter (resistance) was recorded at temperatures of 0 to 90°C in 10°C steps.

Results
The following table of data was obtained from this experiment.

Temperature (°C)	Resistance (kΩ)
0	12.87
10	7.98
20	5.70
30	3.92
40	2.92
50	2.07
60	1.51
70	1.11
80	0.84
90	0.63

Using the data in the table, a graph of resistance of the thermistor against temperature was plotted.

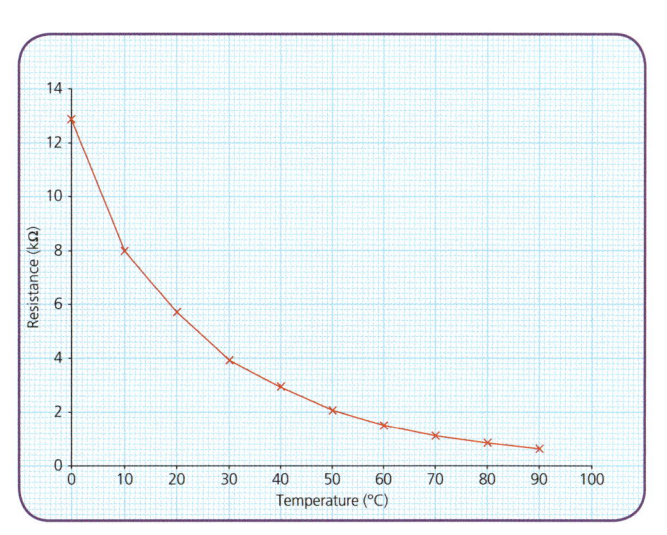

Relevant data from Source 2 was taken from the Data Sheet for the thermistor used in the experiment and is shown in the table below.

Temperature (°C)	Resistance (kΩ)
0	13.29
10	8.84
20	6.01
30	4.18
40	2.96
50	2.14
60	1.57
70	1.17
80	0.88
90	0.68

National 4 Added Value Unit

The graph I plotted shows that the resistance of the thermistor decreases as the temperature increases.

Impact on environment/society

In cars the information detected by the thermistor allows any problems to be easily detected and remedied. This makes the car more efficient and saves the motorist money. In thermostats, the thermistor allows heating (or cooling) to be controlled efficiently. This saves the user money and the more efficient use of energy will have a positive impact on the environment.

The data sheet table for the thermistor I used in the experiment is shown below.

Temperature (°C)	Type					
	102AT	202AT	502AT	103AT	203AT	503AT
−50	24.46	55.68	154.6	329.5	1253	3168
−45	18.88	42.17	116.5	247.7	890.5	2257
−40	14.43	32.34	88.91	188.5	642.0	1632
−35	11.23	24.96	68.19	144.1	485.8	1166
−30	8.834	19.48	52.87	111.3	342.5	872.8
−25	6.998	15.29	41.21	86.43	253.6	646.3
−20	5.594	12.11	32.44	87.77	190.0	484.3
−15	4.501	9.655	25.66	53.41	143.2	364.6
−10	3.651	7.763	20.48	42.47	109.1	277.5
−5	2.979	6.277	16.43	33.90	83.75	212.3
0	2.449	5.114	13.29	27.28	64.88	184.0
5	2.024	4.188	10.80	22.05	50.53	127.5
10	1.684	3.454	8.840	17.96	39.71	99.99
15	1.408	2.862	7.267	14.69	31.36	78.77
20	1.184	2.387	6.013	12.09	24.96	62.56
25	1.000	2.000	5.000	10.00	20.00	50.00
30	0.8466	1.684	4.179	8.313	16.12	40.20
35	0.7229	1.424	3.508	6.940	13.06	32.48
40	0.6189	1.211	2.961	5.827	10.65	26.43
45	0.5316	1.033	2.509	4.911	8.716	21.59
50	0.4587	8.8854	2.137	4.160	7.181	17.75
55	0.3987	0.7620	1.828	3.638	5.941	14.64
60	0.3446	0.6587	1.567	3.020	4.943	12.15
65	0.3000	0.5713	1.350	2.588	4.127	10.13
70	0.2622	0.4976	1.168	2.228	3.464	8.482
75	0.2285	0.4343	1.014	1.924	2.916	7.129
80	0.1999	0.3807	0.8835	1.668	2.468	6.022
85	0.1751	0.3348	0.7722	1.451	2.096	5.105
90	0.1536	0.2949	0.6771	1.268	1.788	4.345
95			0.5961	1.108	1.530	3.712
100			0.5265	0.9731	1.315	3.185
105			0.4654	0.8572	1.134	2.741
110			0.4128	0.7576	0.9807	2.369

Rearranging physics equations

You are required to solve numerical problems in National 4 Physics. There are two methods of doing this:

A Equation, substitute the values, if required rearrange, then calculate the answer.
B Equation, if required rearrange, substitute the values, then calculate the answer.

These two methods are shown in the example below.

Worked example

Example

The resistance of an electrical component is 30 Ω. The voltage across the component is 6.0 V. Calculate the current in the component.

Solution using method A

$V = IR$	equation
$6 = I \times 30$	substitution of values
$I = \dfrac{6}{30} = 0.2$ A	rearrange and calculate answer

Solution using method B

$V = IR$	equation
$I = \dfrac{V}{R}$	rearrange equation
$I = \dfrac{6}{30} = 0.2$ A	substitution of values and calculate answer

It is very important when you are solving numerical problems that you use a method that you understand and are happy with.

This book uses method B along with the use of a 'maths triangle'.

Using a 'maths triangle'

A 'maths triangle' can be used to find the different forms of an equation:

- Cover up the symbol for the quantity that you are trying to find.
- If the remaining symbols are side by side, this means multiply them.
- If the remaining symbols are one over the other, this means divide them.

Example 1

Using the triangle on $V = IR$ gives:

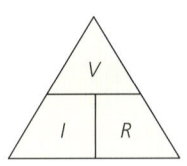

$$V = I \times R \qquad I = \frac{V}{R} \qquad R = \frac{V}{I}$$

Example 2

Using the triangle on $F_{un} = ma$ gives:

$$F_{un} = m \times a \qquad m = \frac{F_{un}}{a} \qquad a = \frac{F_{un}}{m}$$

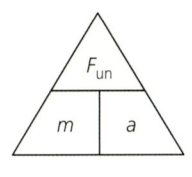

Example 3

Using the triangle on $v = f\lambda$ gives:

$$v = f \times \lambda \qquad f = \frac{v}{\lambda} \qquad \lambda = \frac{v}{f}$$

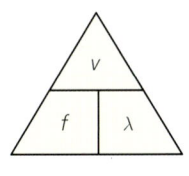

Data sheet

Speed of light in materials

Material	Speed in m/s
air	3.0×10^8
carbon dioxide	3.0×10^8
diamond	1.2×10^8
glass	2.0×10^8
glycerol	2.1×10^8
water	2.3×10^8

Speed of sound in materials

Material	Speed in m/s
aluminium	5200
air	340
bone	4100
carbon dioxide	270
glycerol	1900
muscle	1600
steel	5200
tissue	1500
water	1500

Gravitational field strengths

	Gravitational field strength on the surface in N/kg
Earth	9.8
Jupiter	23
Mars	3.7
Mercury	3.7
Moon	1.6
Neptune	11
Saturn	9.0
Sun	270
Uranus	8.7
Venus	8.9

SI prefixes and multiplication factors

Prefix	Symbol	Factor
giga	G	$1\,000\,000\,000 = 10^9$
mega	M	$1\,000\,000 = 10^6$
kilo	k	$1000 = 10^3$
milli	m	$0.001 = 10^{-3}$
micro	µ	$0.000\,001 = 10^{-6}$
nano	n	$0.000\,000\,001 = 10^{-9}$

Relationship sheet

$V = IR$

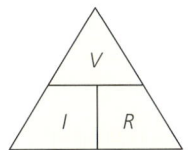

$R_T = R_1 + R_2 + R_3 ...$

$P = \dfrac{E}{t}$

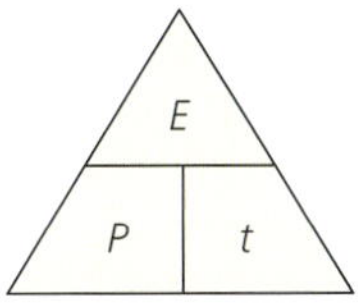

$\text{efficiency} = \dfrac{\text{useful energy output}}{\text{total energy input}} \times 100\%$

$\text{efficiency} = \dfrac{\text{useful power output}}{\text{total power input}} \times 100\%$

$\dfrac{n_S}{n_P} = \dfrac{V_S}{V_E}$

$\bar{v} = \dfrac{d}{t}$

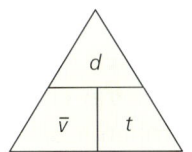

$v = f\lambda$

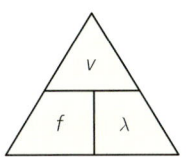

$a = \dfrac{v - u}{t}$

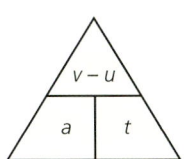

$W = mg$

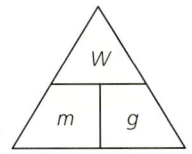

$F_{un} = ma$

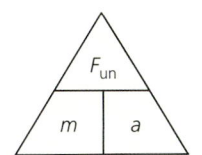

147

Key areas for National 4 Physics

Key Areas for Electricity and Energy

Practical electrical and electronic circuits (Chapters 1–4)

Use of an appropriate relationship to solve problems involving voltage, current and resistance.

Measurement of current and voltage using appropriate meters in series or parallel circuits.

Knowledge of the circuit symbol, function and application of standard electrical and electronic components including cell, battery, lamp, switch, resistor, variable resistor, voltmeter, ammeter, LED, motor, microphone, loudspeaker, solar cell, fuse, relay, LDR.

Identification of analogue and digital input and output devices.

Use of an appropriate relationship to solve problems involving the total resistance of resistors in series circuits.

Use of AND, OR and NOT logic gates in electronic circuits.

Electrical power (Chapter 5)

Definition of electrical power as a measure of the energy transferred electrically by an appliance every second.

Comparison of power consumption of heat producing and non-heat producing appliances, qualitative and quantitative.

Use of an appropriate relationship to solve problems involving power, energy and time.

Awareness of energy efficiency as a key factor in conserving resources and the environment.

Use of an appropriate relationship to solve problems involving efficiency given input and output power/energy.

Electromagnetism (Chapter 6)

Sketch of magnetic field patterns between magnetic poles.

Knowledge of the magnetic effects of electricity.

Knowledge of some practical applications of magnets and electromagnets.

Use of transformers in high voltage transmission.

Generation and distribution of electricity (Chapter 7)

Knowledge of advantages and disadvantages of different methods of electricity generation.

Knowledge of the potential role of different methods of electricity generation in future sustainable energy supply.

Awareness of the concept of energy efficiency and energy efficiency issues related to generation, distribution and use of electricity.

Knowledge of energy transformations and basic components of power stations.

Gas laws and the kinetic theory (Chapter 8)

Knowledge of the kinetic model of a gas.

Qualitative knowledge of the effects of varying pressure, volume or temperature on a fixed mass of an ideal gas.

Awareness of applications of the kinetic model of a gas using knowledge of pressure, volume and temperature (for a fixed mass of gas).

Key Areas for Waves and Radiation

Wave characteristics (Chapter 9)

Comparison of longitudinal and transverse waves.

Definition of frequency as the number of waves per second.

Key areas for National 4 Physics

Use of an appropriate relationship to solve problems involving frequency, number of waves and time.

Identification of wavelength and amplitude of transverse waves.

Use of an appropriate relationship to solve problems involving wave speed, frequency and wavelength.

Use of an appropriate relationship to solve problems involving distance, speed and time for waves.

Sound (Chapter 10)
Analysis of sound waveforms including changing amplitude and frequency.

Knowledge of methods of measurement of speed of sound in air.

Knowledge of sound level measurement, including decibel scale.

Awareness of noise pollution and risks to human hearing.

Knowledge of methods of protecting hearing.

Awareness of noise cancellation as a means of reducing the risk of damage to hearing.

Awareness of applications of sonar and ultrasound.

Awareness of sound reproduction technologies.

Electromagnetic spectrum (Chapter 11)
Knowledge of applications and hazards associated with electromagnetic radiations.

Knowledge of approaches to minimising risks associated with electromagnetic radiations.

Description of how invisible parts of the EM spectrum can be detected.

Description of refraction in terms of change of direction (where angle of incidence is greater than 0°).

Nuclear radiation (Chapter 12)
Knowledge of natural and artificial sources of nuclear radiation and associated medical and industrial applications.

Consideration of the pros and cons of generating electricity using nuclear fuel.

Comparison of risk due to nuclear radiation with risk due to other environmental hazards (e.g. global warming) and the management of this risk.

Key Areas for Dynamics and Space

Speed and acceleration (Chapter 13)
Use of an appropriate relationship to solve problems involving speed, distance and time.

Determination of average and instantaneous speed.

Interpretation of speed–time graphs to describe motion including calculation of distance (for objects which are speeding up, slowing down, stationary and moving with constant speed). Motion in one direction only.

Use of an appropriate relationship to solve problems involving acceleration, change in speed and time.

Relationships between forces, motion and energy (Chapter 14)
Use of Newton's first law and balanced forces to explain constant speed for a moving object, making reference to frictional forces.

Use of Newton's second law to explain the movement of objects in situations involving constant acceleration.

Use of an appropriate relationship to solve problems involving force, mass and acceleration in situations where only one force is acting.

Use of an appropriate relationship to solve problems involving weight, mass and gravitational field strength.

Knowledge of the risks and benefits associated with space exploration including challenges of re-entry to a planet's atmosphere and the use of thermal protection systems to protect spacecraft on re-entry.

Satellites (Chapter 15)
Knowledge of the range of heights and functions of satellites in orbit around the Earth, including geostationary and natural satellites.

Knowledge of the qualitative relationship between the altitude of a satellite and its period.

Knowledge of the use of parabolic reflectors to send and receive signals.

Use of the relationship between distance, speed and time applied to satellite communication.

Awareness of a range of applications of satellites including telecommunications, weather monitoring, their use in environmental monitoring and developing our understanding of the global impact of mankind's actions.

Cosmology (Chapter 16)

Description of planet, moon, star, solar systems, exo-planet, galaxy and universe.

Awareness of the scale of the solar system and universe measured in light years.

Awareness of space exploration and its impact on our understanding of the universe and planet Earth.

Consideration of the conditions required for an exo-planet to sustain life.

Index

A
a.c. supply 8
acceleration 111–13
air bags 123
airport security 91
alpha particles 94–6, 97
ammeters 4
amplitude 71
analogue signals 21
AND-gate 30–1
Apollo missions 125–6, 137
aqualungs 65
atmospheric pressure 64
atom 'model' 94

B
background radiation 97
balanced forces 119
beta particles 94–6, 97
biomass (plants) 54
brakes 121
branches 3

C
circuit current 5
circuit symbols 3, 8–9
circuits 3
combined heat and power stations 57
conductors 2–3
conservation of energy 58
cosmology 135–8
crest 71
crumple zones 123
current
    description 2–3
    measuring 4–5
curved reflectors 130–1

D
d.c. supply 8
decibels 82
demand (of electricity) 49–51, 53
digital processing devices 30–2
digital signals 21
dish aerials 130–1
diving 65

E
the Earth 135
efficiency 37, 57
electric bells 42
electric motors 24–5
electric shocks 9
electrical energy 35
electrical systems 20–1
electricity
    circuit symbols 3
    conductors 2–3
    current 2
    generating 44–6
    supply and demand 49–51, 53
electromagnetic spectrum 87–92
electromagnetism 41–3, 46
energy 92
energy conversions 17, 35
energy labels 37

F
filament lamps 26
film badges 91
forces
    balanced 119
    frictional 120–1
    measuring 118–19
    unbalanced 119–20
fossil fuels 49, 56
fracking 50
frequency 71, 76, 92
frictional forces 120–1

G
galaxies 135
gamma cameras 92
gamma rays 91–2, 94–6, 97
gas
    kinetic model 60–1
    pressure and kinetic theory 63–4
    pressure and temperature 62, 63–4
    pressure and volume 61–2, 64
    volume and temperature 63, 64
gas pressure 60–1
Geiger counters 96
generation of electricity 49–58
generators 44–6
geostationary satellites 129–30
geothermal power 55
GPS (Global Positioning System) 132
gravitational field strength 124–5
gravity 124

H
head restraints 123
hearing 80
heat 35
Hubble Space Telescope 137–8
human hearing 80
hydroelectric power stations 52

I
infrared radiation 88–9
input 20
input devices 21–4
instantaneous speed 108–11
insulators 2–3
International Space Station (ISS) 132, 137
ionisation 95–6
ISS (International Space Station) 132, 137

J
joulemeters 36

K
kinetic energy 35
kinetic model of gas 60–1, 63–4

L
LDRs (light-dependent resistors) 23, 24
LEDs (light-emitting diodes) 26
light 35
light-dependent resistors (LDRs) 23, 24
light-emitting diodes (LEDs) 26
light waves 89
light years 136–7
logic gates 30–2
longitudinal waves 70
loudspeakers 24
lubrication 120

M
maglev trains 43
magnetic relays 43
magnetic resonance imaging (MRI) 43
magnets 40–1
mass 123–4
'maths triangle' 145
medical uses (of radiation) 98–9
microphones 21–2, 23
microwaves 88
Milky Way 135, 136
MRI (magnetic resonance imaging) 43–4

N
National Grid 57
Newton balance 119
Newton's first law 121
Newton's second law 121–2
noise cancellation 82–3
noise pollution 82
NOT (inverter) gate 30
nuclear accidents 100
nuclear power stations 51, 56–7, 99–100
nuclear radiation
    background 97
    detecting 96
    effect of 97
    ionisation 95–6
    sources 97–8
    types of 94–6
    use in medicine 98–9
nuclear waste 100

O
ohmmeters 13
OR-gate 31
oscilloscopes 76–7
output 20
output devices 24–8

P
parallel circuits 3, 5, 7, 8, 9
photons 92
planets 135–6
plants (biomass) 54
power 36–7
power stations 49–51, 56–7, 99–100
power supplies 8–9

Index

power transmission 57–8
pressure (gas) 61–2, 63–4
process 20

R

radiation *see* nuclear radiation
radio waves 87
radioactive tracers 92, 99
radiotherapy 98–9
rating plates 35
re-entry 125–6
receiving dishes 130–1
refraction 89
relays 25
renewable energy sources 51–5
resistance 13–17
resistors 14–17

S

satellites 128–32
SCUBA diving 65
seat belts 123
series circuits 3, 4, 6, 8, 9
seven-segment displays 27
sight defects 89

solar cells 22, 23
solar power 54
Solar System 135, 136
solenoids 25
sound
    definition 75–6
    and electrical energy 35
    measuring 82–3
    oscilloscopes 76–7
    production 83
    speed of 77–8
    using 80–2
sources
    of nuclear radiation 97–8
space disasters 126
space exploration 125–6, 137
space observatories 137–8
space probes 137
Space Shuttle 126, 137
speed
    average speed 106–8
    instantaneous speed 108–11
    of sound 77–8
    of a wave 71
speed cameras 110–11
speed–time graphs 114–15
Sputnik I 128, 137

sterilisation 99
stethoscopes 80
streamlining 120
supply (of electricity) 49–51
supply voltage 6
switches 23, 24

T

temperature, gas 62–3, 64
thermistors 22, 24
tidal power 55
transformers 45–6, 57–8
transmission (electrical energy) 57–8
transmitting dishes 131
transverse waves 70
trough 71
TV waves 87–8

U

ultrasound 80–1
ultraviolet 90
unbalanced forces 119–20
the universe 135, 136

V

variable resistors 14
visible light 89
voltage 5–8
voltmeters 5
volume (gas) 61–2, 63, 64

W

waste, nuclear 100
wave power 54–5
wavelength 71
waves
    light 89
    microwaves 88
    radio 87
    speed 71–3
    terms 71
    TV 87–8
    types 70
weight 124
wind farms 53
wind power 53

X

X-rays 90

Answers

Answers to Unit 1

1 Electrical circuits

1. a) ammeter
   b) battery
   c) switch
   d) voltmeter
   e) lamp
   f) fuse
2. A = source, B = electrons, C = positive, D = current, E = amperes, F = heat, G = light (answers F and G can be either way around)
3. A = one, B = parallel, C = branches, D = current, E = series, F = voltmeter
4. a) series
   b) parallel
   c) series
   d) series and parallel – P and Q in series, R and S in series, P and Q in parallel with R and S
5. a) P is an ammeter
   b) Q is a voltmeter
6. a) Ammeter connected in series anywhere in circuit.
   b) Voltmeter connected in parallel with lamp Z.

   (i) [circuit diagram]
   (ii) [circuit diagram]

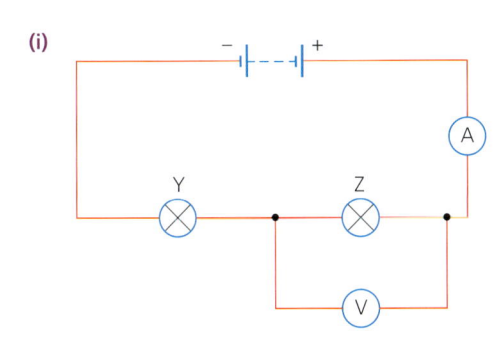

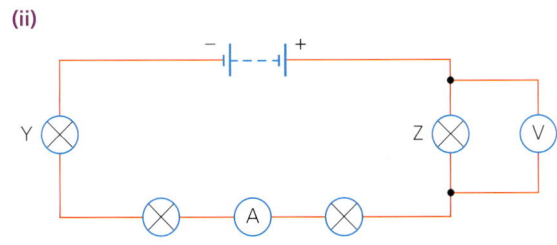

7. a) $A_1 = A_2 = A_3 = 2$ A
   b) $A_4 = 1.5$ A, $A_5 = 3$ A, $A_6 = 2$ A
8. $V_1 = 5$ V
9. a) $A_1 = 2$ A, $A_2 = 3$ A
   b) $V_1 = 4$ V, $V_2 = 12$ V
10. [circuit symbols a–f]

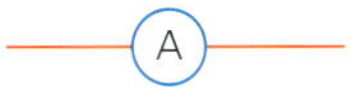

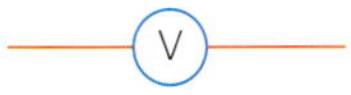

2 Resistance

1. a) lamp
   b) resistor
   c) battery
   d) variable resistor
   e) switch
   f) ohmmeter
2. For example: volume control on a radio; dimmer control on a light; speed control on a food mixer
3. A = resistance, B = ohmmeter, C = ohms, D = decreases, E = electrical, F = heat
4. a) $V = IR = 2 \times 115 = 230$ V
   b) $V = IR = 0.05 \times 100 = 5$ V
   c) $I = \dfrac{V}{R} = \dfrac{10}{4} = 2.5$ A
   d) $I = \dfrac{V}{R} = \dfrac{5}{50} = 0.1$ A
   e) $R = \dfrac{V}{I} = \dfrac{10}{2} = 5\ \Omega$
   f) $R = \dfrac{V}{I} = \dfrac{12}{4} = 3\ \Omega$ 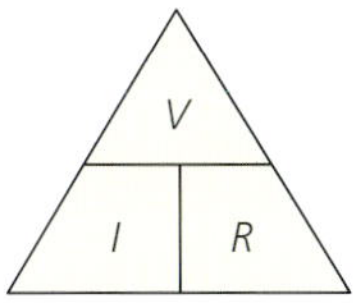
5. $V = IR = 1.5 \times 5 = 7.5$ V
6. $V = IR$

   $I = \dfrac{V}{R} = \dfrac{1.5}{7.5} = 0.2$ A

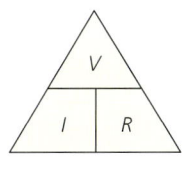

Answers

7. $V = IR$
   $R = \dfrac{V}{I} = \dfrac{12}{2} = 6\ \Omega$

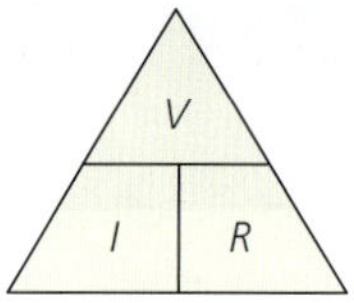

8. $V = IR$
   $R = \dfrac{V}{I} = \dfrac{12}{3} = 4\ \Omega$

9. a) Circuit A
   b) $V = IR$
      $R = \dfrac{V}{I} = \dfrac{10}{2} = 5\ \Omega$ 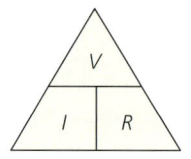
   c) $V = IR$
      $R = \dfrac{V}{I} = \dfrac{6}{3} = 2\ \Omega$

10. a) $V = IR$
       $I = \dfrac{V}{R} = \dfrac{230}{46} = 5\ A$ 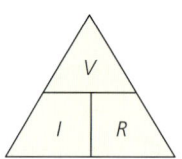
    b) electrical energy to heat

11. $R_T = R_1 + R_2 = 33 + 82 = 115\ \Omega$

12. $R_T = R_1 + R_2 + R_3 = 10 + 15 + 30 = 55\ \Omega$

13. toaster, hairdryer, kettle, etc.

14. a)  switch symbol
    b) 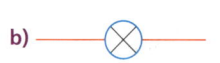 lamp symbol
    c) 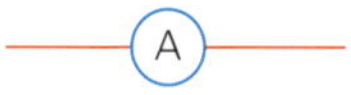 ammeter symbol
    d)  resistor symbol
    e) 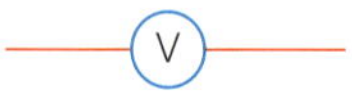 voltmeter symbol
    f) 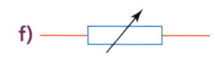 variable resistor symbol

15. a) circuit diagram
    b) Take a value for V and corresponding value for I,
       e.g. 1.0 V and 0.2 A
       $V = IR$
       $R = \dfrac{V}{I} = \dfrac{1}{0.2} = 5\ \Omega$

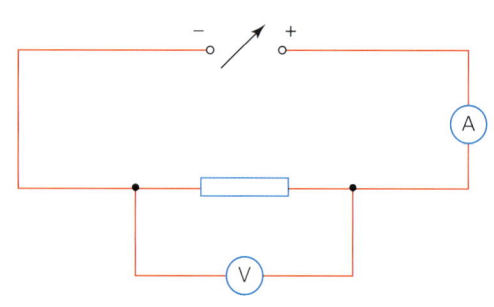

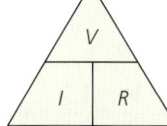

3 Electrical systems and components

1. a) Diagrams Q and S are digital.
   b) Diagrams P and R are analogue.
2. a) sound to electrical
   b) light to electrical
3. a) thermistor
   b) LDR or solar cell
   c) microphone
4. a) $V_{thermistor} = (IR)_{thermistor}$
      $R_{thermistor} = \dfrac{1.8}{0.0036} = 500\ \Omega$ 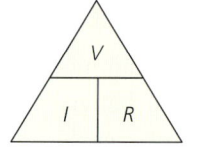
   b) $V_R = V_{supply} - V_{thermistor} = 4.5 - 1.8 = 2.7\ V$
      $R_R = \dfrac{2.7}{0.0036} = 750\ \Omega$
   c) Resistance of the thermistor decreases so the ammeter reading will increase to, for example, 0.0040 A.
5. a) electrical to kinetic
   b) electrical to light
   c) electrical to sound
6. a) 2 = a, b, g, e, d
   b) 5 = a, f, g, c, d
   c) 7 = a, b, c
7. a) buzzer or lamp
   b) motor
   c) relay
8. a) (i) relay and solenoid (electric motor, LED and loudspeaker could be digital)
      (ii) any two from light-dependent resistor (LDR), microphone or thermistor
      (iii) sound to electrical
   b) (i) There will be a larger reading on the ammeter.
      (ii) As the temperature rises, the resistance of the thermistor decreases, so the current in the circuit will increase.

4 Digital processes

1. high voltage = logic '1' and low voltage = logic '0'
2. a) NOT gate symbol

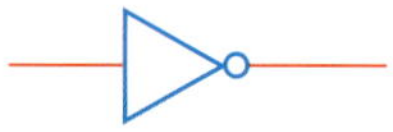

   b)
Input	Output
0	1
1	0

Answers

3 a) A, B → AND gate → output

b)
Input A	Input B	Output
0	0	0
0	1	0
1	0	0
1	1	1

4 a) A, B → OR gate → output

b)
Input A	Input B	Output
0	0	0
0	1	1
1	0	1
1	1	1

5 NOT-gate

6 a) (i) P = AND-gate
(ii) Q = NOT-gate

b)
A	B	C	D
0	0	0	1
0	1	0	1
1	0	0	1
1	1	1	0

7 a) (i) R = OR-gate
(ii) S = NOT-gate

b)
A	B	C	D
0	0	0	1
0	1	1	0
1	0	1	0
1	1	1	0

8
A	B	C	D
0	0	1	0
0	1	1	1
1	0	0	0
1	1	0	0

9 Buzzer on when light switch on AND ignition switch off (ignition switch NOT on).

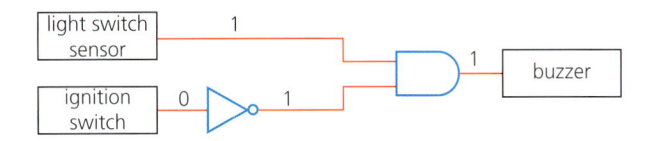

light switch sensor → 1 → AND gate → 1 → buzzer
ignition switch → 0 → NOT gate → 1 → AND gate

10 a) (i) X = OR-gate
(ii) Y = AND-gate

b)
D	E
0	0
1	1
1	1
1	1

5 Electrical power

1 a) electrical energy to heat
b) electrical energy to kinetic
c) electrical energy to heat
d) electrical energy to kinetic

2 a) clock (7 W)
b) electric drill (as it has the highest power rating of 750 W)

3 electrical energy to heat and light

4 $P = \dfrac{E}{t}$

$E = P \times t = 2200 \times 1 = 2200$ joules

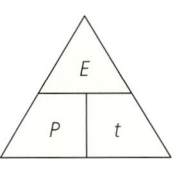

5 a) $P = \dfrac{E}{t} = \dfrac{1050}{30} = 35$ watts

b) $P = \dfrac{E}{t} = \dfrac{6000}{2000} = 3$ watts

c) $P = \dfrac{E}{t}$
$E = P \times t = 900 \times 500 = 450\,000$ joules

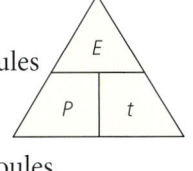

d) $P = \dfrac{E}{t}$
$E = P \times t = 2200 \times 120 = 264\,000$ joules

e) $P = \dfrac{E}{t}$
$t = \dfrac{E}{P} = \dfrac{18\,000}{60} = 300$ seconds

f) $P = \dfrac{E}{t}$
$t = \dfrac{E}{P} = \dfrac{200\,000}{100} = 2000$ seconds

6 $P = \dfrac{E}{t} = \dfrac{216\,000}{720} = 300$ watts

155

Answers

7. $P = \dfrac{E}{t}$

   $t = \dfrac{E}{P} = \dfrac{135\,000}{900} = 150$ s

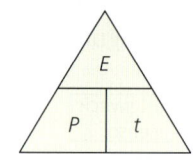

8. $P = \dfrac{E}{t}$

   $E = P \times t = 14 \times 1800 = 25\,200$ J

9. % efficiency $= \dfrac{\text{useful energy output}}{\text{total energy input}} \times 100\%$

   $= \dfrac{5760}{7200} \times 100\% = 80\%$

10. % efficiency $= \dfrac{\text{useful power output}}{\text{total power input}} \times 100\%$

    $= \dfrac{6}{20} \times 100\% = 30\%$

11. % efficiency $= \dfrac{\text{useful energy output}}{\text{total energy input}} \times 100\%$

    $= \dfrac{12}{48} \times 100\% = 25\%$

12. % efficiency $= \dfrac{\text{useful power output}}{\text{total power input}} \times 100\%$

    $= \dfrac{810\,000\,000}{1\,800\,000\,000} \times 100\% = 45\%$

6 Electromagnetism

1. A = north; B = south; C = attracts; D = like; E = unlike
2. Magnetic field lines must go from north to south – see Figure 6.5.
3. a) There is a magnetic field surrounding the current-carrying wire.
   b) (i) Compass needles would return to their original positions as shown in diagram A.
      (ii) Compass needles would point in the opposite direction, i.e. anti-clockwise.
4. Increase the current in the wire (by increasing the supply voltage); wind more turns of wire around the nail.
5. Increase the current (by increasing the supply voltage); increase the number of turns of wire; place an iron core through the turns of wire.
6. Move the loop of wire faster through the magnetic field; increase the number of turns of wire that pass through the magnetic field; increase the strength of the magnetic field of the magnet.
7. X = primary coil; Y = iron core; Z = secondary coil
8. Note $V_P = 16$ V, $n_P = 4800$ turns and $V_S = 12$ V

   $\dfrac{n_S}{n_P} = \dfrac{V_S}{V_P}$, $\dfrac{n_S}{4800} = \dfrac{12}{16}$

   $n_S = \dfrac{12}{16} \times 4800 = 3600$ turns

7 Generation and distribution of electricity

1. a) coal, oil and gas
   b) They are the chemical remains of plants and animals that lived millions of years ago.
2. a) fit loft insulation, fit draught-excluders, etc.
   b) use public transport, walk, etc.
3. renewable: biomass, solar, water, wind; non-renewable: coal, gas, oil
4. Renewable sources of energy will not run out, i.e. they are infinite, such as wind and waves. Non-renewable sources of energy cannot be replaced, i.e. they are finite, such as fossil fuels.
5. For example: Wind: clean source but unreliable due to variations in wind speed. Solar: clean source but only available during daylight hours. Wave: clean source but unreliable due to the fact that you do not always have waves.
6. a) on top of a windy hill
   b) electrical power = 30 × 1.5 million
      = 45 million units
7. Length $= \dfrac{20\,000\,000}{10\,000} = 2000$ m
8. % efficiency $= \dfrac{\text{useful power output}}{\text{total power input}} \times 100\%$

   $= \dfrac{23}{25} \times 100\% = 92\%$

9. % efficiency $= \dfrac{\text{useful power output}}{\text{total power input}} \times 100\%$

   $= \dfrac{18\,000}{24\,000} \times 100\% = 75\%$

10. % efficiency $= \dfrac{\text{useful power output}}{\text{total power input}} \times 100\%$

    $= \dfrac{42}{60} \times 100\% = 70\%$

11. % efficiency $= \dfrac{\text{useful power output}}{\text{total power input}} \times 100\%$

    $= \dfrac{750\,000}{1\,000\,000} \times 100\% = 75\%$

12. % efficiency $= \dfrac{\text{useful power output}}{\text{total power input}} \times 100\%$

    $= \dfrac{846}{1800} \times 100\% = 47\%$

8 Gas laws and the kinetic theory

1. a) 32 units (any value greater than 31 units)
   b) As the temperature of the gas increases during the journey, the average kinetic energy of the particles increases, so the particles speed up.

They hit the walls of the container more often and with a larger force. This means that there is more particle bombardment of the walls, so the pressure exerted by the gas increases.

2 The average kinetic energy of the particles increases as the temperature of the gas in the can increases, so the particles speed up. They hit the walls of the can more often and with a larger force. This means there is more particle bombardment of the walls of the can, so the pressure exerted by the gas increases until the can explodes.

3 The average kinetic energy of the particles decreases as the temperature of the gas decreases, so the particles slow down. They hit the walls of their container with a smaller force and less often. This means there is less particle bombardment of the walls, so the pressure exerted by the gas falls.

4 a) The temperature of the air in the squash ball at the end of the game is greater than the temperature at the start of the game.
b) The temperature of the air inside the ball has increased. The kinetic energy of the particles has therefore increased, so the particles speed up. They hit the walls of the ball with a larger force and more often (more times per second). This means there is more particle bombardment of the walls of the ball, so the pressure exerted by the gas increases and the ball is harder to compress.

Unit 1 exam practice

1 a) hydroelectric, nuclear or wind
b) any one from: solar, biomass, geothermal, wave, tidal
c) (i) For example: the wind does not always blow; wind farms may spoil areas of natural beauty.
(ii) For example: difficulty of safely disposing of nuclear waste; risk of an accident.

2 a) nuclear
b) 20 years
c) any one from: hydroelectric, wind, solar, biomass, geothermal, wave, tidal

3 a) secondary coil
b) % efficiency = $\frac{\text{useful power output}}{\text{total power input}} \times 100\%$
= $\frac{18}{20} \times 100\% = 90\%$

4 a) 46 watts
b) the hairdryer (since it has the larger power rating)
c) $P = \frac{E}{t}$
$E = P \times t = 1200 \times (10 \times 60)$
= 720 000 joules

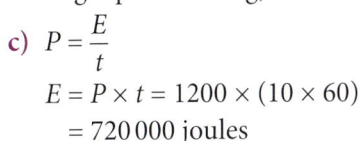

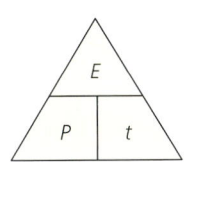

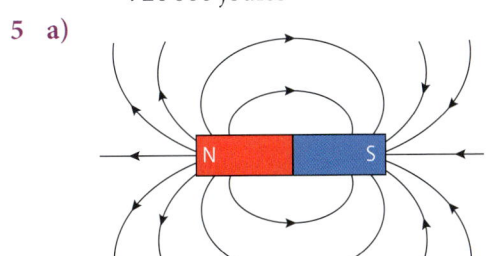

5 a)

b) (i) The changing magnetic field in the coil causes a voltage across the coil of wire.
(ii) any two from: turn the handle (magnet) more rapidly; use a stronger magnet; have more coils of wire on the iron core

6 a) As the spindle rotates, the magnet rotates, which gives a changing magnetic field in the coil. This gives a voltage across the coil of wire.
b) any two from: larger plastic cups to 'collect' more wind and rotate the spindle faster; stronger magnet; more coils of wire on the iron core

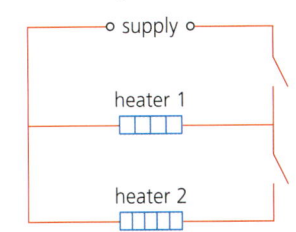

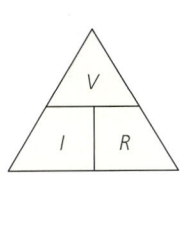

7 a) $V = IR$
$R = \frac{V}{I} = \frac{230}{5} = 46\ \Omega$
b)

8 a) 0.25 A (since a series circuit)
b) Voltage across R_2 = 12 − 5 = 7 V
$V = IR$
$R = \frac{V}{I} = \frac{7}{0.25} = 28\ \Omega$

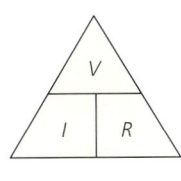

9 a) input device
b) $V = IR$
$R = \frac{V}{I} = \frac{4}{0.02} = 200\ \Omega$
c) For instance, 100 Ω (any value between 25 Ω and 560 Ω)

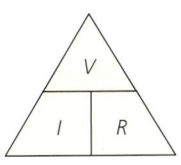

Answers

10 a) (i) process
    (ii) output
  b) (i) X = NOT-gate; Y = AND-gate
    (ii)

P	Q	R	S
0	0	1	0
0	1	1	1
1	0	0	0
1	1	0	0

11 As the bubble rises, the pressure on the bubble decreases. This means that the volume of the bubble will increase.

12 When the gas is heated, the temperature of the gas increases. This means that the average kinetic energy of the gas particles increases and so their speed increases. The gas particles will hit the container walls harder (with more force) and more often, so increasing the particle bombardment. This increases the pressure exerted by the gas.

Answers to Unit 2

9 Wave characteristics

1 a) waveform X
  b) waveform Y
2 a) The frequency of a wave is the number of waves produced in one second.
  b) The speed of a wave is the distance travelled in one second.
3 a) any one from: light, microwaves or water
  b) sound
4 a) $2A = 0.5$
$$A = \frac{0.5}{2} = 0.25 \text{ m}$$
  b) Frequency = $\frac{\text{number of waves}}{\text{time to produce waves}}$
$$= \frac{4}{0.4} = 10 \text{ Hz}$$
(Note that there are four waves between X and Y)
  c) $4\lambda = 2$
$$\lambda = \frac{2}{4} = 0.5 \text{ m}$$
  d) $v = f\lambda = 10 \times 0.5 = 5 \text{ m/s}$
or $v = \frac{d}{t} = \frac{2}{0.4} = 5 \text{ m/s}$
5 a) $v = f\lambda = 50 \times 1.2 = 60 \text{ m/s}$
  b) $v = f\lambda = 0.25 \times 4.8 = 1.2 \text{ m/s}$

c) $v = f\lambda$
$$f = \frac{v}{\lambda} = \frac{340}{0.25} = 1360 \text{ Hz}$$ 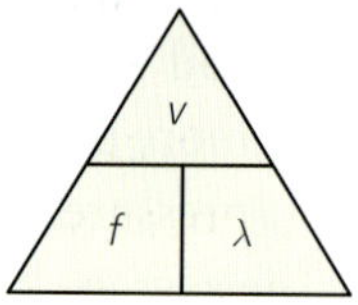
d) $v = f\lambda$
$$f = \frac{v}{\lambda} = \frac{270}{4.5} = 60 \text{ Hz}$$
e) $v = f\lambda$
$$\lambda = \frac{v}{f} = \frac{1500}{5000} = 0.3 \text{ m}$$ 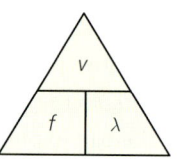
f) $v = f\lambda$
$$\lambda = \frac{v}{f} = \frac{340}{200} = 1.7 \text{ m}$$
6 $v = f\lambda = 0.25 \times 6000 = 1500 \text{ m/s}$
7 $v = f\lambda$
$$\lambda = \frac{v}{f} = \frac{270}{500} = 0.54 \text{ m}$$ 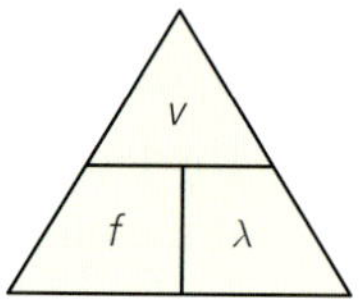
8 $v = f\lambda$
$$f = \frac{v}{\lambda} = \frac{1600}{0.32} = 5000 \text{ Hz}$$
9 a) $2A = 4$
$$A = \frac{4}{2} = 2 \text{ m}$$
  b) 5 waves in 2.5 s
frequency = $\frac{\text{number of waves}}{\text{time to produce waves}}$
$$= \frac{5}{2.5} = 2 \text{ Hz}$$
  c) $\lambda = \frac{8}{2} = 4 \text{ m}$
  d) $v = f\lambda = 2 \times 4 = 8 \text{ m/s}$
10 a) frequency = $\frac{\text{number of waves}}{\text{time to produce waves}}$
$$= \frac{80}{10} = 8 \text{ Hz}$$
  b) $v = f\lambda$
$$\lambda = \frac{v}{f} = \frac{0.6}{8} = 0.075 \text{ m}$$

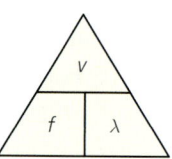

10 Sound

1 A = vibrates; B = wave; C = one; D = frequency; E = hertz; F = pitch
2 a) C
  b) D
  c) A
  d) B
3 a) frequency decreases
  b) frequency increases
4 The new sound has a higher frequency.

Answers

5 The sound that produced trace b) has twice the frequency of that which produced trace a). The sound that produced trace a) is louder than the sound that produced trace b).

6 a) B
  b) B
7 D
8 B
9 E
10 a) same height of wave but fewer than three waves on the screen
   b) increase length of string or make string looser
11 For example: The sound of thunder from a lightning strike takes longer to reach you than the sight of the lightning flash.
12 a) $v = \dfrac{d}{t} = \dfrac{24}{6} = 4$ m/s
   b) $v = \dfrac{d}{t} = \dfrac{1000}{40} = 25$ m/s
   c) $v = \dfrac{d}{t}$
      $t = \dfrac{d}{v} = \dfrac{120}{1500} = 0.08$ s 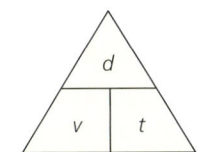
   d) $v = \dfrac{d}{t}$
      $t = \dfrac{d}{v} = \dfrac{1700}{340} = 5$ s
   e) $v = \dfrac{d}{t}$
      $d = vt = 270 \times 2.5 = 675$ m
   f) $v = \dfrac{d}{t}$
      $d = vt = 5200 \times 0.12 = 624$ m
13 $v = \dfrac{d}{t} = \dfrac{469}{1.4} = 335$ m/s
14 $v = \dfrac{d}{t} = \dfrac{2210}{6.5} = 340$ m/s
15 $v = \dfrac{d}{t}$
   $d = vt = 1500 \times 0.52 = 780$ m 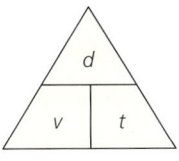
16 a) distance travelled by sound $= 2 \times 255 = 510$ m
   b) $v = \dfrac{d}{t} = \dfrac{510}{1.5} = 340$ m/s
17 the distance between the two students
18 a) reflection of the sound wave from the canyon wall
   b) there is an echo from both sides of the canyon walls
19 $v = \dfrac{d}{t} = \dfrac{170}{0.5} = 340$ m/s

20 a) and b) diagram and description of any one of the three methods described in this chapter (or another suitable method)
   c) Use speed $= \dfrac{\text{distance travelled}}{\text{time taken}}$
21 A = gases; B = particles; C = vacuum
22 A = frequencies; B = ultrasound; C = decibel; D = damage
23 Any value above 20 000 Hz, for example 21 000 Hz
24 a) [bar chart showing frequency of upper limit of hearing (Hz) for cat ~45 000, dog ~30 000, human ~20 000, whale ~80 000]
   b) cat and whale
25 For example: to obtain an image of an unborn baby; to obtain an image of a crack in a metal object
26 For example: heavy lorries; loud music, etc.
27 90 dB
28 ultrasound
29 To reduce the loudness of the sound the engineer is exposed to below 90 dB. (For comfort the loudness heard by the engineer should be reduced to about 70 dB.)
30 a) Distance = distance from surface to oil + distance from oil back to surface = 750 + 750 = 1500 m
   b) Speed $= \dfrac{\text{distance}}{\text{time}} = \dfrac{1500}{0.3} = 5000$ m/s
   c) The ear protectors reduce the loudness of the sound at the ears and prevent damage to the physicist's hearing.

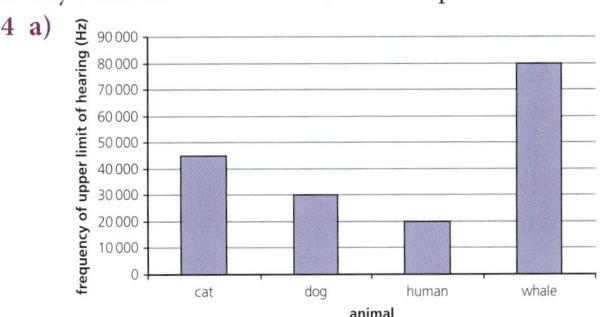

11 Electromagnetic spectrum

1 infrared
2 a) sunburn or skin cancer
  b) suggestions could include: use sun cream; cover the body with clothing and a hat; stay in the shade
  c) for example: to produce vitamin D or to treat some skin conditions such as acne
3 to heat damaged muscle so it heals more quickly
4 a) P = infrared; Q = X-rays
  b) to kill cancerous tumours in the body
  c) for example: to heat food; to communicate by mobile phone

Answers

5 X-rays damage healthy cells. The lead apron prevents the X-rays reaching the radiographer's body.
6 Gamma rays cannot be detected by our eyes as they have a shorter wavelength than visible light.
7 damage and kill the cells

12 Nuclear radiation

1 The diagram should look similar to Figure 12.1. There is a nucleus consisting of protons (positively charged) and neutrons (neutral). Surrounding the nucleus are electrons, which are negatively charged.
2 a) Ionisation is the breaking up of a neutral atom into positive and negative pieces.
   b) (i) alpha radiation
      (ii) gamma radiation
3 a) The amount and type of radiation the wearer has been exposed to must be carefully checked, as it could be harmful.
   b) The open window and the plastic (0.1 mm thickness) will be affected. Beta particles are absorbed by a few mm of aluminium and by lead. Therefore the 3 mm aluminium may or may not be affected – it depends on the strength of the beta radiation. The 1 mm lead will be unaffected.
4 The gamma source, as it will be able to penetrate through the body and so be detected outside the patient's body. Alpha and beta radiation will be absorbed by the body.
5 Place each source, in turn, close to a GM tube. Place the thin paper between each source and the GM tube. For the gamma and beta sources the count rate will be unaffected by the paper. For the alpha source the count rate will fall almost to zero.
Next, place the remaining two sources, in turn, close to the GM tube. Place the 5 mm-thick aluminium between the source and the tube. For the gamma source, the count rate will be unaffected by the aluminium. For the beta source, the count rate will fall almost to zero.
6 Gamma rays would pass through both the wooden and aluminium boxes.
7 a) either cosmic rays coming from outer space or radon gas coming from the ground
   b) either gamma rays in a radiotherapy treatment or an X-ray of a bone fracture

8 a) No carbon dioxide or gases that cause air pollution are produced; or nuclear fuel will last a long time; or the same mass of nuclear fuel produces more energy than fossil fuels.
   b) Disposal of the nuclear waste produced is difficult; or there is the possibility of an accident causing a nuclear explosion; or there are limited resources of nuclear fuel (uranium).
9 Initially the high-level waste is stored in cooling ponds. Much later it is sealed in drums and these are then stored in vaults.

Unit 2 exam practice

1 a) A wave is described as a transverse wave when the particles of the medium vibrate at right-angles to the direction the wave is travelling in.
   b) Frequency = $\dfrac{\text{number of waves}}{\text{time to produce waves}}$
      = $\dfrac{5}{1}$ = 5 Hz
   c) $v = \dfrac{d}{t} = \dfrac{30}{7.5}$ = 4 m/s
      $v = f\lambda$
      $\lambda = \dfrac{v}{f} = \dfrac{4}{5}$ = 0.8 m 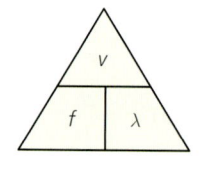
2 a) crest
   b) amplitude = $\dfrac{1.2}{2}$ = 0.6 m
   c) Between O and X there are five complete waves.
      Frequency = $\dfrac{\text{number of waves}}{\text{time to produce waves}}$
      = $\dfrac{5}{2.5}$ = 2 Hz
   d) Wavelength = $\dfrac{4.5}{3}$ = 1.5 m
   e) $v = f\lambda = 2 \times 1.5$ = 3 m/s
3 a) 1020
   b)

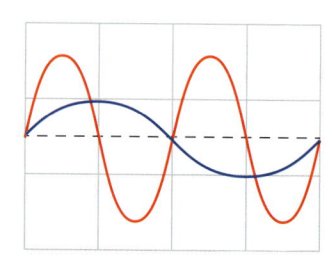

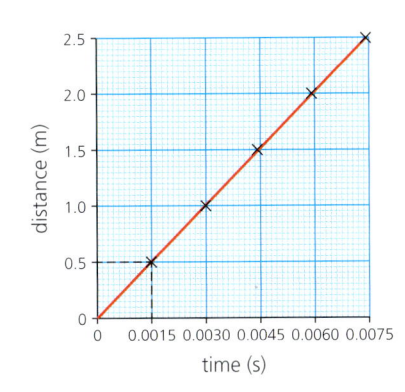

4 a) [graph: distance (m) vs time (s), linear through points up to 2.5 m at 0.0060 s]

b) $v = \dfrac{d}{t} = \dfrac{2}{0.0059} = 339$ m/s

5 a) $v = f\lambda$

$f = \dfrac{v}{\lambda} = \dfrac{340}{0.2} = 1700$ Hz

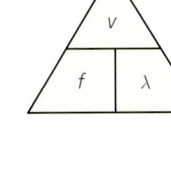

[triangle: v over f, λ]

b) [waveform diagram]

6 a) P
   b) ultraviolet
   c) (i) For example: to heat damaged muscles so they heal more quickly
      (ii) For example: to kill cancerous cells inside the body; to sterilise medical equipment

7 a) X-rays
   b) (i) ultraviolet
      (ii) skin cancer (or sunburn)

8 a) 3 cm (a few cm)
   b) radioactive materials or the Sun
   c) security systems or remote control (other answers are possible)
   d) eye, photographic film or light dependent resistor
   e) Any two from radio, TV, microwaves

9 a) (i) alpha
      (ii) gamma
   b) The short range of alpha particles means that they cannot pass through the body and be detected. They are very ionising and would cause serious damage to living cells inside the body.

10 a) (i) radon, gamma rays from the ground and buildings, cosmic rays, or internal from food and drink
       (ii) medical radiotherapy and diagnostics
    b) (i) 10%
       (ii) 12%

11 a) For example: no carbon dioxide is produced (a greenhouse gas); no other polluting gases are produced
    b) (i) For example: Fewer people would be affected if there was a radioactive spillage.
       (ii) For example: Marshy ground would make it difficult to clear up a radioactive spillage.

Answers to Unit 3

13 Speed and acceleration

1 Note initial distance reading (from odometer) before journey commences. Note final distance reading (from odometer) after completing journey. Start stopwatch when journey starts and stop stopwatch when journey is completed. Note time taken for journey.
Calculate distance travelled from final distance reading minus initial distance reading.
Calculate average speed $= \dfrac{\text{distance travelled}}{\text{time taken}}$

2 a) $\bar{v} = \dfrac{d}{t} = \dfrac{25}{10} = 2.5$ m/s

b) $\bar{v} = \dfrac{d}{t} = \dfrac{3200}{400} = 8$ m/s

c) $\bar{v} = \dfrac{d}{t}$

$t = \dfrac{d}{\bar{v}} = \dfrac{1000}{4} = 250$ s

d) $\bar{v} = \dfrac{d}{t}$

$t = \dfrac{d}{\bar{v}} = \dfrac{1.6}{0.2} = 8$ s

e) $\bar{v} = \dfrac{d}{t}$

$d = \bar{v} \times t = 3.5 \times 50 = 175$ m

f) $\bar{v} = \dfrac{d}{t}$

$d = \bar{v} \times t = 2.4 \times 1500 = 3600$ m

3 $\bar{v} = \dfrac{d}{t} = \dfrac{1.8}{4.5} = 0.4$ m/s

[triangle: d over $\bar{v}$, t]

Answers

4. $\bar{v} = \dfrac{d}{t}$

   $d = \bar{v} \times t = 0.8 \times 800 = 640$ m

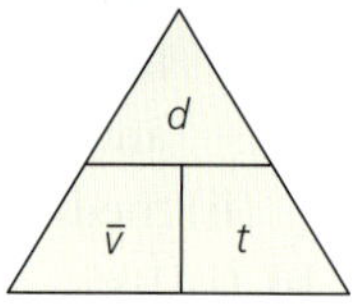

5. $\bar{v} = \dfrac{d}{t}$

   $t = \dfrac{d}{\bar{v}} = \dfrac{100}{8} = 12.5$ seconds

6. Mark a line on the road. Start the stopwatch when the front wheel of the bicycle passes this line and stop the stopwatch when the rear wheel of the bicycle passes the line. Measure the length of the bicycle.

   Calculate: speed = $\dfrac{\text{length of bicycle}}{\text{time on stopwatch}}$

   This is taken as the instantaneous speed of the bicycle, as the time is short.

7. $a = \dfrac{v - u}{t} = \dfrac{15 - 0}{12} = \dfrac{15}{12} = 1.25$ m/s²

8. $a = \dfrac{v - u}{t} = \dfrac{4 - 0}{5} = \dfrac{4}{5} = 0.8$ m/s²

9. $a = \dfrac{v - u}{t}$

   $t = \dfrac{v - u}{a} = \dfrac{0 - 30}{-1.5} = \dfrac{-30}{-1.5} = 20$ s

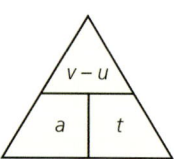

10. $a = \dfrac{v - u}{t}$

    $t = \dfrac{v - u}{a} = \dfrac{9.5 - 2}{2.5} = \dfrac{7.5}{2.5} = 3$ s

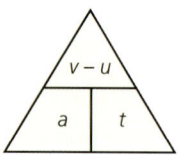

11. a) $a = \dfrac{v - u}{t} = \dfrac{18 - 0}{6} = \dfrac{18}{6} = 3$ m/s²

    b) distance = area under speed–time graph
       distance = area of triangle = ½ × 6 × 18 = 54 m

    c) $\bar{v} = \dfrac{d}{t} = \dfrac{54}{6} = 9$ m/s

12. a) Constant negative acceleration (or constant deceleration) for 10 s

    b) Note that $u = 12$ m/s and $v = 8$ m/s

       $a = \dfrac{v - u}{t} = \dfrac{8 - 12}{10} = \dfrac{-4}{10} = -0.4$ m/s²

    c) distance = area under speed–time graph
       = area of rectangle + area of triangle
       = (10 × 8) + (½ × 10 × 4)
       = 80 + 20 = 100 m

       $\bar{v} = \dfrac{d}{t} = \dfrac{100}{10} = 10$ m/s

13. a) [speed–time graph: rises from 0 to 5 m/s at t=4 s, then drops to 2 m/s at t=7 s]

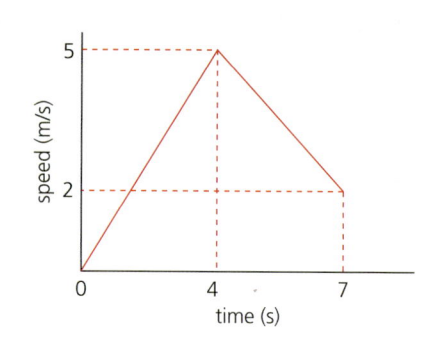

    b) $a = \dfrac{v - u}{t} = \dfrac{5 - 0}{4} = \dfrac{5}{4} = 1.25$ m/s²

14. a) (i) uniform acceleration from rest for 10 s
       (ii) constant speed of 20 m/s for 15 s

    b) (i) $a = \dfrac{v - u}{t} = \dfrac{20 - 0}{10} = \dfrac{20}{10} = 2$ m/s²

       (ii) $a = \dfrac{v - u}{t} = \dfrac{20 - 20}{15} = \dfrac{0}{15} = 0$ m/s²

    c) distance = area under speed–time graph
       distance = area of triangle + area of rectangle
       = (½ × 10 × 20) + (15 × 20)
       = 100 + 300 = 400 m

    d) $\bar{v} = \dfrac{d}{t} = \dfrac{400}{25} = 16$ m/s

14 Relationship between forces, motion and energy

1. Since the car is moving at constant speed, the forces acting on the car must be balanced (Newton's first law), i.e. the resistive force is equal in size but opposite in direction to the forward force from the engine.

2. 6 N (to the right)

3. a) resistive force ← car → engine force

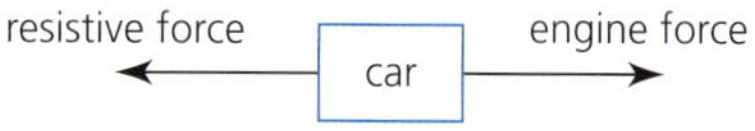

   b) (i) The forces are balanced, or the engine force is equal in size but acts in the opposite direction to the resistive force.
      (ii) The engine force is larger than the resistive force.

4. a) A = air resistance, B = lift force (from wings), C = engine force, D = weight

   b) (i) A and C are equal in size but opposite in direction.
      (ii) B and D are equal in size but opposite in direction.

Answers

5 $F_{un} = ma = 5000 \times 0.12 = 600$ N

6 $F_{un} = ma$

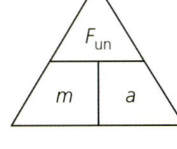

$a = \dfrac{F_{un}}{m} = \dfrac{0.2}{0.40} = 0.5$ m/s^2

7 $F_{un} = ma$

$m = \dfrac{F_{un}}{a} = \dfrac{5400}{2.7} = 2000$ kg

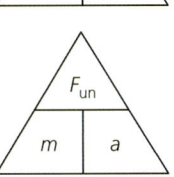

8 $W = mg = 0.2 \times 9.8 = 1.96$ N
(Note g for Earth from Data sheet)

9 a) 150 kg (the number and type of particles making up the probe have not changed so its mass remains the same)
   b) (i) $W_{Earth} = mg = 150 \times 9.8 = 1470$ N
   (Note g for Earth from Data sheet)
   (ii) $W_{Mars} = mg = 150 \times 3.7 = 555$ N
   (Note g for Mars from Data sheet)

10 $W = mg$

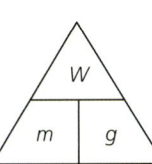

$m = \dfrac{W}{g} = \dfrac{4.9}{9.8} = 0.5$ kg

(Note g for Earth from Data sheet)

15 Satellites

1 Y will have a longer period.
2 a) A satellite that appears to stay above one point on the Earth's surface OR a satellite with a period of 24 hours.
   b) You do not need to reposition the transmitter or receiver, as the satellite appears to be always in the same position.
3 a) Satellite Q
   b) (i) Any value greater than 2000 km but less than 36 000 km, for example 10 000 km.
   (ii) Any value greater than 24 hours, for example 26 hours.
4 a) and b)

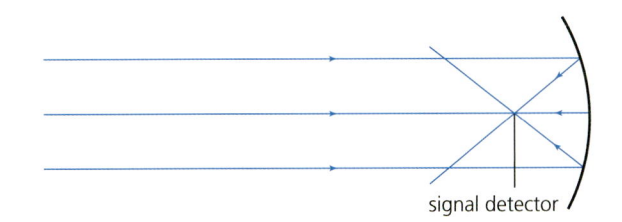

   c) focus
5 a) at the focus
   b) The signal would be stronger, as more energy or waves would be reflected from the larger dish to the signal detector at the focus.

6 $d = 345\,000$ km $= 345\,000\,000$ m

$v = \dfrac{d}{t}$

$t = \dfrac{d}{v} = \dfrac{345\,000\,000}{300\,000\,000} = 1.15$ s

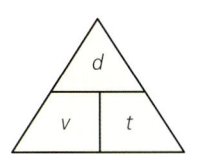

7 $v = \dfrac{d}{t}$

$t = \dfrac{d}{v} = \dfrac{180\,000}{300\,000\,000} = 0.0006$ s

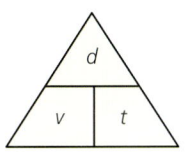

8 a) $v = \dfrac{d}{t}$

$d = v \times t$

$d = 300\,000\,000 \times 0.24$

$d = 72\,000\,000$ m, but this is the distance to the satellite and back

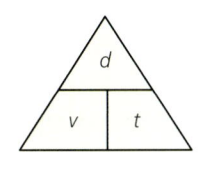

height of satellite $= \dfrac{72\,000\,000}{2} = 36\,000\,000$ m

   b) 24 hours, since the satellite is in a geostationary orbit

9 a) 35 600 km
   b) Period of satellite = 12 hours
      From graph, height = 20 000 km

16 Cosmology

1 A = Sun, B = planets, C = satellite, D = moons, E = stars, F = Solar System, G = galaxy, H = universe

2 $v = \dfrac{d}{t}$

$t = \dfrac{d}{v} = \dfrac{1.5 \times 10^{11}}{300\,000\,000} = 500$ seconds

$t = \dfrac{500}{60} = 8.3$ minutes

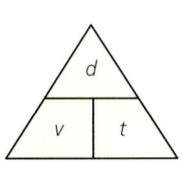

3 a) time $= \dfrac{2.3}{2} = 1.15$ seconds
   b) $v = \dfrac{d}{t}$

$d = v \times t = 300\,000\,000 \times 1.15$

$d = 345\,000\,000$ m

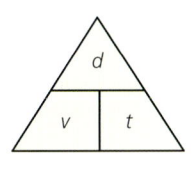

4 a) 1 light year $= 300\,000\,000 \times (365 \times 24 \times 60 \times 60)$
      $= 9.5 \times 10^{15}$ m
   b) 1 light year $= 9.5 \times 10^{15}$ m
      8.6 light years $= 8.6 \times 9.5 \times 10^{15} = 8.17 \times 10^{16}$ m

5 a) a planet orbiting a star outside our Solar System
   b) liquid water

Answers

Unit 3 exam practice

1 a) Use a stopwatch and a metre stick. Measure the distance between X and Y with the metre stick. Use the stopwatch to measure the time the trolley takes to travel from X to Y. Calculate the average speed using:

$$\text{average speed} = \frac{\text{distance from X to Y}}{\text{time on stopwatch}}$$

b) The average speed is the steady or constant speed that the trolley would need to travel at, all of the time, in order to cover the distance between X and Y in the time taken. However, since the object is accelerating, it will actually have a greater speed at Y compared to any other point between X and Y.

2 a) (i) constant acceleration for 3 s
(ii) constant speed of 6 m/s for 4 s

b) (i) $a = \frac{v-u}{t} = \frac{6-0}{3} = \frac{6}{3} = 2$ m/s²

(ii) $a = \frac{v-u}{t} = \frac{6-6}{4} = \frac{0}{4} = 0$ m/s²

c) distance travelled = area under speed–time graph
= (½ × 3 × 6) + (4 × 6)
= 9 + 24 = 33 m

d) $\bar{v} = \frac{d}{t} = \frac{33}{7} = 4.7$ m/s

3 a) Stellar
b) (i) Rocketry
(ii) Rocketry takes the shortest time to go from 0 to 60 miles per hour.

4 a) $F_{un} = ma = 3 \times 2 = 6$ N
b) 12 N (= 18 − 6)
c) (i) As the value of X increases, the unbalanced force acting on the object will decrease. This will mean that the acceleration will decrease.
(ii) The object travels at a constant speed. The forces acting on the object are balanced.

5 a) (i) engine force and resistive force
(ii) balanced
b) (i) resistive force (or air resistance)
(ii) For example: give it a smoother shape

6 a) Y
b) (i) geostationary
(ii) 300 000 000 m/s
(iii) $v = \frac{d}{t}$

$t = \frac{d}{v} = \frac{36\,000\,000}{300\,000\,000} = 0.12$ s

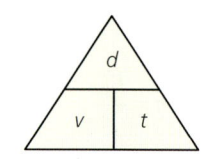

7 a) The weak signal coming from Earth reflects off the dish and this leads to a much stronger signal being received by the aerial.
b) (i)

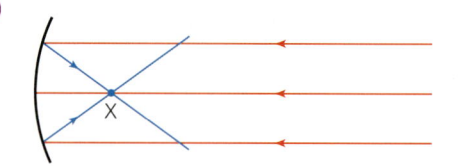

(ii) The focus is the point where the strongest signal is received.

8 a) $W = mg = 12 \times 7.6 = 91.2$ N
b) it increases
c) Rodgl

9 a) the Milky Way
b) a cluster
c) spiral
d) 100 billion
e) radio
f) Stars that are nearer to the centre of the galaxy than our Solar System appear to move in the opposite direction to those that are further away than our Solar System.

10 a) a planet circling a star outside our Solar System
b) (liquid) water